© 2019 by Rhonda K. Oliver

All rights reserved. No portion of this book may be reproduced, stored in a retrieval system, or transmitted in any form or by any means electronic, mechanical, photocopy, recording, scanning, or other except for brief quotations in critical reviews or articles, without the prior written permission of the author.

Scripture quotations are taken from the Holy Bible

King James and New International Version

ISBN 978-0-578-55457-0

Library of Congress Cataloging in Publication Data

Self-Published by Rhonda K. Oliver

Front and Back Cover: Jonnika Allen

www.jondidesign.com

Photographer: Shamya J'nel

Printed in the United States of America

Text: Rhonda K. Oliver

You Got Time to Get It Right

You GOT TIME
to Get It Right

Rhonda K. Oliver

ACKNOWLEDGEMENTS

I would like to give my Lord and Savior, Jesus Christ all the glory, honor, and praise for using me to write this book. It is my prayer that my beautiful daughter Reiona and my grandsons Riley and Euro never give up on anything, never settle for mediocrity, and always reach for the stars.

My love for all of you is limitless!

♥

♥

Success is for the Best

Don't tell people what you're doing, show them what you've done

It's not the end, when you can begin again

Don't allow past decisions to thwart your vision

Our Children Belong to God

Psalm 24:1
The earth is the LORD's, and everything in it, the world, and all who live in it;

I believe all inmates with children would agree the hardest thing about being in prison is being away from our kids. This was a pill I was unfortunately forced to swallow, and it did nothing to relieve me of the pain of being separated from my daughter.

After the judge sentenced me to 20 years and remanded me to prison, I was devastated. My mind was filled with so much at one time. I began to think about what would happen to my child: I wondered about who would care for her, who would protect her from strangers, who would nurture and love her the way I do? My list of concerns went on and on. Finally, I received an answer after hearing Warden Johnnie Jones quote Psalm 24:1 at a volunteer's banquet.

Although being away from my daughter still hurt, I must admit I gained some comfort after reading everyone who dwells in this world we live in belongs to God (Psalm 24:1). This includes my daughter. This includes your children, too. God has only blessed us with our children for a period of time; we love them dearly, but God loves them so much more than we ever can.

We are in prison and not in a position to be there for our children the way we would like to. Moreover, once we are released we still cannot be there for our children every moment -- this is why we must give our children back to God and trust him to carry out His will in their lives.

Know What Your Business Is

1 Thessalonians 4:11
And to make it your ambition to lead a quiet life. You should mind your own business and work with your hands, just as we told you

As Christians we should live quiet lives and mind our own business. However, before we can do this successfully we must be able to discern between business we should be involved with and business we should avoid. We need to know how to distinguish between the two.

There have been several occasions when I observed an inmate steal from their job. We all know stealing is a sin, as the Bible clearly commands us not to steal (Exodus 20:15). Although this is wrong, I don't believe it is our business to 'tell' on someone who has chosen to do so.

Often I would witness an inmate sneak into their dormitory to sleep when they were supposed to be working. It is very tempting to bring attention to someone who does this, especially when you are out in extremely hot or cold weather and wishing you could be sleep yourself, but this is not your business so you shouldn't get involved.

When I say it is wrong to tell on someone who is stealing from their job, or someone who skips work to sleep, I mean it is not your business to volunteer such information. However, it becomes your business if you are directly asked about these things because you are obligated to tell the truth. Moreover, you are obligated to love these people and live a Christian life before them. It's going to be very difficult to witness to people if you are known as someone who reveals all you see and hear. The very next time someone does something wrong, humbly reach out to them regarding their actions, let them know you love them, and above all else pray for their

deliverance.

What Are You Watching?

Ephesians 4:27
And do not give the devil a foothold.

We must be mindful of everything we do. Satan doesn't care who or what he uses to cause us to lose focus; watching television may seem small, but this could be a tool of the enemy to keep you in bondage.

Television in itself is not bad -- it's what we choose to watch. Unfortunately, to those of us in prison, usually this choice is not a personal one.

What's watched on television is determined by a majority vote. Sadly, the majority often choose movies that promote sin. So many inmates spend most of their time in front of the television -- it doesn't matter how ungodly or degrading the movie is, they watch it anyway.

It was very tempting for me to go into the tv room and watch tv like everyone else; this was a temptation I fought constantly. Okay I must admit that sometimes I gave into the temptation, but for a good cause: the New Orleans Saints were playing! All jokes aside, no matter how tempting it was for me to pass time by watching television, I decided against it. Before my incarceration I spent a lot of time in front of the television set. Watching television was something I always enjoyed doing. In fact, I loved it. Now, I was determined to be different. I was determined to live the word of God. I was determined to be a light in a dark place. Most of all, I was determined not to allow the enemy to use the ungodliness shown on television, to give place to him.

I encourage you to stop wasting time watching television. Instead, start spending that time reading and studying the word of God or doing something else productive. In doing this you will avoid a lot of trouble, and you won't find yourself giving the devil a place in your life.

So-Called Friends

Galatians 1:10
Am I now trying to win the approval of human beings, or of God? Or am I trying to please people? If I were still trying to please people, I would not be a servant of Christ.

Don't call everyone you associate with your friend. This is not a word you just throw around. If you would like to find out who your true friends are, stop pleasing man and start pleasing God and in no time, you will know who's who.

One of the inmates, who I'll call Lezly, came to me one day and confessed that she had been giving her friends extra food from the cafeteria serving line. She admitted that she had been doing this for years. Lezly went on to say that she knows her actions were wrong and that she wasn't going to do it anymore. When I saw Lezly again she told me she had stopped giving her friends extra food, and as a result her friends had decided not to speak to her anymore. This bothered her so much she started giving her so-called 'friends' extra food again just so they would start back speaking to her.

True friends will never ask you to do something that may get you in trouble. Friends should be selfless, not selfish; friends should always have your best interests in mind. If you stop trying to please people and start pleasing God instead, you will see who your true friends are. True friends don't mind being told no and will not influence you to do wrong.

Stop trying to buy friends! If you have friends who do not accept you for who you are without wanting to know what you can do for them, those are friends you do not need. Live to please God and your so-called friends will disappear. Those who remain may truly be called friends.

Your Name Matters

Proverbs 22:1
A good name is more desirable than great riches; to be esteemed is better than silver or gold.

It does not pay to accumulate canteen items and store up all kinds of illegal foods at the expense of your name, yet this is very common. Sadly, incarcerated individuals who do not have Jesus as their focus, live to accumulate items from the canteen and store up unjust gains by any means necessary.

The most popular means by which to profit illegally is theft of sugar, ham, smoke sausage, or some other hot item from the kitchen -- these items are always demanded and sold throughout the compound. If an inmate is not stealing or carrying out some other ungodly act, they are not considered cool. They are labeled as fake or scary. Instances of stealing from the kitchen are so bad that kitchen workers getting off shift are searched before leaving to return to their living areas. Many times, when kitchen workers are caught with some stolen item in their possession, they do not have enough sense to be embarrassed or ashamed. Instead, they brag about the whole ordeal.

Many times, opportunities arise for inmates to travel offsite to places such as the Governor's Mansion, churches, or to functions held at various hotels. When the time comes to decide who will be eligible to make these trips, inmates are chosen by their character (usually one of the 'uncool' inmates).

The crime we chose to commit caused us to have a bad name, yet this is not the end of the world. Right now is a good time to start making a good name for yourself. So do your part and the Lord will do the rest, after all your name matters.

Abandoned by Loved Ones

Romans 8:28
And we know that in all things God works for the good of those who love Him, who have been called according to His purpose.

A common concern shared by most inmates is not hearing from their family and friends. This often causes discouragement. Yet, if you look at the situation from a broader perspective, you may see this as a blessing and instead be encouraged.

Claire, who had not heard from her husband in some time, was very upset about his lack of communication and expressed this to me; this gave me the opportunity to minister to her. I reminded her that whomever the Lord put together no man can separate (Mark 10:9). I told her that if this is the man God has for her then nothing else, including prison, could cause her marriage to end. I then went on to say that if God didn't put the two of them together, it won't last. I assured her the spouse the Lord has for her will be longsuffering, will bear all things, will hope all things, and will endure all things. The spouse the Lord has for you will not fail you (1 Corinthians 13:4-8).

If it is other family members you are longing to hear from, and if you know where they are, do your part by writing them. If you don't know where they are just pray to the God who does, and leave the outcome to Him.

People who you consider friends are really not if they have abandoned you in such times. After all, a friend loveth at all times (Proverbs 17:17, KJV). Thank God for using your situation to reveal to you who will be there for you when you are down and out.

Today, make a decision to do what I did: thank God for allowing you to see the true colors of all those in your life. Then, if you must, make up your mind to go on without them, as their part in your life may be over.

Tell the Truth Regardless

John 8:32
Then you will know the truth, and the truth will set you free.

Witnesses should always be willing to tell the truth; be sure you do so if ever called upon. Telling the truth shouldn't be based on what others may say or do, but on the word of God.

Just a few days ago as I sat on the bunk assigned to me, I could hear two people arguing in the room two doors down the hall. The argument became more intense, and the next thing I know it had escalated into a fist fight. By the time security realized something was going on, the fight was over. As an attempt to prevent the fighters from going to lock down, several people on the hall stated they had not been fighting, just arguing. Several minutes later security began going from room to room asking, 'were the two ladies fighting'? When they made their way to me, I said yes, they were fighting. When security asked if I would sign a form to that effect, I said no, I already told you what I saw. When they left, one of the inmates thanked me for not signing the form, telling me it was the right thing to do. I took this as a perfect opportunity to minister.

I told the lady I didn't sign the form but I did tell the truth about what I witnessed, because I want to please Jesus, and I know He is always pleased with the truth. I said lying is never the answer.

Don't allow anyone to cause you to think that your right is wrong, and their wrong is right. Go to the word and allow God to be the judge. After all, He is the righteous one, and wants us to tell the truth regardless.

Settle the Debt

Romans 13:8-9

Let no debt remain outstanding, except the continuing debt to love one another, for whoever loves others has fulfilled the law. The commandments, "You shall not commit adultery," "You shall not murder," "You shall not steal," "You shall not covet," and whatever other command there may be, are summed up in this one command:"Love your neighbor as yourself."

Seeing people be mistreated is a common practice in prison. No one has a right to wrong another individual -- in fact, we are obligated to love people.

We are not allowed to pick and choose who we will love. The word of God requires us to love everyone. This means you must love your roommate who murdered her child, you must love the rapist who sleeps in the bunk next to you, and you even have to love the child molester down the hall. People like this are often picked out to be picked on because man has a tendency to weigh sin. Yet, in the eyes of God there is no sin greater than the other.

We do not deserve the love of God, but God loves us anyway. He knows us better than we know ourselves, He knows about everything we have ever done, He knows all about the sinful lifestyle we once led, and yet He still loves us. He does not limit his love to only you and me, He also loves your roommate although she murdered her child, He loves your bunkmate who is charged with rape, and the child molester down the hall. If a Holy God can love these people, then who are you not to do the same? Besides, if these people have accepted Jesus Christ as their Lord and Savior, He no longer sees them as they were (1 Corinthians 6:9-11).

One thing I absolutely hate is debt. This is why I strive to walk in love with my neighbor. You should consider doing the same. If you are not then you are in debt, so take this time to settle it by walking in love with everyone.

I See You

James 2:13
Because judgment without mercy will be shown to anyone who has not been merciful. Mercy triumphs over judgment.

Before I gave my life to the Lord, there were so many times God showed me mercy. Not only was I showed mercy by God, there were times that man even showed me mercy. Now that I am a believer, I am expected to do the same.

There is so much that goes on in a prison setting. With the inmate-to-security ratio being so much greater, it is impossible for security to see everything that goes on. I, however, saw too much. I got so tired of seeing women who had absolutely no respect for themselves openly degrade themselves by practicing sexual immorality. This went on in the dorm, on the job, on the yard, in the shower area, etc. There wasn't any place such acts did not occur.

So many times, I wanted to head straight to security and inform them of everything I had seen, yet I never did. My Spirit never led me to do so. I knew God would soon expose their evil deeds, because what is done in the dark will come to the light. Besides, these people are unbelievers and are acting as such. I, on the other hand, confess to be a believer and should therefore act like one by loving these people and treating them with compassion. If I tell on them, this wouldn't be showing them love and may even ruin my chances of witnessing to them.

God is a merciful God; He does not hold back his mercy from us. Let us follow his example by not hesitating to extend mercy to others.

Believe the Impossible

Matthew 19:26
Jesus looked at them and said,
"With man this is impossible, but with God all things are possible."

There are so many people incarcerated who has been sentenced to spend the rest of their lives in prison. There are others who have been sentenced to serve 25 or more years. Regardless to how much man sentenced these people to, I make sure to encourage these people by reminding them of the God who specialize in impossibilities.

It always was discouraging to me when I would hear a lifer or a long timer ask someone who was expected to be released a year later, to leave them their property. To me this was saying I have 50, 60, 70 years and will still be here when you leave 12 months from now, because God is limited and can't possibly help me get out of this mess I got myself into, so think about me when you leave by giving me what you don't want. Besides, I'm going to be here a long time. A person who talks like this is focusing on how things look in the natural. It doesn't matter how much time man gave you, you must believe that God is able to turn your situation around. You must believe this now, even before you see. Thomas had to see the evidence before he believed that Jesus had risen from the dead. Jesus told him blessed are they that have not seen, and yet have believed (John 20:29).

One day one of the ladies here, who man sentenced to life, asked me could she have one of my gospel cd's when I go home. I told her, if I go home before she does, I will leave the cd with her, I then stated that, "there is no guarantee that I'm going home before you, you could very well be released before me." She didn't say a word she just looked at me like I was crazy; I could clearly see that she didn't understand so I elaborated by saying, "Vacating a life sentence is nothing to God." She blessed me with a smile.

The next time you have the chance to talk with a person who has life or a long prison term, remind them that with God all things are possible (Matthew 19:26). Let them know that God can do anything. Because nothing is too hard for God not even releasing you from the sentence man handed down.

Home Talk

Luke 6:31
Do to others as you would have them do to you.

As much as I miss my family and desperately want to go home, whenever I am around people sentenced to life, I avoid discussing this topic. I know for some this is a very sensitive subject, especially for someone serving a life sentence. Therefore, I'm mindful not to initiate such a conversation.

In prison you hear a lot of talk about going home. To many of us, this is like soothing music to our ears. Although there is nothing wrong with chatting about home, I have noticed how such talk quickly silences those sentenced to life, who have no idea when they will be released, or if they ever will. I'm always mindful of my company. If someone starts a conversation about home, I'm quick to change the subject if a 'lifer' is present and I see they are uncomfortable. This may seem very trivial to you, but it's not, to me it is a Big Deal. To me it is an opportunity to show someone I care. If avoiding conversations about home will help someone keep their spirits up, then I'm all for it.

You should be willing to do whatever it takes to help someone. The Apostle Paul said it perfectly: "To the Jews I became like a Jew, to win the Jews. To those under the law I became like one under the law (though I myself am not under the law), so as to win those under the law." (1 Corinthians 9:20). I'm not saying you have to become a 'lifer' to understand, but in order to reach them you must be sensitive to their situation. Allow God to use you to make a difference through your very own words. Be determined to edify in all you say or do, even if it means putting some conversations on hold.

What's A Life Sentence?

James 4:13-14
Now listen, you who say, "Today or tomorrow we will go to this or that city, spend a year there, carry on business and make money." Why, you do not even know what will happen tomorrow. What is your life? You are a mist that appears for little while and then vanishes.

While in the cafeteria one morning, I encountered two inmates engaging in a verbal confrontation. One of the women had about two years left to serve, the other was serving a life sentence. The first woman was taunting the second woman, insinuating she would never be allowed to go home and would die in prison. She went on, bragging about how she had a release date and that she was getting ready to leave.

Since my incarceration I've witnessed at least eight 'lifers' walk out the doors, despite some judge sentencing them to 'natural life'. I have also witnessed at least five inmates who did not have life sentences take sick and die in prison (one of these ladies was due to be released within six months).

Simply because the justice system did not sentence you to life in prison does not give you the right to throw someone else's sentence in their face. You may believe you have a reason, but that doesn't make it right. Throwing someone's time in their face is wrong.

Tomorrow is not promised to anyone. You have no way of knowing when you will breathe your last breath, neither do you know for certain if you will spend the rest of your life in prison. After all, a life sentence is not living in prison but dying there.

Obedience Is Better Than Going to Church

1 Samuel 15:22
But Samuel replied: "Does the LORD delight in burnt offerings and sacrifices as much as in obeying the LORD? To obey is better than sacrifice, and to heed is better than the fat of rams.

In prison there are many rules by which we are supposed to abide. Some of these rules are okay but there are some we simply don't like. No matter how much we may not like the rules, we are still expected to obey them as long as they are in line with the word of God.

I recall turning my library book into the library 12 hours late. The book was supposed to be brought back before the close of the business day, which was at 8:00 p.m. However, I didn't bring it back until 8:00 a.m. the next morning as I had forgotten the book was due. As a result, I received a disciplinary report causing me to be placed on two weeks of Yard and Recreation. I was very upset with that punishment because it meant I could no longer attend church several times a week, but instead only once.

For hours I struggled with the question of whether I should violate Yard and Recreation and go to church. Finally, I decided to be disobedient and sneak to church for two weeks. I had convinced myself that is was okay for me to disobey, since I was fellowshipping.

I went to church, but I couldn't enjoy it. I was extremely miserable. Then to top it all off, the Holy Spirit reminded me that obedience is better than sacrifice (1 Samuel 15:22).

Never would I have thought that going to church could ever be wrong. However, in this situation it was. I didn't have a roommate at this time and had a room all to myself. God could have been setting things up for me to be alone with him but I allowed my disobedience to get in the way, not realizing that God would rather I be obedient than to go to church.

Conduct Yourself Accordingly

1 Corinthians 14:40
But everything should be done in a fitting and orderly way.

God loves you. He welcomes you to come to church just as you are and yet, you should still have some order about yourself when you get there.

At LCIW we are blessed to have several different church services from which to choose, and the choice of which to attend is totally up to us. There are many reasons inmates choose to go to church: some go just so their name may appear on the annual dinner list, some go to meet with friends and some because bad weather is keeping them from hanging out in the yard. However, there are still those such as myself who go to fellowship with other believers simply to hear the word of the Lord. No matter what our reason is for going to church, we should always show reverence for God and respect whomever God sends to bring the word. We are not showing respect when we show up at church late and/or leave early. We are not showing respect when we are holding a conversation with someone, we are not showing respect for God when we are constantly going in and out of the sanctuary, disrupting the flow of the Holy Spirit.

Don't stop going to church just because you may be going for the wrong reasons. Even then, you might find God can still move on your behalf. Now that you know better, practice doing better so that we may have some order in the church.

Practicing the Sin You Once Condemned

1 Corinthians 10:12
So, if you think you are standing firm, be careful that you don't fall!

When I first entered prison, I noticed a lady in church who appeared to be very strong in the Lord. This lady spoke in tongues, preached sermons, and was always out in the yard ministering to others. She had much knowledge of the Bible; ask her where a scripture was, and she was able to tell you. A short time later, this lady and I began to hold fellowship together. It was then I discovered that she was not who she appeared to be. This lady constantly condemned those who were in bondage to homosexuality. It got to the point where every time she and I got together she would focus on the homosexual couples, constantly going on about how disgusting these people were. Not too long afterward, she had become one of these people herself.

As Christians, we must understand that temptation is common to man (1 Corinthians 10:13). We shouldn't assume we can't fall victim to those same temptations, because we can and we will if we don't resist the devil and take the escape routes provided. When we ignore the escape route, we will find ourselves in the same mess as those we have judged.

There are many people bound by sin. Regardless what sin it is, it is still sin. Whenever you come across those who are in bondage don't talk about it, pray about it, and remember you too can fall.

Wait Your Turn

Galatians 5:22-23
But the fruit of the Spirit is love, joy, peace, forbearance, kindness, goodness, faithfulness, gentleness and self-control. Against such things there is no law.

In prison, there are only a few showers in each dorm and we don't have the luxury of showering whenever we want to, therefore some of us just have to wait.

On the wing to which I was assigned, there were two regular showers, one handicap-accessible shower, and one tub for 66 inmates to share. We were allowed to take showers anytime between the hours of 5:30 a.m. and 10:00 p.m., the only exception was count time. Most inmates finish work at approximately 3:00 p.m., and nearly everyone is ready to shower at that time.

There are some inmates assigned to jobs requiring them to work much harder than other inmates and/or to work outdoors; those inmates believe they should always be allowed to take their showers first. Inmates who think like this are selfish and impatient.

Ultimately, we are serving time in prison because we committed a crime. However, I am more than confident that God allowed us to come to prison so that he could work on us spiritually. If you are one of those inmates who makes a big deal over waiting for the shower, then I can tell you that you lack patience. Allow God to work patience in you the next time you are waiting for the shower.

Everyone would like a shower to be available when they are ready to take one. Unfortunately, incarceration makes this impossible. The next time you find yourself waiting in line for a shower, allow patience to work in you and simply wait your turn.

Discipline Is Not Harassment

Romans 13:1
Let everyone be subject to the governing authorities, for there is no authority except that which God has established. The authorities that exist have been established by God.

If a security guard instructs you to do or not do a particular thing, please just obey them. It doesn't matter if you've never been given such an order before, you are being ordered now, so be obedient.

In prison there are many guards who have a lackadaisical character and don't enforce rules as they should, but there are also a small number of guards who do their jobs and ensure all of the rules are enforced.

One day I overheard an inmate accuse a guard of picking on her because she was not allowed to wear what she had on. This inmate based her accusation on never having been told this before by any other officer. I am very familiar with the rules, and make it a practice to read everything I am given. This is how I knew this inmate was not being picked on; the guard was only enforcing a rule.

The word of God commands us to obey authority. Whether we like it or not, the prison guards have rule over us and we must obey them. If you practice doing this, you will save yourself from much trouble.

The very next time security tells you to do something, comply immediately. If you make yourself familiar with the rules, you will see that he or she is only doing their job. Knowing this will keep you from making false accusations, as well as keeping you out of a lot of trouble.

It Is Okay to Say No

Matthew 25:9
"No," they replied, "there may not be enough for both us and you. Instead, go to those who sell oil and buy some for yourselves."

Christianity does not obligate you to financially take care of others. There are some who may disagree. You do not have to take care of people who are financially able to take care of themselves but refuse to do so.

Prison is a place where people live closely to one another; because of this, you often run across inmates who will try to take advantage of you. Unfortunately, many times these people are successful.

When incarcerated, you meet inmates who receive a lot of financial support, and those with little financial support. Some get absolutely no funds at all. Often those inmates who only get a little, mismanage their money, spending it on cigarettes or other things they don't need. They then expect you to take care of them with money received from your family.

If you have a bunkmate or someone in the dorm with you who spends their money foolishly and then expects you to take care of them with what you have, don't do it. I am reminded of the five wise virgins who refused to give the five foolish virgins some of their oil (Matthew 25:9). The five wise virgins were right not to give up their oil; after all, if the five foolish virgins had not misused theirs, they wouldn't have found themselves in such a dilemma.

I realize saying no is difficult for some to say. Unfortunately, we must tell some people no or they will continue to take advantage of our kindness. We want to help them if we can, but we must understand that if we decide to say no, this may just cause them to start helping themselves.

Choosing to Be in Need

Psalm 23:1
The Lord is my Shepherd; I shall not be in want.

God promises in his word to meet our needs (Psalms 23:1) and the answer to his promises are 'Yes' and 'Amen' (2 Corinthians 1:20). If your needs are not being met then check yourself, because God can not lie (Hebrews 6:18).

Inmates often came to me with their problems and I would always minister to them by offering biblical advice. If they wanted me to pray for them, I would do just that. I began to notice that most of the inmates who came to me with a problem were actually the reason for it.

I recall one inmate who came to me complaining that she was tired of doing without and that she believed God would bring a financial blessing. She went on to say how she was in need of personal items and that she would like to be able to purchase snacks sometimes. I knew this individual was a cigarette smoker, so I asked her how she gets cigarettes at $4.00 a pack. She responded by stating, "I get incentive pay and I iron clothes for people and they pay me."

Again, I stress to you that the Lord is our shepherd and we shall not be in want (Psalm 23:1). This means God will provide for all of our needs. When God makes a way for our needs to be met, we choose to neglect our needs and meet our wants instead, then we pray to God for a financial blessing but miss it when it comes.

Are you currently in need? If so, think back and see if you have neglected your needs for your wants. If you find that you have, take this time to start over and stop choosing to be in need.

Be Considerate

Psalm 41:1
Blessed are those who have regard for the weak; the Lord delivers them in times of trouble.

God wants to deliver you from the trouble you are in; your deliverance depends on you and it may be contingent upon whether you are considering the poor.

Some people are never satisfied, always looking for ways to gain more and more. I've encountered many of these people at LCIW.

It's not often inmates get to eat good food from the outside. Whenever the inmate organizations sell food, certain inmates are chosen to work food sales; as a result, they get all kinds of good food for working.

There are many events that require food preparation. Many of the kitchen workers are called on to serve food, and usually the same workers are chosen time and again.

All throughout the word of God provisions are made for the poor. In the book of Ruth, Boaz considered Ruth and allowed her to glean in his field. He even commanded his young men to purposefully drop extra food so Ruth could have even more (Ruth 2:15).

The next time you are given the opportunity to work a food sale or serve food for some special function, be considerate and suggest that someone who never goes to the canteen is chosen instead. Some of these people are forced to go to bed hungry because they have no outside support. You may make a real difference in someone's life if you consider the poor, then the Lord can deliver you in time of trouble.

On Call Witness

Matthew 5:16
In the same way, let your light shine before others,
that they may see your good deeds and glorify your Father in Heaven.

Practicing what you preach will cause you to have a good reputation. People will start seeing you as someone with integrity and once they see this, God will start building a bridge for you to witness to these people.

One day, Sheena was asked to share a word from the Lord at a church service. Sheena began to tell the church that the Lord said we need to come out of our comfort zones and start going out on the yard to witness to unbelievers. She went on to say that these people were hurting, and the Lord wants us to show them love.

There is not a doubt in my mind the Lord gave this word to Sheena. I believe he gave her this word because he wanted her to walk the compound and witness to unbelievers. God never told me to do this. For the most part, I've been led to witness by living the word of God one day at a time -- the Spirit will do the rest.

Jesus went about doing his Father's business and his good reputation grew until people did whatever it took to get to him. The woman with the issue of blood pressed her way through the crowd to touch the hem of Jesus' garment (Mark 5:27). The lame man got his friends to cut a hole in the roof and lower him down to where Jesus was (Mark 2:4), and Zacchaeus climbed up a tree (Luke 19:4).

Often, I'm called on by an unbeliever who wants me to pray for them, while others call on me just to talk. Whenever they call I am always ready to witness, and they are always ready to receive. God may tell you to witness one way and tell me to witness in another; regardless of how, just make sure you are always ready to answer the call.

Content with Change

Philippians 4:11
I am not saying this because I am in need, for I have learned to be content whatever the circumstances.

Changes are always being made in prison. Today you may be allowed to have something that you may not be able to have tomorrow. One day you may be allowed to do something that you will be prohibited from doing the very next day. If you learn to expect change, you will be content when it happens.

Here at LCIW. there are not any open dorms; instead, you have rooms shared by two or three inmates. After being in prison for several years we were informed that soon, the doors to each room would have to be open at all times and this open-door rule is now in effect. No matter where I went on the compound, I heard inmates express how much they hated this new rule. I was even asked to join with others in writing a correspondence to the warden, asking him to reconsider this rule. I politely declined.

I liked being able to close the door, as it allowed us to have a little more privacy. However, leaving the doors open does not bother me one bit.

The word of God tells us we should be as a tree planted by the rivers of water (Psalm 1:3). This means that a new rule or anything else should not cause us to be moved. After all, as believers we shouldn't have anything to hide, so gladly open the door and allow God to help you grow content with change.

Your Approach Counts

Galatians 5:16
So I say, walk by the Spirit, and you will not gratify the desires of the flesh.

When you say you are a Christian, people are going to test you; your approach to these tests are extremely important, as it will determine how others see you.

There were many times throughout my incarceration when I was verbally attacked. I don't remember exactly why these individuals lashed out at me, but I believe it was for righteousness' sake. I was adamant about taking a stand for what was right but sadly, I discovered the majority hated me for this.

One day I can recall taking a stand against Ms. Kaley. Again, I don't remember what went on but I do know that Ms. Kaley was always practicing unrighteousness -- this woman had very evil ways. The stand I took caused her to cuss at me, calling me very ugly names. Although I yearned to fight back, instead I chose to follow the Spirit and not say a word. A few days later this same woman came to me and admitted that she was illiterate. She also told me she didn't know how to open her combination lock and would I please open it for her. I smiled and politely went into her room to open her lock.

The same lady who called me all those ugly names now trusted me enough to give me her lock's combination. This woman had so call friends, a social circle, and she was even in a homosexual relationship, yet she didn't trust any of these people with her number.

As Christians, we will be attacked. The next time it happens to you, remember that how you handle the situation will determine how people define you. We will be sure to handle the situation we are faced with the way Jesus would if we are mindful of our approach.

Don't Come as You Are

1 Corinthians 14:40
But everything should be done in a fitting and orderly way.

We should be very careful how we enter the presence of God. This was so important to God that he instructed the priests on how to do so (Leviticus 8:13). Although we no longer need a priest, we can still take heed of the instructions given them by preparing ourselves before entering his presence.

When I first came to prison, I would roll my hair before going to church. I did this because it was convenient. I rolled my hair after I got off from work at 3:00 p.m. instead of rolling it after I got out of church at 7:00 p.m. It was better for me to enter God's presence any kind of way, than to sacrifice by staying up late to roll my hair.

One day the Lord convicted me about wearing rollers to church. I wouldn't be caught dead with rollers in my hair at my daughter's graduation or at a wedding. It is very important to me how I groom myself when going to non-Christian events. Therefore, it should be even more important how I am attired when going to church.

The word of God encourages us to come as we are. This is not speaking of physical appearance, it means God wants you to come to him in the spiritual condition in which you find yourself. You don't have to stop stealing before you come. You don't have to stop fornicating before you come. Neither do you have to be properly attired, but as a Christian you should want to be.

No Right

Hosea 4:6
My people are destroyed from lack of knowledge.
"Because you have rejected knowledge, I
also reject you as my priests; because you
have ignored the law of your God, I also
will ignore your children.

It is extremely important that we know how to distinguish rights from privileges. Sadly, in prison, many inmates do not know how to differentiate between the two. Because they lack this knowledge, they fight many losing battles.

Here at LCIW, smoking is prohibited indoors. Outdoors it is allowed only in designated areas. It has been said that smoking will be stopped all together if smoking continues where it is prohibited. Whenever inmates would hear this, their response was always, 'they can't stop us from smoking, and if they do it won't last long because everyone will file a grievance'. This is a battle everyone was going to lose.

You do not have a constitutional right to smoke a cigarette. Smoking harms the smoker and others. Smoking is a privilege, not a right.

Maybe you are complaining about cold showers. If this is so, then you need to know there are several court rulings stating an inmate does not have the right to shower in hot water. The food you are served may not be what you want or prepared how you want it. Maybe if you knew that the state is only required to provide you with two meals a day, you would learn to appreciate the three you get.

Knowledge is most definitely power; a lack of knowledge causes you to be powerless. Make it your business to know as much as possible about what you plan to do before you do it. This way you will be able to distinguish privileges from your rights and begin winning battle

Suffering the Consequences

James 2:9
But if you show favoritism, you sin and are convicted by the law as lawbreakers.

Elderly people also experience punishment. Those who punish the elderly are often looked at as evil, wrong and even uncaring. However, everyone has to suffer the consequences behind his or her actions. Besides, the word of God tells us that we should not have respect of persons.

Usually, when we think of not having respect of persons we relate this to God blessing the righteous and unrighteous. Some stand on God rains on the just and the unjust (Mathew 5:45). Yet, we shouldn't limit respect of person to the blessings of God, because God also punishes the righteous and the unrighteous alike.

One day I recall hearing much negative talk against security. Supposedly, an elderly inmate was handcuffed and placed on lockdown for threatening a guard. Inmates accused security of being heartless and commented, "They didn't have to lock up that little old lady."

Many times in the Bible we see where God killed numerous people because of their actions or bad choices (Numbers 16:31-33, Exodus 32:27-28). It didn't matter if these people were babies, adults, or the elderly, they all experienced the wrath of God. God had absolutely no respect as to who he killed.

Give security a break - they have a job to do! They should not be looked at as evil. They are doing the job they are being paid to do. If an elderly person is acting out and making threats, then that person must be punished. If God is no respecter of persons, then we cannot be either.

Answered Prayer

Galatians 6:7
Do not be deceived: God cannot be mocked. A man reaps what he sows

Prayer is very essential in my life. I practice covering my daughter through prayer on a daily basis and I believe the parents of the inmates here are praying for their children as well. God may be using you to answer that prayer, so don't fail at your assignment.

We can't be with our children every second of the day. Even if we were not incarcerated, there would still be times when we would be separated from our children. Therefore, we should cry out to God through prayer for him to direct our children to people who will lead and guide them in the right direction. Your roommate or coworker may be led to you so that you can minister to them, but instead you encourage this child to lie, cheat, and steal. You may even introduce someone else's child to homosexuality.

How can you pray and ask God to protect your child, but then fail to allow him to use you to protect the child of another? If you want others to treat your child right, don't you dare mistreat the children you are around. After all, the word of God teaches that you reap what you sow.

Someone is praying that God will lead their children to the right person; you may very well be that person. Do not lose the opportunity for God to use you to answer someone's prayer.

Believer at Fault

Galatians 6:1
Brothers and Sisters, if someone is caught in a sin, you who live by the Spirit should restore that person gently. But watch yourselves, or you also may be tempted.

As Christians, we are to go to other believers in love if we find them in fault. Even if you've had bad experiences doing so, don't allow this to prevent you from doing what the word of God instructs us to do.

Recently, I was led to confront someone who claimed to be a Christian. It was alleged that this person was stealing from the chapel. Several people had approached me on different occasions regarding this matter. I don't know their motives for telling me, but I knew I had to ask this person, who just happened to be my coworker, if these allegations were true. Finally, I approached her and asked if there was any truth regarding these allegations. She denied that there was, and so I left it alone. However, she did not. This woman began telling lies about me, stopped speaking to me, and succeeded in turning others against me.

One day I overheard this person telling another co-worker of ours about all she had stolen and how she distributed it as Christmas gifts. This is why she reacted the way she did. I confronted her with the truth, and that hurts.

We should never have to think twice when it comes to obeying the word of God. Neither should we be concerned about what people say or think about us for doing so. When you see or hear about a believer being caught up in a fault, you need to go to that individual in love. Do your part and leave the rest up to God.

Sick Call Abuse

Proverbs 13:4

A sluggard's appetite is never filled, but the desires of the diligent are fully satisfied.

No one wants to be sick. Unfortunately, most of us are faced with it at some point in our lives. When we are faced with sickness, we want medical attention, but sometimes it is difficult to get this attention when people who are not sick abuse the system.

To the best of my knowledge, everyone serving time in a state facility was sentenced to hard labor. This hard labor does not include a vacation plan and is carried out for a few to no cents an hour. Offenders who don't want to work usually pretend to be sick and head to the infirmary in order to get some time off work. Then someone who really is sick is checked and sent on their way without the No Duty slip they really need.

We were sent to prison to work. This is a debt we owe society for the crime we committed. It shouldn't matter that you aren't getting paid, you should work as unto the Lord (Colossians 3:23). His pay is far greater than anything man can give you. Moreover, not wanting to work is a sign of laziness. If you leave prison with this same attitude, you will find it almost impossible to be able to provide for yourself and your family.

There are people in this world who wish they could work but can't because some medical condition has handicapped them; these people would probably give anything to be able to work.

The next time you are tempted to fake a sickness, think about that sick person who really needs the medical attention that you don't need, then go to work, and thank God for being able to do so.

Re-Count

Galatians 6:3
If anyone thinks they are something when they are not, they deceive themselves.

Don't give security a hard time if they have to do a recount. You don't know the reason behind it, neither is it your business. Your business is to quietly stand up and be counted. As easy as we think counting is, it takes concentration and we all miscount from time to time.

When the numbers don't add up to what the inmate population should be, you can expect to be counted again. Your complaining will not stop this. You will be counted until the count is accurate.

In retrospect, there were times I can recall when the inmates would deliberately mess up the count. They would get in the wrong line so the count wouldn't clear. This way they didn't have to go back to work. Sometimes the count doesn't clear because inmates are so engrossed in a conversation they fail to get in line because they didn't hear it called.

One day, my supervisor told me and another inmate to count crates of vegetables. I counted 57, while the other person counted 58. When I counted again, I also got 58. I had made a mistake with something as easy as counting.

When you are trying to put security down for recounting, you are lifting yourself up. What you are saying is I can do it and get it right, because I'm above making a mistake. Remember, you are no better than anyone else and can always miscount, too.

Who Are You To Judge?

Matthew 7:1
Do not judge, or you too will be judged.

We shouldn't assume that someone is faking a sickness merely because so many inmates do so regularly; there are many inmates who are truly ill and need our help. Stop acting on your assumptions and extend a helping hand.

The majority of inmates who bombard the infirmary with fake illnesses are those who are classified for field work. I've seen inmate after inmate go out into the field and pass out or pretend to be dizzy, overheated, etc. Although most of these inmates are pretenders, this was not always the case.

I recall one field worker who passed out every time she was in the field to work. Once, she even passed out while standing at the door for count. This lady was teased and talked about by other inmates who accused her of faking and trying to get out of working. This woman was treated very badly. One day, this lady was sent to the hospital and when she came back her head was shaved bald; it was discovered that she had a brain tumor and as a result she had to undergo a very serious surgery.

There was another young inmate who worked in housekeeping and was always sick. She was also ridiculed and talked about and accused of being lazy. This young girl served her time and was released. About two weeks later she died in Children's Hospital.

Being in prison is bad enough, but to be sick also is even worse. Don't waste precious time trying to figure out if a person who always seems to be sick, really is. Instead, spend this time in prayer for the person and stop trying to judge out of ignorance. After all, God is the only one who can judge a person's motives.

No Comment

1 Thessalonians 4:11
And to make it your ambition to lead a quiet life:
You should mind your own business and work with your hands, just as we told you.

In prison roommates come and go. I've had many of them throughout my incarceration. It seemed like every time someone would get a new roommate, there were always those ready to give a negative report on that person. Don't allow yourself to react negatively to bad reports; when you do, it says a lot about you.

There will always be certain people who seek to get into the ear of the new person to inform them of what they want them to know about another person. You should never allow what you hear about someone to cause you to form an opinion, neither should you voluntarily share your opinion about a difficult person.

One day I asked Ms. Reba how she was doing. She responded by saying, "I am not doing well because I do not like the dorm they moved me to." I then asked her who her two roommates were, after she told me, she looked at me, as if she was waiting for negative feedback but I just smiled and walked away.

One of the roommates Ms. Reba mentioned was no stranger to me. This lady and I had an earlier encounter and I was well aware of her evil ways. However, I did not add to the current situation between the two ladies by voicing a negative opinion. If you are faced with such a situation, make it your business to do the same. After all, if you don't have anything good to say, then just don't comment at all.

What's Good About It?

Malachi 2:17

You have wearied the Lord with your words. "How have we wearied him?" you ask. By saying, "All who do evil are good in the eyes of the Lord, and he is pleased with them" or "Where is the God of justice?"

The devil has deceived so many people into thinking that good is evil, and evil is good; it is time for us to stop confusing the two. When we do this, we will be able to differentiate good from evil.

Many inmates spend their time reading books and watching television. It is common to hear someone yell out that a good movie is about to come on, or ask, "does anyone have a good book?" Usually the inmates would get on their bunks and discuss what these 'good' books are about. The books they read and the movies they watch are always about using and selling drugs, rape, murder, fornication, homosexuality, lying, cheating, stealing, adultery, etc. I can go on and on, but I'm sure you get my point. All of the above are sins, and sin is never good. Satan has blinded us, and cunningly deceived us into thinking that all the trashy books we read and dirty movies we watch are good.

It is time for us to see good as good and evil as evil. However, this will be hard for us to do if we continue to put evil in our spirit. We have to make a decision to stop looking at movies and reading books that are filled with evil, and start reading the word of God which is "The Good Book". Once we fill our spirit with the truth inside the word of God, then we will immediately be able to recognize what is really good.

Honesty Is the Best Policy

Romans 12:17b
Be careful to do what is right in the eyes of everyone.

You have no right to give some inmates more than you give to others. If you are in a state facility, everything except for the few possessions in your locker belong to the state. Therefore, if you find yourself in a position that allows you to distribute to other inmates, you should always give the amount you are told.

One of my responsibilities as a prison chapel worker was to pass out greeting cards to inmates upon their request. It grieved my spirit when I saw one of my coworkers, who claims to be a Christian, handle this task dishonestly. All of the chapel workers were instructed to give each inmate seven cards. However, I watched my coworker hand out 13 and 14 cards again and again to friends of hers, or to those who buy stolen goods from her. Yet, whenever she came across a request from an inmate who was not a friend of hers, who was not popular by man's standards, who didn't have financial support or who was just someone she couldn't benefit from, she made sure they received seven of the most plain, least favorite cards that were hardly ever requested.

The word of God teaches us that we are not to have respect of persons (James 2:9). There are no exceptions to this. You may be making many people happy, but you are doing so at the expense of your reputation. When it comes down to it, these people see you as the dishonest person you are. Your coworkers will see you as someone who can't be trusted, but if you repent of your evil ways and start treating everyone equally, God will see you as if you had never done anything wrong.

Order in the Church

1 Corinthians 14:40
But everything should be done in a fitting and orderly way.

Disrespectful behavior is all too common. Sadly, this is even the case during church services. It is almost necessary to hand out a list of rules before entering the chapel.

Every time I go to church I go expecting. I go expecting answers to prayers through the speaker, I go expecting Confirmation, a rhema word and anything else God has for me.

When the word of God is being preached, we should give the man or woman of God the respect they deserve. It is impossible to do this when we are engrossed in a conversation. The Lord may be trying to speak to us through the speaker; if we are busy talking, we will miss what God is trying to say to us.

Popping gum is another thing we shouldn't do in church. On several occasions. I was moved to ask an inmate to please stop popping their gum in church. Even one of the volunteers had to ask one of the inmates not to pop gum in church. Popping gum in church is rude and a distraction and this is why we shouldn't do it.

I have witnessed inmates gather in the gym to watch the Drama Club perform or inmates perform in a talent show and no one would get up to use the restroom because they didn't want to miss anything. Yet as soon as the preacher starts to preach, one after the other gets up to use the restroom. It is understandable that sometimes we must excuse ourselves, but most times we can avoid this. Getting up and down interrupts the flow of the Spirit and this can also send a negative sign to the speaker. The word of God tells us to do everything decently and in order (1 Corinthians 14:40, KJV). We are totally out of order when we are talking, eating, popping gum and moving around in church. Let us come to order and listen with undivided attention.

True Rest

Matthew 11:28
Come to me, all you who are weary and burdened, and I will give you rest.

Street drugs hold many people in bondage. Most of the time God has to step in and lock them away, just to free them. Maybe this is the case with you; if it is, fight to stay free and don't allow Satan to deceive you into taking a substitute.

There are a large number of inmates at LCIW who take medicine for depression. Most of these people admit they have never before taken medication for depression and the only reason they claim to take them while in prison is to sleep. They believe their nights are restless without these drugs.

Before you came to prison, Satan was trying to use drugs to destroy you. However, God intervened on your behalf. Satan is not about to give up on you, he wants to kill you (John 10:10), this is why he is causing you to think you can't rest without medicine. This is a trick of the enemy. If you never took depression medication before your incarceration, your only reason for taking it now is to substitute your drug of choice for any drug that is available.

Stop choosing to allow drugs to trouble your heart (John 14:1). The Lord has set you free and who the Son makes free is free indeed (John 8:36). Drugs can't give you rest but Jesus can. In fact, this is his promise to you, all you have to do is come to him (Matthew 11:28). His arms are wide open and he's waiting on you to come and experience the only true rest there is.

A New Life

2 Corinthians 5:17
Therefore, if anyone is in Christ, the new creation has come: The old has gone, the new is here!

Taking drugs not prescribed to you can be very dangerous, maybe even fatal. Besides, as a new creature in Christ, your old lifestyle of drugs has passed away and should not be a part of your new life.

One of the ladies who was formerly a drug addict continued to keep such a mindset even in prison. There wasn't anything this woman wouldn't sell to purchase pills from another inmate. She allowed nothing to stop her from getting pills from someone who was foolish and cunning enough to sneak their pills during medication call.

Ninety-nine percent of those incarcerated have actually committed a crime. However, I believe the real reason God allowed us to be caught is so we could be saved from the wicked ways that were leading us to destruction. Drug abuse is the testimony of so many and now they are in no position to get the drugs of their addiction, they have decided to buy prescription drugs from others.

If drugs controlled your life on the streets, you cannot continue to let drugs control your life now that you are incarcerated. As a new creature in Christ Jesus, you can no longer be associated with your old lifestyle. Make up your mind to celebrate the new creature you are: say no to drugs and yes to Jesus.

To God Be the Glory

1 Corinthians 10:31
So whether you eat or drink or whatever you do, do it all for the glory of God.

Our past miry clay experiences aren't anything to boast about. Yet often we do so anyway. We shouldn't be caught talking about the sins of our past unless it is done to the glory of God.

It is almost impossible to get through the day without hearing someone brag about the terrible, sinful life they once lived. Sin is very serious, and nothing to laugh about. I believe it is safe to say that your perspective in life has not changed if you still get a kick out of talking about the people you robbed or about all the drugs you used, or how much you stole from merchants or whatever sinful life you lived. There is absolutely nothing funny about sin; in fact, it is something you should be ashamed of.

When I first started serving my prison term, I found myself telling people about the theft of goods charge I was convicted of. It wasn't done for fun and games, but so that people could see where I used to be and where I am now. I was one of the few inmates who had earned an excellent reputation and I was very proud of how God had changed my life. I rightfully directed all Glory to God. I would minister to some of the ladies I worked with, the ones I knew were stealing. I told them they must resist the temptation to steal while in prison because if they can't do it while inside, they won't be able to do it once released.

We are not condemned because of our past. God doesn't condemn us, neither should we condemn ourselves (Romans 8:1). This doesn't mean we should give glory to the devil by bragging about our mess. The next time you catch yourself talking about your past, make sure it's for the good of others and to the Glory of God.

Forgiven

Mark 10:27
Jesus looked at them and said, "With man this is impossible, but not with God; all things are possible with God."

Are you serving time for taking the life of another? If you are, I want you to know that if you have repented, God has forgiven you. Amazingly, He can also soften the hearts of the victim's family and cause them to forgive you, too.

Losing a family member to murder is a very hard pill to swallow. Unfortunately, so many families have been forced to swallow this pill. We have all probably seen or heard about the tears of angry loved ones, either on television, in courtrooms, or at pardon board hearings as they pour out their hearts while remembering the life of their deceased loved ones. The hatred and lack of forgiveness these families express for the perpetrator is all too real. Fortunately, God is real too and hatred is nothing for him to heal.

After Ava had served 15 years in prison, she received a letter from the sibling of her victim. This sibling wanted her to know that God had taken away the hate he had toward her and that he had forgiven her a long time ago. This sibling went on to say he believed in second chances and that he would do everything in his power to help her regain her freedom.

Usually, when someone convicted of murder goes before the pardon board, it is a very slim chance for the pardon to be granted when the victim's family is against the inmate's release. Most families find it hard to get past this hatred. This is why you should make it your business to sincerely pray for your victim's family. Don't ever think the hatred they feel toward you is impossible for God to change. Remember, God is a God who specializes in impossibilities. Nothing is too hard for God (Genesis 18:14), not even causing your victim's family to forgive you.

We Can't Be Friends

1 Thessalonians 5:22
Reject every kind of evil.

The devil is very cunning. He can make it look like our actions are harmless. The things we are doing may not be evil in themselves but the appearance may very well be; if this is the case, we must abstain from these things.

Two ladies who were once in a homosexual relationship with each other both accepted the call for salvation yet continued to hang out together every day. The first one to arrive at the cafeteria would always save a seat for the other. After observing the behavior of these two for a while, I was led to ask them about their relationship. They expressed that they were just friends and went on to say nothing was wrong with them hanging out together. This is so far from the truth.

As Christians, we are obligated to live right before others and to live the same when we are all alone. If the Lord has delivered you from homosexuality you have no business tampering with this lifestyle. It is not wise to be friends with someone you were once in a homosexual relationship with, neither is it wise to be in the company of other homosexual couples. Your association with these people may be totally innocent, but you must agree that it doesn't appear that way.

Wherefore let him that think he stand take heed lest he fall (1 Corinthians 10:12, KJV). You will fall if you continue to play around with sin. It will behoove you to start choosing who you surround yourself with carefully. Start hanging out with other believers who can help you to stand strong.

A Problem Washed Away

Proverbs 21:5
The plans of the diligent lead to profit as surely as haste leads to poverty.

Hard work has its benefits. A diligent behavior will always pay off. Try putting this into practice and you will avoid many self-made problems.

In prison, laundry day always ends up in confusion. Some complain that their clothes did not come back or that they were not cleaned properly. Others complain their laundry was returned wet and then you have those who murmur that their white clothes are no longer white. These are just a few of the complaints made by inmates who send their clothes out to be washed.

Throughout my incarceration, the Holy Spirit always admonished me regarding any decision I had to make. The Holy Spirit warned me not to send my clothes out to be washed with the general compound. Instead, I was led to practice diligence by washing my clothes by hand. There were many times I didn't feel like hand washing, but I didn't give in to what I felt. I knew if I had chosen the easy way I would have found myself in the same boat as everyone else.

I understand that hand washing isn't always possible. Large and /or heavy garments have to be sent out because there is no way to dry them but definitely do so for those items that can be easily washed by hand. Don't allow petty problems that can be avoided to bother you. Eliminate these problems by making diligence a part of your life.

How Soon Do We Forget

Deuteronomy 8:14
Then your heart will become proud and you will forget the Lord your God, who brought you out of Egypt, out of the land of slavery.

We may be able to fool people, but we can't ever fool God although sometimes we act as if we can. The God we serve is omniscient; He knows everything, even our reason for attending church.

Looking back, when one of the ladies was very ill, I can recall her going back and forth to the infirmary with terrible migraines. Despite how she felt, she made sure she attended church and Bible study. After several visits to the infirmary and fainting a few times, this inmate ended up going to the hospital where it was discovered she had an aneurism. When this young lady came back from the hospital one section of her head was shaved and she had stitches but she looked so much better. She said she felt better, too. After that, there was no need for this girl to return to the infirmary, neither did she see a need to continue going to church. After all, she was healed.

In Deuteronomy 8:14, God had to remind the Israelites about all that he had brought them through. God knew how quickly we forget after we receive a blessing. This lady had no problem calling on God during her illness but as soon as she received her healing, God was out of the picture.

We can't fool God -- God knows our heart. He already knows that after He heals you He will not hear from you again until you need him. The good news is God doesn't bless you based on who you are but because of who He is.

Ungodly Counsel Divides

1 Corinthians 6:1
If any of you has a dispute with another, do you dare to take it before the ungodly for judgment instead of before the Lord's people?

There will be times when believers may engage in a dispute; this shouldn't be, but it happens. As Christians, we should strive to keep peace with everyone, especially other believers. If you ever find yourself disputing, be sure not to seek counsel from the ungodly.

My spirit is always grieved whenever I see a believer go to an unbeliever for counsel on how to handle a situation regarding another believer. Whenever we do this we are opening up the door for Satan to bring division among the body of Christ -- when this happens, it is difficult for the body to function as a whole. After all, a house divided against itself can't stand (Matthew 12:25, KJV). It is okay for believers to disagree, as we all have opinions and different beliefs. With this in mind, we must respect one another.

Coming up, I can recall disputing with my siblings. Whatever was said in our home was not discussed with our neighbors; as a family unit we dealt with any problems we had in the privacy of our home, without the help of outside intervention.

Christians are not perfect. There may come a time when a Christian may wrong you in some way. If this happens to you, don't make matters worse by going to the ungodly for counsel. If you simply must talk to someone, ask God to lead you to a strong believer or take it to God and leave it there.

Keep Hope Alive

Romans 4:19-21

Without weakening in his faith, he faced the fact that his body was as good as dead since he was about a hundred years old and that Sarah's womb was also dead. Yet he did not waver through unbelief regarding the promise of God but was strengthened in his faith and gave glory to God, being fully persuaded that God had power to do what he had promised.

Some of us are faced with lengthy sentences. Don't allow Satan to use your long prison term to discourage you. Don't listen to him when he tells you that you are never going home.

There were many times that Satan tried to use the 20-year sentence that man gave me to make me lose focus. However, I didn't let him succeed. I believed with everything in me that I wasn't going to serve 20 years in prison. Never once did I say when I go home I'll be 49 years old. Every Christmas that came I said that it was my last. When I found myself still incarcerated yet another Christmas, I still was confident I would not spend 20 years in prison, and that this Christmas will be my last one spent in prison. Well, seven more Christmases have passed since then and I still believe my time to be released is coming soon.

Abraham didn't doubt God. God told him that he was going to father a child. Abraham was 100 years old when his son, Isaac was born (Genesis 21:5). The Bibles says Abraham didn't even stagger at the promise (Romans 4:20, KJV).

My bags are packed and I'm ready to go. I know that man may say I have ten more years to serve but I refuse to believe this. I am standing on the promises of God regarding my legal situation. I'm absolutely sure that my release is drawing nigh. It doesn't matter to me what it looks like, every second I'm expecting.

Regardless of how much time you're serving, God is a God of many chances. If it is God's will, he can turn your situation around. Just take him at his word and don't you dare stagger.

Facing Reality

2 Samuel 12:18a
On the seventh day the child died.

For the most part, we all are incarcerated because of some crime we committed. As difficult as it may be to face, the consequences of some of our crimes will be unto death. I know this is not easy to accept, but God can help you to do so anyway.

God told Moses to speak to the rock. Moses disobeyed God and instead he struck the rock. As a result, Moses was not allowed to enter the Promised Land (Numbers 20:7:12).

David was known as a man after God's own heart (Acts 13:22). David wanted Bathsheba so badly that he conspired to have her husband Uriah killed (2 Samuel 11:14-17). As a result of David's sin, the son he had with Bathsheba died. David fasted and prayed but God still allowed his son to die.

Paul went to God regarding something in his life that was not easy for him to bear. Yet, whatever this thing was God did not remove it. God assured Paul that his grace was sufficient (2 Corinthians 12:9, KJV).

There are many who are serving time for very serious offenses. Although man judges crime differently, in God's eyes they all are sin. Nonetheless, if you have given your life to Jesus Christ, whatever you did is under the blood. Unfortunately, being under the blood does not erase the consequences you may have to face.

The fact of the matter is God will not deliver everyone from incarceration. Some inmates will spend the rest of their lives in prison. If by chance this is your situation, cry out to God and ask him to help you face reality.

Don't Hate

Romans 12:15
Rejoice with those who rejoice; mourn with those who mourn.

It is so easy to succumb to the tricks of the enemy. Discouragement and bitterness are just two of the many tricks Satan uses. Don't allow the devil to cause you to become discouraged and/or bitter over someone else's good report.

One day I received some really good news from the court. I was so excited, I went around telling everyone about the good news. To my surprise, it became obvious that not too many people were happy for me. I was elated because of my good news and I had assumed others wanted to share in my excitement, but this was not the case. The reactions I got from the majority saddened me deeply and caused me to want to keep my good news to myself in the future. In fact, I will be going back to court soon and I am certain I will be released, but this time I refuse to broadcast the news.

The majority of those who are incarcerated would like to go home; this is truly understandable. However, your season may not be my season and my season may not be yours.

Whenever someone gets a time cut or immediate release, don't allow the enemy to cause you to become bitter or angry. God can do the same for you and he will if you just stop hating on the next person. Sincerely rejoice with this individual and know that you could very well be next in line for a miracle.

Partaker

1 Corinthians 10:21
You cannot drink the cup of the Lord and the cup of demons too; you cannot have a part in both the Lord's table and the table of demons.

Homosexuality is prevalent in the prison system. Although this is true, it is not our place to condemn those who practice this sin. As Christians, we must love these people, but loving them does not require partaking in their lifestyle.

When I first arrived in prison, I recall going to work one morning and having an inmate tell me to tell her girlfriend that she loved her. I could have kept silent, gone to work and not passed the message on, but I didn't want my silence misinterpreted. Therefore, it was important that I take the opportunity to minister. I told the girl that I would not give her girlfriend the message. I expressed to her that if I was to do so then I would be partaking in her sin. The girl didn't say anything in response, she just looked at me as if though I was crazy.

All too often I have witnessed people who said they are Christians pass such messages and relate to females as males and vice versa. God did not make any mistakes. He said that everything he created was good (Genesis 1:31). Now that you know this, stop referring to females as your brother or daddy, and stop calling men, women. There is no place for lukewarm Christians in the kingdom; besides, Jesus says he will spit you out of his mouth (Revelation 3:15-16, NIV).

Be a bright light where you are. Give God glory with the way you live. In order for you to do this, start by refusing to partake in the sins of others.

We Are One

1 Corinthians 12:12
Just as a body, though one, has many parts, but all its many parts form one body, so it is with Christ.

God can use anyone. He used David, who was an adulterer (2 Samuel 11:4) and a murderer (2 Samuel 11:1517). He used Rahab who was a prostitute (Hebrews 11:31). Believe it or not, he will use you, too if you let him. There is no need for you to be envious of what he's called another believer to do. Their calling is not your calling, neither is your calling theirs. For we are many members in one body, and all members have not the same function (Romans 12:4, NIV). You are the body of Christ, and each one is a part of it (1 Corinthians 12:27, NIV).

We don't all have the same gifts. God has given me various gifts, one of which is singing. Fortunately, he has also given this same gift to many others. Although many of us all have the gift of song, our gifts are still unique. When we all put our gifts together and lift up the Lord, it is then we are bringing him glory.

Stop concerning yourself with what someone else is doing or not doing and do your part. We all have a part in the body and we all need to do that which we are gifted to do. The gifts you possess are designed just for you, so use them wisely and don't concern yourself with the talents you don't have.

Who Is The Leader?

Deuteronomy 17:15
Be sure to appoint over you a king the Lord your God chooses. He must be from among your fellow Israelites. Do not place a foreigner over you, one who is not an Israelite.

I miss being able to make choices for myself. In the past, I made many unfortunate decisions. Now, with the few choices that I do have, I am sure to make them wisely.

There are several different organizations an inmate can choose to be a part of. I was all set to do the right things and get myself involved in positive activities. I checked out some of the clubs that were available, and even decided to join one of them. It didn't take long before I realized I didn't want to be a part of that group; from the outside everything looked okay, but this was not the case. The leader was not a Christian. I knew I couldn't have this individual leading me and as a result, I chose to leave this group.

In the book of Deuteronomy, God gave the Israelites some guidelines for choosing a king; the main thing he said was that the king could not be a stranger (Deuteronomy 17:15). In other words, the Lord told them the leader they chose must be a believer; God knows the outcome of placing an unbeliever in a position of authority.

Don't just join different clubs because your friends are in them -- it is important that you look into them first. Besides, if what you are a part of does not have a Christian leader in place, I then question whether you are a part of anything at all.

God Is Watching

Deuteronomy 6:18
Do what is right and good in the Lord's sight, so that it may go well with you and you may go in and take over the good land the Lord promised on oath to your ancestors

Security is not always present to watch inmates. Whenever they are not, this is when inmates sneak around doing everything they are not supposed to. They act as if they are not being watched at all.

People such as myself are determined to obey the rules. We are those who are tired of doing the same old foolish things and getting the same foolish results. We are the people who, deep down inside, just know there has to be a better way and have decided to go that direction by accepting Jesus Christ as our Lord and Savior. We know that although security may not be around at all times, God is omnipresent and we are commanded to do that which is right and good in the sight of the Lord (Deuteronomy 6:18).

When Moses left the people to go up to Mount Sinai to receive the Ten Commandments from the Lord, the people decided to make a golden calf idol and engage in all kind of ungodliness. God knew exactly what they were doing, even if Moses did not. God saw every evil thing they had done (Exodus 32:1-9).

We are all adults. Security shouldn't have to be around for us to do that which is right and good. We are commanded to do so. Next time you decide to sneak around committing all types of ungodliness, remember that the God who never slumbers is all-knowing; He sees all and He is watching.

To God Be the Glory

1Peter 5:6
Humble yourselves, therefore, under God's mighty hand, that he may lift you up in due time.

People who volunteer are useful and needed in a church service. Volunteering in itself is good. There is absolutely nothing wrong with willingly being active in church unless we are only doing so to exalt ourselves.

God has blessed many of us with gifts and talents. Singing, dancing, preaching, and teaching are just a few of those gifts. He has given all of us abilities.

There may be times when you are truly led to get up and sing or dance at a church service. There are other times when people ask a volunteer to allow them to sing or dance just for show. They want people to know how well they can sing or dance as though they gave themselves the gift. God is the one who gave you the gift and you should use it to glorify him (1Peter 4:11). Don't always be so quick to jump up to sing or dance; keep your seat and wait to be called upon. Wait on God to exalt you and stop trying to exalt yourself. Exalting yourself is pride and it will cause you to be humbled (Luke 14:11, KJV).

Your flesh will take over if you let it, so don't allow it to do so. Stop being the one to always get up in church to do something, sit down and let someone else share their gifts. But again I express that you please do get up if you are led and if you are doing it to give glory to God. When God exalts you there is no coming down, but whenever you try to exalt yourself, you may succeed momentarily but be sure to prepare yourself for the fall.

Judging Other Believers

Matthew 7:1-2
Do not judge, or you too will be judged. For in the same way you judge others, you will be judged, and with the measure you use, it will be measured to you.

We are all expected to judge. Judging others is never easy. This is why you should be sure to use a righteous standard anytime you find yourself in a position to judge.

Living in such close proximity with other believers, we witness much ungodly behavior; and these actions should never be ignored. We are responsible for going to a believer who we find in fault (Galatians 6:1, KJV).

In 1 Corinthians 5 we read that there was a believer in the church who was involved in sexual immorality. The members of the church tried to ignore the sin of this believer instead of dealing with it. Paul, on the other hand, refused to ignore the sin of this man. Paul didn't condemn this man but he used the righteous measure which is the word of God to deal with this man's sin. After all, we are called not to judge by how things appear but to make a righteous judgment (John 7:24, KJV).

Believers are called to judge other believers (1 Corinthians 5:12-13, KJV). The measure a believer uses to judge should be one of love and humility. If we use this measure to judge someone, then this same righteous measure will be used to judge us.

Judgment and condemnation are two different things. We should not condemn people because it tears them down. However, a righteous judgment will help build them up.

If you are using the word of God in context as your standard and not worldly measures, then you have nothing to worry about. The next time you find yourself in a position to judge be sure to check the measure you are using before you proceed. Oh, and check yourself too.

God Awaits Your Return

Deuteronomy 4:30-31
When you are in distress and all these things have happened to you, then in later days you will return to the Lord your God and obey him. For the Lord your God is a merciful God; he will not abandon or destroy you or forget the covenant with your ancestor, which he confirmed to them by oath.

Don't ever think that someone is too far gone for Christ to reach. The farther away we are makes the miracle even greater. The same God who reached us still has his hand outstretched for others to come in.

Sins practiced by unbelievers are known by everyone. There is no such thing as privacy when serving time in prison. Everyone knows what everyone does. Many of the unbelievers I have encountered live very degrading lifestyles. Sometimes we may be reluctant to reach out to these people, thinking that there is just no hope for them. Well I have news for you, there is hope for these people so don't give up on them. Besides, God didn't give up on them and he most certainly didn't give up on us. It is our responsibility to show the love of Christ to these individuals through how we live before them. God doesn't want anyone to perish (2 Peter 3:9, KJV). We must continue to win souls for the kingdom. Don't concern yourself with not seeing any change. You can't change anyone so leave this up to God, the only one who can. Just allow God to use you to minister to lost souls and he will draw them (John 6:44). The same God who saved you from the mess you were in will most definitely save them from their mess. Remember, he is the same God, yesterday, today, and forever (Hebrews 13:8).

God loves you so much. He will take you back just as you are. You don't have to clean yourself up first either, he is willing to do it for you.

Transformed Little by Little

Deuteronomy 7:22
The Lord your God will drive out those nations before you, little by little. You will not be allowed to eliminate them all at once, or the wild animals will multiply around you.

No one came into this world walking and talking. We went from being carried, to crawling, then finally we were able to walk. This was all a process that gradually came to pass.

When my daughter was born she was 5lbs. 8ozs. and 19 inches long. On a regular basis I took her to see a pediatrician. Every time she visited her doctor I noticed that her weight and height had changed. At the writing of this book, my daughter is 18 years old, 110 pounds and 5'7" tall. My daughter didn't go from being the little person she was at the time of her birth to her present weight and height overnight, it was a process that took almost two decades.

The Lord told Moses that the children of Israel would inhabit the Promised Land. Before they were able to do so, the Lord was going to put out the nations before them little by little (Deuteronomy 7:22).

Here at LCIW there are many church services to choose from. It is very common to see inmates get up and go to the altar for the call to salvation. It is also common to see these same people, who said they accepted Christ as their Lord and Savior living the same way they were before they were saved. The reason for this is that they are still babes. It will take time for them to grow spiritually – a gradual process, just like physical growth.

Before my daughter was able to walk properly, she fell down quite a lot, yet I was always right there to pick her up. We believers should be the same with the babes in our spiritual family.

Don't Give in to Jealousy

1 Corinthians 13:4c
……love does not envy

To be envious or jealous-hearted is serious. Many people may deny feelings of envy or jealousy yet, when you make a negative accusation against someone based on what you think they think, you are walking in jealousy.

Does this statement ring true to you?

'She thinks she's too much.'

If this is something you find yourself saying about someone, you are jealous of that individual. It is impossible for you to know the thoughts of someone else, only God is capable of knowing our thoughts.

Usually, when someone makes accusations against you based on their thoughts, this is because they have no solid evidence on which to base their accusations on. The lifestyle they see you living is an upright one, the words they hear you speak are edifying. When people who right out refuse to apply the Word to their life witness you doing so, it intimidates them. They desperately want to walk the same walk but just can't seem to do it, therefore they begin to walk in envy and jealousy and, as a result, they make up lies to try to tear you down. This is the only way these people can feel good about themselves.

Allowing yourself to succumb to envy and jealousy is very dangerous. God considered David an upright man, a man after God's own heart (Acts 13:22, KJV), yet this didn't stop King Saul from wanting to kill David. Saul was so jealous of David that he wanted him dead (1 Samuel 18:9-11). This very dangerous sin caused Saul to lose complete control and it will do the same to you if you yield to it.

Destruction of Property

Ecclesiastes 10:18
Through laziness, the rafters sag: because of idle hands, the house leaks.

Many problems can be eliminated if we simply learn how to practice diligence every day of our lives. This is not a hard thing to do; in fact, not doing it makes things much harder.

Throwing foreign objects into the toilets are common among inmates -- I've seen inmates flush both paper and plastic. Female inmates have a bad habit of flushing sanitary napkins. This can cause serious plumbing issues requiring the city or state to spend money unnecessarily, funds that can most definitely be better spent. You may be wondering why on earth am I concerned about the state and its plumbing problems. As Christians we should all share this concern. We shouldn't misuse anything, especially if it doesn't belong to us. The Word of God says if you be faithful in that which is another man, I'll give you your own (Luke 16:12, KJV). You don't want to be looked upon as slothful or lazy. Whenever you don't take the time to properly dispose of your sanitary products this is exactly what you are.

Ladies, when that time of the month comes around again don't throw your pads in the toilet, or in the little trash pal in your room or cell. Instead dispose of these items properly by wrapping them in paper and walking to the garbage can to throw them away. This may require a little more work but it will prevent plumbing issues and problems with your roommate or the people on your dorm so just be diligent and stop destroying property.

Forgive and Remember No More

Jeremiah 31:34
…….for I will forgive their wickedness and will remember their sins no more.

We should all practice walking in forgiveness. This is not optional; it is required of us. Moreover, you do not have to forget about what someone did to you to forgive them.

Often times I have heard people say I forgive but I won't forget. Usually such a statement is made tritely but in reality, this is the truth: we can't forget, nor are we designed to forget something just because we want to. We can, however, choose to remember no more. Remembering takes so much energy. It is the act of memory, it is recalling a thought back to our mind so we can think about it.

When I was about 12 years old, myself and several other kids who lived in my neighborhood were approached by a man who saw that one of the girls with me had money in her hand. He ran toward us and snatched my friend's money. Sometime later I saw him in a store. Immediately, I recognized him and began to think about that night again. I didn't forget what this man did but I didn't have to ponder on the memory either.

If God would allow us to forget everything someone did to us then he wouldn't be able to test us in this area. If we forgot every bad thing done to us, there would be no need to forgive. God doesn't expect you to forget but when you see the person who wronged you he wants you to choose not to call that thing back to memory. God doesn't forget our sins. The Bible says he will remember them no more (Jeremiah 31:34). Let's follow this perfect example by no longer remembering what was done to us.

Dismiss the Slander

Proverbs 14:15
The simple believe anything, but the prudent give thought to their steps.

We shouldn't be so quick to believe a bad report told to us about someone. Some bad reports may be true but if you don't have facts, consider it false. Learn how to be adamant about not believing foolishness.

Much talk is heard about others when living in a prison environment, most of which is usually negative. We shouldn't believe everything we hear. If we do, the word of God says that we are simple (Proverbs 14:15). When I first came to prison I quickly noticed that people like to slander other people. Once, I remember talking with someone who told me that a certain individual has AIDS. I told that lady I wasn't going to believe her simply because she had said it, because I wasn't simple. I went on to tell her no one would be aware of that person's medical diagnosis unless she chose to reveal it herself and even if she did tell you, you don't have the right to tell me. The fact that she would tell me this says way more about her character than it did about the lady.

Don't entertain anyone who tells you bad things about another. More importantly, don't believe it. What the person tells you could very well be the truth, but it still doesn't give you a reason to go around spreading a bad report.

Believe the Good

1Corinthians 13:7b
……love always trusts.

My word is very valuable to me. When I speak, I have no reason to expect that people think I'm lying, nor do I think people are lying to me. When we take our brethren at their word we are walking in one of the characteristics of love.

One of my sisters-in-Christ who worked in the kitchen had a problem with stealing from her job. Over and over again she gave in to this temptation. One evening she got up at a church service and confessed this sin to the congregation. She appeared to be very sorrowful and asked everyone to pray that she would stop taking things out of the kitchen -- not too long after this, my sister told me she was no longer practicing this sin and was really proud of herself for not giving in to temptation.

A few weeks later it was brought to my attention that my sister was stealing out the kitchen again. Immediately, I went to her, told her what I heard and asked if it was true. With tears in her eyes, she assured me she had not taken anything from the kitchen since the time she and I had last spoken about it. After hearing this, I had no more to say; I told her that I loved her and I believed her.

The next time your Christian sister or brother tell you something, believe what they say. Don't be quick to doubt them, especially if you love them as you say you do. Besides we should always be ready and willing to believe a good report.

Who's My Neighbor?

Luke 10:27
He answered, 'Love the Lord your God with all your heart and with all your soul and with all your strength and with all your mind'; and, 'Love your neighbor as yourself'.

When I came to prison I thought I was pretty okay with loving people. I learned that I had to love my neighbor. At first I thought it would be easy, until I saw in the Bible who my neighbors were.

I know, you're thinking about the neighbor who lives right next door to your home. Yes, this is still your neighbor, but let's deal with the neighbors in prison with you right now. Like the neighbor who sleeps on the bunk over you who never likes to shower, or the one they moved into the room with you who spits in the sink and doesn't clean it out. How about the one who takes it upon themselves to use your personal things without permission. Yes, even the one who slams the lockers while you are sleeping and constantly calls you out of your name. All of these people are your neighbors; they may do things you don't like and may very well be difficult people to deal with, but God already knows all of this and he still says: Thou should love the Lord your God with all your heart, and with all your soul, and with all your strength, and with all your mind, and your neighbor as yourself (Luke 10:27).

We are all in prison at the present time and we can't allow ourselves to let the things people do or say stop us from loving them. We are commanded to love. Make up your mind to push past the faults of others -- don't allow their actions to define yours. Besides, if God loved us based on what we did we would all be in bad shape.

Respect the Mean Guards, Too

Romans 13:1
Let everyone be subject to the governing authorities, for there is no authority except that which God has established. The authorities that exist have been established by God.

None of us are children. We are all adults who do not like to be ordered around by other adults, especially when some of the adults ordering us around are young enough to be our children. However, we have placed ourselves in a position where we are required to follow orders. When security give us an order, it should be obeyed: not when we feel like obeying it, but immediately. Even when a guard is very mean to us, we are still required to respect and obey them.

Throughout my incarceration, I have encountered many guards with terrible attitudes. They would scream at inmates for absolutely no reason, harassing us just because they knew they could. Some would even use other inmates to pick on you to get you in trouble. All these things are wrong and no one should be subjected to such, especially by someone who has authority over you. Sadly, such abuse does take place, but regardless of what the guards do we must give them respect.

After Saul heard the women singing a song glorifying David for having a greater slaughter than Saul, this caused Saul to become jealous of David (1 Samuel 18:6-9). Saul became so jealous of David that he tried to kill him on more than one occasion (1 Samuel 18:11, 23:8). David had the opportunity to kill Saul but refused to do so; it didn't matter to him how badly Saul wanted him dead, because he respected Saul as God's anointed (1 Samuel 24:10).

Servants are to be subjects to their masters with all fear, not only to the good and gentle, but also to the froward (1 Peter 2:18 KJV). We are obligated to respect the guards no matter how they treat us. We just have to trust God to deal with them. After all, vengeance is his and he will repay (Romans 12:1, KJV). We must believe this and continue to do our part, trusting God to do his.

Stop Hindering Your Prayers

John 9:31
We know that God does not listen to sinners.
He listens to the godly person who does his will.

Prayer is extremely important in my life; in fact, prayer **is** my life, my only means of communicating with God. We shouldn't do anything that will cause this line of communication to be blocked, yet when we live in sin this is exactly what we are doing.

In the first chapter of the book of Isaiah we find that Isaiah brought a message of divine judgment for both Israel and Judah. Israel and Judah were so far into their mess that God wouldn't even hear their prayers. 'And when you spread forth your hands, I will hide mine eyes from you: yea, when you make many prayers, I will not hear: your hands are full of blood' (Isaiah 1:15, KJV). 'Therefore thus said the Lord, Behold, I will bring evil upon them, which they shall not be able to escape; and though they shall cry unto me, I will not hearken unto them' (Jeremiah 11:11, KJV). It is imperative that God hear us when we call. As you can see, there were times when he didn't hear the Israelites. We are no different from them. Moreover, they were his chosen people, but he still refused to hear their cry because of their sinful lives. The same God who didn't hear them is the same God who won't hear us if we are living a life of sin.

All too often I have witnessed inmates openly living a lifestyle of sin and who then have the audacity to think they can go to God, who they refuse to serve, in prayer. The only way God will hear our prayers is if we are praying a prayer of repentance; any other prayer he will not hear if you are practicing sin.

Don't gamble when it comes to prayer. Be certain your prayers are being heard. You can be confident of this when you are not practicing sin.

Guard Your Heart

John 14:1
Do not let your hearts be troubled. You believe in God; believe also in me.

We are responsible for the condition of our hearts. God knows we can handle this responsibility through the Holy Spirit. God has given us the power over our own hearts so why don't you stop allowing it to be troubled.

If your heart is troubled, maybe it's because of your belief system: people do act on what they believe. If you are faced with a sickness today, and if you believe you serve the God who heals, your heart shouldn't be troubled. Maybe you are allowing your heart to be troubled due to lack, then you just need to believe that God is your Jehovah-Jireh, who makes all grace abound in you and generously provides all you need (2 Corinthians 9:8, KJV). Maybe your heart is troubled because you have been wronged by the judicial system. You need to believe that you serve the God of justice, who is just and the one who justifies those who have faith in Jesus (Romans 3:26, KJV).

Whatever reason we are letting our hearts be troubled is not a good one. God allows us to be in charge of our hearts because He knows that He has already given us what it takes for our hearts not to be troubled. Trouble may be around you but it doesn't have to reside in your heart.

Mistreating Others

Romans 12:16a
Live in harmony with one another.

Finances should never play a part in how we treat people. As Christians, we should treat everyone with love and respect. When we don't, we lack stability. This is very important in your Christian walk; to remain stable we must strive to treat everyone the same.

Just because your Bunkie or your roommate does not get visits or have any financial support is no reason to mistreat them. Over and over again, I have witnessed people bond quickly with their Bunkie or roommate. Usually, this is because they are visited regularly and are fortunate enough to have money on their books. This individual could be an obnoxious person, doing all those irritating things most roommates hate; regardless of how many bad habits this person may have, her money will cause them to be overlooked. On the other hand, you can move someone with a beautiful attitude and a pleasant spirit in the room with this same person and she will make sure she does everything in her power to make her roommate's life miserable if she doesn't get any money.

The word of God tells us to do unto others as we would like them to do unto us (Matthew 7:12, KJV). You would not want someone mistreating you because of your lack of money, so you shouldn't be mistreating them, either. God does everything for a reason. Everyone who God allows us to come in contact with is for a reason and a purpose. This person could very well be an answer to your prayer. Are you praying to pass The GED test? Maybe your roommate is a GED tutor. Are you struggling with algebra or some other subject? Your roommate may be able to help you with these courses. If you need help learning how to read, perhaps your roommate can teach you. Stop looking at what a person doesn't have; your roommate may be an angel unaware (Hebrews 13:2, KJV).

Praise God for Your Possessions

Deuteronomy 5:6-7

I am the Lord your God, who brought you out of Egypt, out of the land of slavery. You shall have no other gods before me.

Sadly, many of us are incarcerated because we didn't have God as our focus. Instead we were focused on many little gods that were acting as idols in our lives; some of those gods are the reason we ended up in prison.

Unfortunately, too many of us are still allowing things to take our attention away from God. Whatever that thing is, is an idol. What may be an idol in your life may not be the same as someone else's, but if we don't have God as the center of our life who are whatever is, is an idol.

We must start understanding that God is the reason for everything we have. Your mother's name may very well be on the outside of the money order you received, but God is the one who allowed her to get the job she has and enabled her so that she can perform her duties and earn a paycheck. Don't begin praising your mother, start praising the God who allowed it to happen.

Your spouse may have sent you money to purchase things from the canteen to stock your lockers, but you shouldn't allow any of these things to become idols in your life. You have to humbly recognize the true source. It is good to have our needs met and to have the things we want, as long as we don't allow these things to have us.

Prophesying

1 John 4:1
Dear friends, do not believe every spirit, but test the spirits to see whether they are from God, because many false prophets have gone out into the world.

Only a fool wouldn't want someone to speak well of their life. However, anyone can talk a good talk. Just because someone is telling you what you want to hear does not make it true, you must try the spirit by the Spirit.

Throughout my incarceration I have heard many so-called 'prophecies' given at church services. The Bible tells us we shouldn't despise prophesying and I was mindful not to do so. Yet, I carefully listened to what was being prophesied. I wanted desperately to accept what was being predicted as truth but I had to handle the prophecy according to the word of God. "And if thou say in thine heart, how shall we know the word which the Lord hath not spoken? When a prophet speak in the name of the Lord, if the thing follow not, nor come to pass, that is the thing which the Lord hath not spoken, but the prophet hath spoken it presumptuously; thou shalt not be afraid of him" (Deuteronomy 18:21-22, KJV).

I am an inmate just like you are, and I would love to hear someone prophesy to me that I am going home after doing only nine years of my 20-year sentence. However, if this is not a word from the Lord I could hear this prophecy over and over again, and still find myself completing my entire sentence. I cannot express to you enough how badly I want to go home, but this will not cause me to believe I could get released in 30 days simply because it had been prophesied to me.

I truly believe in prophecy. Still, I am wise enough to know some prophesies are false. Do not get caught up with what someone has prophesied, but rather if what was prophesied actually comes to pass.

Peace Depends on You

John 14:27
Peace I leave with you; my peace I give you. I do not give to you as the world gives. Do not let your hearts be troubled and do not be afraid.

At some time, troubles will visit our lives. It will come to each and every one of us who live on this earth and it will come whether we are ready or not. Nevertheless, if we choose, even in the midst of the trouble we could have peace.

Your peace is not based on the roommate you have or on the dormitory to which you are assigned, the job you're classified to or the right warden being placed over the institution.
`These things I have spoken unto you, that in me you might have peace. In the world you shall have tribulation: but be of good cheer; I have overcome the world` (John 16:33). These are the words of Jesus himself, the only one who can give you peace. Your peace is found in him and no other. `This is the peace of God, which passes all understanding, this peace will keep your hearts and minds through Christ Jesus` (Philippians 4:7). God has already left you with the peace, now it is up to you to let the peace of God rule in your hearts, to the which also you are called in one body; and be thankful (Colossians 3:15, KJV).

The next time someone slanders your name, or your roommate says something ugly to you, remember that Jesus has left you with His peace and this is your opportunity to operate in it. Don't focus on what they said or did to you because this will cause you to take matters into your own hands. Instead, keep your focus on Jesus and pray for these people; this way you can still keep your peace.

Don't Focus on How Things Look

2 Corinthians 5:7
For we live by faith, not by sight.

Worrying about the time man gave you won't make it go away. We will only discourage ourselves if we constantly allow our thoughts to be consumed with how things appear. Although our situation may look as if there is no way out, walking by faith will allow your entire perspective to change.

While sitting in a church service one afternoon, an inmate who was sentenced to life asked if she could share a word with the congregation. This lady went on to say that she was going to appear in front of the pardon board in a couple of weeks and that she would be going home. She then told the volunteers that she would be joining their church upon release. I want you to know that this woman, who had spent almost 20 years in prison on a life sentence, received her pardon and was given immediate release just as she said. This lady didn't allow discouragement to creep into her spirit by allowing her thoughts to be captivated with thoughts of all the lifers who had been denied in the past. She didn't allow what she saw to hinder her faith walk.

This reminds me of a mighty man of faith -- I am speaking about Abraham. God told Abraham to offer up his son Isaac for a sacrifice. Abraham could not see how God was going to work this situation out, yet he believed that God would because Abraham told his servants that he and Isaac would come to them again (Genesis 22:5). This is what you call strong faith.

Inmates all have one thing in common: we all want to go home. If it is God's will we will all go home at the appointed time. Therefore, stop dwelling on how much time you have and put your faith in the all-powerful God who controls all time.

Ungodly Company

2 Corinthians 6:14
Do not be yoked together with unbelievers. For what do righteousness and wickedness have in common? Or what fellowship can light have with darkness?

Christians should not ostracize unbelievers. Neither should Christians casually hang out with them. Any association a Christian has with an unbeliever should be strictly centered on God and not the world.

Unbelievers are quick to say that Jesus hung out with sinners. I don't recall reading that anywhere in the Bible, but he did eat with sinners (Matthew 9:10). Jesus spent quality time with his disciples. Sometimes he kept company with only 12 of them (Matthew 10:14, 12:1) and there were other times when he only hung out with Peter, James, and John (Matthew 17:1).

I used to love to hang out with my so-called friends. Whenever I hung out with them it was usually for one reason -- we would all drink, party, and just have what we all considered a good time.

Jesus was not hanging out with sinners, He only ate with them. You had better believe that Jesus glorified his Father with everything he said and did. Jesus wasn't laughing at their dirty jokes or compromising to please them, not at all, He made sure to let his light shine. He did not let the unbelievers pull him into their way of living; instead, he led them into his.

As Christians, we should do everything we can to win unbelievers to the Lord. Yet, we should not think this means hanging out with them; after all, evil communication corrupts good manners (1 Corinthians 15:33, KJV). Whenever we find ourselves in the company of unbelievers, show them much love and be a Christlike example.

Live Like There Is a God

Psalms 14:1

The fool says in his heart, "There is no God." They are corrupt, their deeds are vile; there is no one who does good.

Atheists openly express that there is no God. Yet morally, atheists live fairly decent lives. What's ironic is many people who say they are Christians, just like atheists, also express that there is no God. The only difference is that the atheists says there is no God with their mouths and those who say that they are Christians say there is no God with their lives.

Do you know that whenever we decide to live like the Bible does not exist and instead live the way we want to live that we are saying there is no God? If you really believe that there is a God then why are you stealing? The Lord is your Shepherd; you shall not want (Psalm23:1, KJV). This means God will supply all of our needs so we must live like we believe this.

If we really believe there is a God then why are we mistreating people when we are commanded to do unto others as we want others to do unto us (Matthew 7:12, KJV). This means we need to stop swearing at people and saying nasty things about them regardless of whether they are true are not.

Security did not put you in prison, your judge did as a result of a choice you made. Security is not your enemy. If you really believed that there is a God you would respect authority. Let every soul be subject unto the higher powers, for there is no power but of God. The powers that be are ordained of God (Romans 13:1).

God deserves our praise. He deserves it because He is worthy of it, not just when we are in church but all the time. Keep this in mind and stop living any way you want and start living in a way that screams, 'there is a God'!

Sow Good Seeds

Galatians 6:7
Do not be deceived: God cannot be mocked. A man reaps what he sows.

Before my incarceration I never planted anything. Yet, when I was classified to work in the field one of my duties was to plant seeds. I'll be the first to admit that I still don't know much about planting but I do know that when my supervisor said she wanted to reap beets, I had to sow beet seeds.

'God is not a man that he should lie; neither the son of man, that he should repent' (Numbers 23:19, KJV). We have been warned through the Holy Scriptures that while the earth remains, seedtime and harvest, cold and heat, summer and winter, and day and night shall not cease (Genesis 8:22, KJV). For the rest of our lives we will harvest, according to the seeds we plant.

Cain killed his brother Abel (Genesis 4:8). As a result, he was punished severely (Genesis 4:11-13). Judas betrayed our Lord and Savior Jesus Christ (Matthew 27:47-49) then later he hung himself (Matthew 27:5). Rahab hid the two men who were sent out by Joshua to spy out the Promised Land (Joshua 2:4). For this courageous act, Rahab the harlot did not perish (Hebrews 11:31, KJV).

When you curse security or try to attack them physically, you will be placed in maximum security. You may even get rebooked. You can pray about it or fast for however long but you still must reap what you sow. Therefore, it will behoove you to sow good seeds.

Inmates are quick to say that security could have let us slide, they could have given me another chance. God gave all of us another chance when he blessed us with our incarceration, yet some of us are still choosing to plant bad seeds. If we want to reap a good harvest it is imperative that we plant good seeds.

Strive to Show Mercy

Luke 6:36
Be merciful, just as your Father is merciful.

When I look back over my life, I can recall countless times when God was merciful to me. Many of us were probably looking at more years than we ultimately received, but because of God's mercy we didn't get the time we deserved. Mercy is freely extended to us over and over again. In the same manner we should be sure to extend mercy to others.

When I came across Luke 6:36 it was very hard for me to apply this scripture. My flesh did not want to cooperate. I was perfectly okay with God supplying me with his mercy; but I had a problem with being merciful with those who wronged me in some way.

One of my roommates insisted on telling lies about me and saying really bad things about me. This girl was known for slandering my name. Every time my roommate lied about me or to me, she always apologized whenever the lie caught up with her. If my roommate wasn't lying about me, she was doing something else to try to attack my character. I even walked up to her several times while she was in the act. This vexed me a great deal, I didn't believe I needed to show mercy to my roommate because I had convinced myself she didn't deserve it. Immediately, the Spirit reminded me how I, too am so undeserving of God's mercy. How could I forget that?

Prison life is not easy. We will encounter people from all walks of life. We will come across people who will lie about us, and for no reason slander our name. Sadly, most of the time this is done by those who claim to be Christians. Whatever the case may be, we have to remember that the light afflictions we go through can in no way be compared with what Jesus went through and yet he was merciful to those who crucified him (Luke 23:34). If Jesus was merciful to those who nailed him to the cross, it shouldn't be hard for us to show mercy to those who talk about us.

Standing through the Storm

2 Thessalonians 2:15
So then, brothers and sisters, stand firm and hold fast to the teachings we passed on to you, whether by word of mouth or by letter.

Down here in The South we are all too familiar with storms and Hurricane Katrina was one of the worst I can remember. This storm caused a great deal of damage, yet despite how serious this storm was, it amazed me to see so many trees still standing after the storm.

It is true that many trees were standing after Katrina, but it is also true that many trees were not. Some of the trees didn't stand a chance and were quickly uprooted. This is the same way it is with some of us when we are faced with the storms of life.

Inmates are faced with so much. We are forced to share a room or a dorm with someone who may be verbally or physically abusive, we sometimes encounter security guards who mistreat us, or we have to cope with the death of a loved one, all by ourselves. Denial after denial from the courts, parole and /or pardon boards. Some of us do not have family support and are forced to go to bed hungry. We are struck with sickness and disease with limited medical care. Whatever our storm may be, we must keep standing.

It's easy to stand when the storm is over but we must learn how to stand like a tree, firmly planted in the midst of the storm (Psalms 1:3, KJV). I am writing this because I am qualified. I lived through the storms and God equipped me to stand. It was difficult at times but with Jesus, I was able to stand strong.

When you are faced with any of the storms of life, I advise you to pray, fast, and stand on the word of God. This will not make the storm less difficult; it will, however, help you to remain standing after the storm.

Speaking Lies

Deuteronomy 5:20
You shall not give false testimony against your neighbor.

For many of us, lying was a part of our lives. However, as new creatures this should no longer be a part of who we are. We should be men or women of integrity. This should be prevalent in the life of every believer; unfortunately, it is just the opposite.

Stop lying! Stop backbiting! Stop bearing false witness! People in prison have enough to deal with without your foolishness. Inmates are separated from loved ones, some have children in state custody. We are not able to be there with our family for important events. These are just some of the issues that inmates have to deal with; don't add to these problems by spreading false information about someone. If you are doing this then you need to do a self- examination.

It would behoove you to find out why you are moved to tell lies about people. I'm talking about people who you don't know, people who never did anything to you. Are you going around telling lies about people because they shop at the canteen and get visits? Is it because the person who you're attacking is living out the scriptures? Is it because this person is holy and sold out for the Lord? Maybe you just can't stand to see someone actually being obedient to the word of God; therefore, you just decide to make up bad things about them.

I don't know why you are lying about others and maybe you don't know, either. God, however, is all-knowing and He knows exactly why you are practicing this sin. Therefore, go to God and ask Him to search your heart (Psalms 139:23) and reveal your motives to you. After He does, cry out to Him and allow God to deliver you from speaking lies.

Father Knows Best

John 16:24
Until now you have not asked for anything in my name.
Ask and you will receive, and your joy will be complete.

There were many things I asked my parents for when I was growing up. Sometimes they gave me what I asked them for, but many times they did not. Today I can thank God that they didn't grant all my requests. Moreover, I thank God that He loves me so much that He doesn't grant them, either.

I know that many inmates cry out to God once they arrive in prison. We ask Him to get us out of the situation into which we got ourselves. When we still find ourselves in the same situation many years later, we start to doubt the word of God. We may begin to wonder why we aren't receiving what we are asking God for.

God is all-knowing. He knows exactly what to give His children, He also knows when to give to His children. God knows if you still desire in your heart to do drugs. God knows that after you don't find a job in two weeks, you will give up on trusting him and go back to your old lifestyle of stealing.

God has not given you what you asked for because it is His will that none should perish (2 Peter 3:9, KJV). God looked into your future and knows that the enemy will kill you if He let you out right now. You are still in prison for your own good.

Stop asking God for what you think you want. Besides, He is more concerned with giving you what you need. If you want God to give you what you ask of Him, ask Him for His will to be done in your life -- He will be sure to grant this request.

By Any Means Necessary

Matthew 18:15
If your brother or sister sins, go and point out their fault, just between the two of you. If they listen to you, you have won them over.

God is a merciful God. He will do whatever it takes to get our attention. It doesn't matter to what extreme, God will reach us by any means necessary. Moreover, we should follow his example and do whatever it takes to reach someone else.

One day a new roommate was placed in the room with me. It didn't take long for me to see what my assignment was with this young lady. After praying, I ended up going to my roommate to talk with her regarding her serious hygiene issues, first it appeared that my roommate had received the words of wisdom, but shortly afterwards I saw this was not the case. I didn't have a problem with my roommate not receiving my wise counsel. I was led to tell her about her hygiene and I did. However, my roommate began to cause problems for herself. She was spreading rumors about me and keeping up confusion, even trying to get into a physical confrontation with me. Security had to get involved several times. Nothing I did worked. Finally, I took the matter before the church (Matthew 18:17) (1 Corinthians 6:1-6). This had to be done because everything I said offended her. I decided to cut off all communication with her because every time I privately spoke the truth to my roommate she became angry. This didn't surprise me at all, and reminded me of the question Paul asked the Galatians: Am I therefore become your enemy, because I tell you the truth? (Galatians 4:16, KJV). As a result of me going before the church, my roommate began to come around a little.

The Bible instructs us to go to the person who trespasses against us and tell them of their faults (Matt. 18:15, KJV). If the person refuses to hear you, then take along with you one or two more people as witnesses (Matthew 18:16). If this does not work, then the word of God commands us to bring the matter to the church (Matt. 18:17). This process is an attempt to reach someone by getting leaders involved.

My roommate did not mind me talking with her as long as it was what she wanted to hear. She didn't want to hear what the word of God had to say because it is quick, and powerful, and sharper than any two-edged sword (Hebrews 4:12, KJV). This is not a case of someone trying to force the word of God on someone, neither should this ever be done. However, this is a case of someone trying to reach another believer. If it means that you have to bring this believer before the church (Matt.18:17), then do whatever it takes. Be sure to pray first for the Spirit's guidance and that your motives are pure.

Hungry but Faithful

Proverbs 23:2
And put a knife to your throat if you are given to gluttony.

We cannot survive without eating food. If we don't eat, soon we will get hungry. Although our physical bodies hunger, this is absolutely no excuse for you to be a person given to appetite, so no matter what, don't give in to yours.

Unfortunately, I didn't have much financial support from the outside. I even had to go to bed hungry a few times. Once while sitting on the bunk assigned to me, I could remember crying out to God. Although I was hungry I was not crying out to God for Him to send someone who would bless me with something to eat. Actually, my tears were tears of joy. Yes, I was hungry but I was filled with joy. I was joyful because God had kept me in the midst of my hunger. You see, I could have violated to get something to eat. I could have compromised some way, somehow to satisfy my appetite. I could have obtained some stolen goods from the cafeteria, yet I did not do any of these things. I know that God preserves the faithful (Psalms 31:23, KJV). God had given me the strength to dominate my flesh and to make no provision for it. I had no desire whatsoever to please my flesh at the expense of compromising my faith. I know that food is a need and I knew this need would be met as soon as breakfast was called the next morning.

God already knew what was in my heart. He allowed me to endure this test so I would know, too. I know hunger has never killed anybody and I also know that not even hunger can make me give in to appetite. God proved to me that I would remain faithful to him even through hunger.

Don't Pass Letters

2 Samuel 11:14
In the morning David wrote a letter to Joab and sent it with Uriah.

At the Louisiana Correctional Institute for Women there are five separate dormitories. Each dorm is named after a zodiac sign and Leo is the dorm that houses maximum custody inmates. Minimum- and medium-custody inmates are not allowed to communicate with those who are placed in maximum security, those who are caught trying must suffer the consequences.

King David wrote a letter to Joab. He ordered Joab to place Uriah on the front line of the hottest battle, so that he could be killed (2 Samuel 11:15, KJV). What's ironic about this letter is that it was delivered by Uriah himself (2 Samuel 11:14). Uriah delivered his own death notice and didn't even know it.

I can recall an inmate who was assigned to bring lunch trays to the lockdown area. In addition to the trays, she had also smuggled in a letter. As soon as she passed the letter to the person for whom it was meant, she was busted by security and placed on lockdown herself.

Even if it's not a lockdown area, don't be the avenue of letter passing. If these letters can't pass through the mailroom then you need to be suspicious of the contents. The letter you are delivering may very well be the cause of someone going outside to be attacked by another inmate. I have seen this happen before.

Don't pass letters for anyone. This may possibly avoid serious problems. The letter you are asked to pass may not be your own death notice, but it may very well cause some kind of destruction.

Keep the Matter Hidden

Proverbs 11:13
A gossip betrays a confidence, but a trustworthy person keeps a secret.

There are many people in prison who are hurting and most of these people need someone to talk to. If you come across someone who trusts you with their hurts don't betray that trust by revealing their secrets. Be a person in which others can confide.

One day, while sitting outside on a bench in front of the dorm, a lady who lived in the same hall with me came to sit beside me. I didn't know this lady and she didn't know me. However, she had been observing me and knew I was a Christian. There was obviously something in her that told her she could trust me. This lady began to tell me about the crime she had committed. She told me that she was involved in a homosexual relationship and that she had been incarcerated for killing her lover. She expressed that she did not mean to do it and I could see the pain in her eyes. She desperately needed someone to talk to, and I was right there to listen. I never discussed the things she confided in me with anyone else; my integrity meant more to me than gossiping about this woman's hardships.

Don't reveal to anyone the secrets that have been entrusted to you. Moreover, beware of anyone who reveals secrets about another to you. The secrets you hold may very well make some juicy gossip but keeping them hidden will show you to be the faithful person you are.

You Are the One

1 Samuel 16:7

But the Lord said to Samuel, "Do not consider his appearance or his height, for I have rejected him. The Lord does not look at the things people look at. People look at the outward appearance, but the Lord looks at the heart."

Complaining about our situation does not change anything. Therefore, stop complaining about your incarceration and start thanking God for it. He has a purpose for allowing us to be where we are.

You may be wondering why God allowed you to be placed in such a situation. You may not be able to see what it is about you that would cause God to use you, but God does; He sees our heart and knows our capabilities better than we do.

When the Lord sent Samuel to anoint the next king after Saul, Samuel thought that Eliab was the one who he was to anoint (1 Samuel 16:6). He thought this because he looked like he could be a king. Jesse made seven of his sons to pass before Samuel, but neither of them was chosen by God. David was the one God wanted Samuel to anoint to be the king over the children of Israel.

God could have allowed any one to get caught up in their mess, but instead He allowed us to get caught up in ours. He chose us. He looked at our hearts and saw that we have what it takes to endure this hardship. He knew that this is exactly what it would take to get our attention so that we can surrender all and use this opportunity to be the man or woman of God we were created to be. It is not a mistake that we are in prison. I realize there are many people who break laws every day and never get caught, yet God didn't choose to use them. Instead he looked at you and said, 'you are the one.'

Forced from a Sinful Lifestyle

Colossians 3:5
Put to death, therefore, whatever belongs to your earthly nature: sexual immorality, impurity, lust, evil desires, and greed, which is idolatry.

Homosexuality is prevalent in our world today, even more so in the prison system. There are many inmates in bondage to this sin. There are some who are not currently practicing homosexuality, yet still are in bondage. You may be wondering how I can make such a statement. Well, I can say this after observing many don't practice this sin due only to their mate being released or rejecting them. This is not good enough. You must be delivered.

We have to mortify our members (Colossians 3:5, KJV). If we do this, then we can no longer be tempted by homosexuality or any other sin. The flesh has to die. Once the flesh is dead we are not going to want to practice sin anymore. It's not good enough that you are not practicing sin for the time being, because someone ended the ungodly relationship in which you were involved; this thing has to be stripped from your heart. Unless you crucify your flesh, you will head right back into this lifestyle as soon as someone else comes along.

Don't fool yourself into thinking that you are delivered from sin. Not engaging in it because your sin of choice is temporarily unavailable is not deliverance. However, if you would just mortify your flesh you will be delivered from sin, instead of just taking short vacations from it.

What's in You?

Deuteronomy 8:2
Remember how the Lord your God led you all the way in the wilderness these forty years, to humble and test you in order to know what was in your heart, whether or not you would keep his commands.

God created us and knows all about us. He knows if we will give up or keep going. He knows whether or not we will compromise. He knows everything we will do or won't do because He knows the very intents of our hearts. His only reason for allowing us to go through the wilderness is so that we can know.

The majority of inmates give in to the temptation of homosexuality. Some of them spend their time writing dirty letters to pen pals. They claim to do these things because they are human and have feelings. Well, the last time I checked I was human and have feelings, too. Yet, with the help of my Lord and Savior Jesus Christ He kept me from both of these sins. He showed me that when placed in a prison with the same sex that I wouldn't succumb to the sin of homosexuality or to writing dirty letters to pen pals, fooling myself into thinking I need to do this to pass time. This is a lie from the enemy.

Some of us would not know what we are capable of and what is in our hearts if it wasn't for our incarceration. The Israelites died in their wilderness experience (Numbers 26:65), but you don't have to die in yours. Let God clean you up, and prove to you, that you too can stand strong in the wilderness.

God Is in Charge

Proverbs 21:1
In the Lord's hand the king's heart is a stream of water that he channels toward all who please him.

Inmates have a tendency to worry about who the governor is, that the right people (by our definition of 'right') are on the pardon and parole boards and in hoping that our sentencing judge somehow gets off the bench and a more lenient judge takes his place. We should not waste time worrying about these things. If you are focusing on any of this then it is obvious you don't know who's in charge.

After 70 years in exile, God worked through Cyrus, King of Persia. God caused him to make a proclamation throughout all his kingdom, by stirring up his spirit (Ezra 1:1). God used Cyrus, who was not even a Jew, to allow the children of Israel to return to Jerusalem. The children of Israel held on to their faith. Their faith was not in King Cyrus, but in the God that has the heart of the king in his hand (Proverbs 21:1).

Do you know that the preparations of the heart in man, and the answer of the tongue, is from the Lord (Proverbs 16:1, KJV)? Do you not know that a man's heart devises his way, but the Lord directs his steps (Proverbs 16:9, KJV)? It doesn't matter what bill man passes or fail to pass, God has the final say. You must grasp the meaning of these verses and take the time to meditate on them until they sink deep into your heart.

Parole, pardon boards, the governor, and judges are all important factors in regaining our freedom, yet your total dependency should not be on any of these people. Now that you know this, get your focus off of man and put all your faith, trust, and hope in the only one who can open up doors that no man, governor or judge can shut (Revelation 3:8).

Mind Your Business

1 Thessalonians 4:11
And to make it your ambition to lead a quiet life: You should mind your own business and work with your hands, just as we told you.

Privacy! I guess you're saying that there is no such thing in prison and I agree with you to an extent. Security has the authority to do shake-downs whenever they choose, and we find ourselves taking showers and using the bathroom facilities in front of others. Although we are subjected to these invasions, we don't have to further invade the privacy of others.

The letters or important papers your Bunkie leaves out is none of your business. Do not take it upon yourself to sneakily read them; this is wrong and you have no right to snoop around someone else's belongings. Do not deprive others of the little privacy they do have.

It is not your job to pass out mail -- this is a task for security. Therefore, when it's time for mail call, don't put all your energy on trying to see what type of mail someone is getting. This has nothing to do with you, so stop intruding.

Study to be quiet, and to do your own business, and to work with your own hands, as we commanded you (1 Thessalonians 4:11, KJV). It's enough that the guards can come and search through personal things at any time, this is not your job. You can't take it upon yourself to go through another person's belongings. Your Bunkie's business is not yours so stay out of it unless he or she gives you an invitation.

In prison it's a wise choice to keep everything locked up. Sadly, there are many offenders who have not turned from their wicked ways and do not mind violating your privacy. If you are this person, pray and ask God to forgive you, then strive to live that quiet life that we are commanded to live and mind your own business.

A Time to Learn

Hosea 4:6
My people are destroyed from lack of knowledge.

Many of us who are incarcerated did not complete high school. Usually, this is because of trying situations, such as lack of family support, the death of parents, teenage pregnancy, or drug addiction, etc. Only God knows exactly what we are going through, but He also knows how to get us back on track. Prison could very well be our golden opportunity.

And we know that all things work together for good to them that love God, to them who are called according to his purpose (Romans 8:28, KJV). This verse does not exclude prisoners. It can work out for our good if we would just apply the Word to our life. It does not matter that we are behind prison walls -- God's Word has no limits.

It always saddens me to see people drop out of school. When I asked a few of those who dropped out why, they told me school was boring and that they were tired of going. Some said they dropped out because they just didn't get it. There is absolutely no reason for an incarcerated individual to drop out of school; you are in prison with nothing but time to apply yourself to getting an education. Besides, other than serving God what else can you do with your time that is more beneficial than going to school?

Take advantage of all the opportunities available to you. Stop settling for ignorance. Knowledge is power, but the lack thereof will destroy us (Hosea 4:6). If you are struggling academically, find someone to help you. Make the best of your situation so that you can be better upon your release. Prison could be beneficial, if we would just take advantage of the opportunities we are given to improve ourselves. Ecclesiastes 3 tells us there is a time for everything. This time in prison may very well be a time to learn.

Unstable Church Goer

James 1:8
Such a person is double-minded and unstable in all they do.

Christians, the time is over for playing games: it's time to get real. We can't just go to church thinking because we are in attendance that we are okay. Everyone knows who the real Christians are. Although some of us may often be called hypocrites or fakes, the ones doing the name-calling know there isn't any truth behind the names.

Just in case you need a little help to know if you are double-minded, let me help you. If you are going to church, singing, dancing, speaking in tongues, falling out, preaching, and teaching, but outside of the church your lifestyle consists of profanity, gossip, stealing, homosexuality or any other sin, you are double-minded.

I'm not saying just because you are a Christian that you won't sin, but I am saying that it shouldn't be your lifestyle. We can't be hot and cold, because this makes us lukewarm and God will spit us out of his mouth
(Revelation 3:15-16).

God has given us all free will. He will not force us to do anything. Choose to be a Christian and stop living a double life. If you do this, you will find that your life will be much better.

Be Hospitable

1 Peter 4:9
Offer hospitality to one another without grumbling.

The same hospitality that we showed to people who came to our homes should also be shown to those who come to the prison. No, we are not in a position to cook for these people, but we can accept them and offer a listening ear. We can give them the utmost respect. We can start practicing this the very next time someone arrives in the dorm to spread the word of God.

When I was housed in Orleans Parish Prison, occasionally volunteers would visit the dorm to minister the Word of God to those who wanted to listen. Unfortunately, there were not many. In fact, when some of the inmates would see the volunteers, they would get angry. You see, they did not want anyone talking about that Bible stuff, disturbing their sleep. There were some inmates watching television who refused to turn down the volume for such a cause. There were others playing cards or dominoes who very rudely continued to slam these objects on the table while talking loudly and using profanity.

If you are housed on an open dorm like I once was, have respect for those who come in to share the gospel. You may not want to listen to what these ministers have to say, but consider those who would like to listen. You can show that you are being considerate by not making noise at the card table. Also, you can turn the television down, if not off.

I know for the time being that your dorm is your temporary place of residence, and you want to make the best of your situation. Nothing is wrong with this, and this is totally understandable. Moreover, you must also understand that others who live with you would also like to make the best of their situation by listening to the Word of God. Do your part and avoid distracting others from doing theirs.

Hearing Is Not Good Enough

James 1:22
Do not merely listen to the word, and so deceive yourselves. Do what it says.

Oftentimes when I am alone, I like to read my Bible where I can hear myself. I just love to hear the Word of God. Hearing the Word of God through preaching and teaching or even by means of reading it aloud yourself are all good, but unfortunately, it is not good enough.

Many of us have been under the care of a physician at some time or another. God has given doctors the knowledge that they have for our benefit. It is extremely important to listen closely to what the doctor says, so we can understand his orders and be able to follow them completely. Doing what your doctor says could very well prolong your life; more importantly, obeying the Word of God is life.

God told Moses to speak to the rock so that they could have water to drink. Moses heard what God had spoken, yet instead of Moses doing what he was told, he decided to strike the rock (Numbers 20:8, 11, KJV). As a result, Moses was only allowed to see the Promised Land, but he could not enter into it.

Inmates are blessed with one thing that people who are not incarcerated just can't find enough of, time! With all the time we have on our hands, none of us should be ignorant of the Word of God. Quite frankly, most inmates know the Word and hear the Word but fail to live it. Jesus said that whosoever hears these sayings of mine, and does them, I will liken him unto a wise man, which built his house upon a rock (Matthew 7:24, KJV). And everyone who hears these sayings of mine and does not do them, shall be likened unto a foolish man, who built his house upon the sand (Matthew 7:26, KJV).

Today is the perfect time to apply the Word of God. We can't continue to play the fool. Therefore, start doing what the Word says so that you may be counted as one who is wise.

Sentenced to Be Watched

James 1:19
My dear brothers and sisters, take note of this: Everyone should be quick to listen, slow to speak, and slow to become angry

Security guards are placed in prisons to watch prisoners; this is the job they are paid to do. We all broke the law and as a result we must be watched. So why are you giving the ones hired to do the watching a hard time?

'Why are you looking at me? I am not your child! I am a grown woman or man! I am not going to let you talk to me this way!' Does any of this sound familiar? Sure it does, you hear this all the time, you may have even said these things yourself. If by chance you are saying these things, then it is time for you to stop it and zip your lip. Security has enough to deal with and should not have to fall victim to your anger.

Just in case you forgot, we were made to stand before a judge because of the crime we committed, as a result we were sentenced to hard labor. This involves being given orders by security. I'll be the first to admit that security are sometimes very ugly and rude. However, two wrongs will never equal right. I understand that you may get angry and nothing is wrong with this, even Jesus got angry (Matthew 21:12) but he didn't sin and we shouldn't, either. We are told in the Word of God, be angry and sin not (Ephesians 4:26, KJV). Regardless of how angry you get, don't argue with security. Listen to them without parting your lips, get rid of the pride, and then respond with a yes or no, Sir or Ma'am. This will make your time much easier to serve.

Security guards are human beings. These people are not working at the prison because they love working. They are here to earn a living so they can provide for themselves and their families. Moreover, security did not put you in prison yet they are paid to watch you as long as you are here.

Trouble Is Just Passing Through

Psalms 34:19
The righteous person may have many troubles, but the Lord delivers him from them all.

Afflictions should never take a Christian by surprise. In fact, we should expect them. When we do this, we are prepared to deal with them when they come.

I've come to realize that most of the trouble I experienced as I lived my Christian life behind prison walls was because of my strong determination to do the right thing. When I worked in the kitchen I was often harassed by other inmates because I refused to give them things security said weren't allowed. I had to experience being cursed at and called all kinds of names. On every job I was classified to there were always inmates who would make demands of me that I refused to honor. Sometimes I was told to let them know when security was coming since I refused to do whatever else they asked of me. I would tell them I couldn't do that either, because to do so would be upholding wrongdoing and would make me a partaker. Of course, this caused me to experience even more grief at the hands of the other inmates.

Jesus was the most righteous man who ever walked on this earth. Yet he too experienced many hardships. A crown of thorns was platted on his head (Matthew 27:29, KJV). They spit on him (Matthew 27:30). He was even crucified (Matthew 27:35). Yet, he endured it all.

You don't have to be afraid to do the right thing, just do it. Live like a Christian and welcome whatever comes with it. Even unbelievers are faced with trouble, but their trouble is usually a result of sin; going through trouble for righteousness' sake makes it much easier to endure. Trouble will come, but with God as the head of your life it won't stay.

Recognizing Love

Psalms 23:4
Even though I walk through the darkest valley, I will fear no evil, for you are with me; your rod and your staff, they comfort me.

Looking back to my childhood, I can remember being chastised by my mother. Sometimes this was done by using a belt. I did not understand as a child why someone who loved me would cause me pain. However, as I grew older I understood my mother's actions and no longer doubted her love for me. Just as I was uncertain about my mother's love, there will be moments when our loving acts will also be misjudged.

Other believers often accused me of not walking in love. I believe they gathered this opinion of my love walk because of my straightforwardness and because I've always been very bold and one who did not mince words. I believe in telling people the truth, no matter how embarrassing it may have been to the both of us.

One day I heard a very popular Bishop say something on television that I really needed to hear. He said, "Just because you are not kissing and hugging someone does not mean that you don't love them". This was a word from God that came just when I was beginning to doubt my love walk.

Yea, though I walk through the valley of the shadow of death, I will fear no evil: for thou art with me; thy rod and thy staff they comfort me (Psalms 23:4, KJV). How could David possibly be comforted by a rod and a staff? I'll tell you how, David had firsthand experience of using a staff and a rod to hit, poke, and push the sheep. This wasn't done to hurt them but to help them and to guide them. This most certainly was an expression of love.

Walking in love is more than treating someone sweet and good. Sometimes it requires telling someone how to care for themselves. Sometimes you may have to use a rod and a staff. Whatever the case may be, just make sure your motives are pure and the truth that you desire to tell is to help someone.

Still Pursued in Prison

Matthew 26:36
Then Jesus went with his disciples to a place called Gethsemane, and he said to them, "Sit here while I go over there and pray."

We are all precious in the sight of God. He loves each and every one of us. He pursued us many times before our incarceration and He still pursues us now. This is why He has called so many men and women of God to do prison ministry.

The Lord has put it in the hearts of ministers to leave their comfortable homes, sometimes even driving in poor weather conditions to minister to us. Yet when they get to where we are, we refuse to walk a few feet or even get up off our bunk to participate in the service. Many of the inmates are watching television or listening to the radio. When service is announced, sadly no one gets up most of the time. Some would even say they are tired, or just don't feel like it. After volunteers drive all the way to the prison we could at least get off our bunks and walk a few feet to join the service. You must understand that this is another attempt to reach you so please don't ignore it.

There were many times when I did not feel like getting up when the church call was made in the dorm. Yet, I always managed to push past feelings that would hinder me if I allowed them to and make my way to the table for Bible study. I did not know much at the time. I was just a baby in the Lord. However, I did know that if I wanted to leave prison better than the way I arrived that I needed to hear what these ministers had to say. Something within me was telling me that I needed to seize the opportunity, and I was glad I did. It will be in your best interests to stop what you are doing to do the same.

God loves us so much, this is why he has put it in the heart of so many to reach us. These people are so determined to accomplish this mission that they have made it their business to come into the dorm to minister the Word of God. Don't continue to ignore all of God's attempts to reach out to you. He desires to reach us so badly that even in prison he is still making house calls.

Man Is Not Your Enemy

2 Corinthians 10:5
We demolish arguments and every pretension that sets itself up against the knowledge of God, and we take captive every thought to make it obedient to Christ.

God is a good God and everything good comes from Him. Satan our enemy is an evil god and everything bad comes from him, even your bad thoughts. Stop thinking about the bad things the devil put in your mind, and start casting them down, you'll find yourself not getting into mess when you do this.

We all are human beings created in the image of God (Genesis 1:27). Therefore, we should not be fighting each other. We are not animals, fighting is expected of them, not of us. Besides, fighting is foolishness and can be avoided if you would just take time to analyze why we choose to do so in the first place.

People don't just walk around deciding they want to get into a physical confrontation with someone. The initiative usually takes place with a bad thought that comes to our mind about a person. Maybe the devil used someone to come to tell you about some ugly thing a person said about you. Maybe this person did you something or you saw something that she done or overheard something she said. Whatever the case may be this all is mess and foolishness. The person is not even our real enemy. We wrestle not against flesh and blood, but against principalities, against powers, against the rulers of the darkness of this world, against spiritual wickedness in high places (Ephesians 6:12, KJV).

People are not our enemies. Satan is our only enemy. The next time he tries to persuade you to hit someone, let him know you recognize his attack and then hit the floor instead with your knees and pray for that person Satan wants you to hit.

You Were Made to Be Courageous

Mark 1:27
The people were all so amazed that they asked each other, "What is this? A new teaching and with authority! He even gives orders to impure spirits and they obey him."

Secondhand smoke is harmful. You don't have to allow anyone to subject you to such harm; if you are a nonsmoker and inmates around you insist on smoking then you need to walk in your boldness.

Inmates have ways of smuggling cigarettes into prisons. Most times it is the new inmates who bring them on the grounds. The prison I'm in does not allow smoking indoors, though it is allowed outdoors. We all know that if a smoker has access to smoking materials they are going to smoke when the timing is right, regardless of where they are or what the rules say.

The children of Israel were given the Promised Land. God told the children of Israel to keep his statutes and his judgments, not to commit any abominations of their own nation nor of any stranger that sojourneth among them (Leviticus 18:26, KJV). It was going to take courage for the Israelites to do everything God told them to do. Just as they were able to walk in their boldness, God will cause us to walk in ours when problems arise.

Many times, I've seen Christians ask their roommates not to smoke, because it bothers them. Some even stress that they have asthma or some other health condition, and that the smoke makes it difficult for them to breathe, yet the smoker insists on smoking. Many of these smokers try to justify their actions by saying that we are all in prison. This is true, but that goes both ways. A non-smoker does not have to be subjected to smoke simply because they are in prison. If a smoker believes you should have stayed home, if you didn't want to smell smoke then it is fair to let them know that they should have stayed home so they could smoke whenever they wanted to without consequences. Then, tell them if they smoke again you will have no other choice but to go to security.

As a Christian, you are to operate in the same authority Jesus did in Mark 1:27 when He commanded the unclean spirits who obeyed him. If your requests are not getting you anywhere, then stop asking and start commanding. You don't have to tolerate secondhand smoke. They will either obey your command or you boldly go and report the violator to security. Sometimes we have to do what we have to do. You have to breathe, but they don't have to smoke.

Take Every Opportunity to Minister

Luke 2:46
After three days they found him in the temple courts, sitting among the teachers, listening to them and asking them questions.

There are many different denominations inside prison facilities. You don't have to avoid these services just because you don't agree with them. Instead, use any invitation as an opportunity to spread the gospel.

Personally, I do not claim to be of any specific denomination. I guess this makes me non-denominational. Besides, it is not about being a part of a man-made religion, it's about having a relationship with Jesus Christ, which I do have.

Once I was invited to a Jehovah's Witness service. I was reluctant to go, but I went anyway. The volunteers who came in to do this service were all beautiful people, and we all respected one another's beliefs. They allowed me to ask questions and didn't have a problem answering them. I wish I could say one of the Jehovah's Witnesses were converted but this did not happen; still, seeds were planted that could very well lead up to a later conversion.

Jesus himself at the age of 12 years old was found in the temple. He wasn't just listening to whatever was being preached but he was also asking questions (Luke 2:46). If someone invites you to a service that you don't usually attend, perhaps because you don't agree with whatever denomination it is, go with them anyway. You don't have to avoid this service. This could be a perfect opportunity for you to minister the Word of God. You don't have to do so arrogantly, or like some know-it-all, just do it. You can listen to what they have to say and write down everything that is not supported by the Word of God. Then request permission to ask some questions. This may very well save souls. It will definitely plant seeds.

Don't ever shun an opportunity to minister to people. If they don't come to the services you attend, then meet them where they are. Someone just may convert from religion to relationship.

Bless Someone

Matthew 10:8
Heal the sick, raise the dead, cleanse those who have leprosy, drive out demons. Freely you have received; freely give.

Blessings are often associated with financial gain; however, this is not the only way God blesses. Money is essential to survive in this world, but there is so much more. Although we are incarcerated, we are not exempt from being blessed, nor from blessing others.

God has freely given us so much. You may be wondering what God has given you. He has given us good health, talents, intellect, ears to hear, eyes to see, and the list goes on and on. However, He didn't just give us these things to keep to ourselves. We are blessed to be a blessing.

Unfortunately, there are many people who are confined to wheelchairs. You can give of yourself to these people by taking time out of your busy schedule to give them a push. After all, the word of God says do unto others as we will have them do unto us (Luke 6:31, KJV). If you were in a wheelchair, I am sure you would want a push sometimes. Maybe you don't know someone who needs a push, but there are those who need you to help them read or write, or to just listen. Whatever the case may be, be willing to freely give of yourself.

God has really blessed us all. He blessed us, now we need to bless others. Make it your business to freely give of yourself today and be a blessing to someone who is a little less fortunate.

Recognizing Holiness

1 Thessalonians 4:7
For God did not call us to be impure, but to live a holy life.

Embarrassment should be the last thing you feel when someone calls you a holy roller. You should not feel shame because someone called you holy. Instead, you should consider this quite an honor.

Before I was saved I can remember being called names that I was not fond of at all. In fact, I hated some of those names. Yet although I hated those names, I was not embarrassed even though I should have been.

For I am not ashamed of the gospel of Christ: for it is the power of God unto salvation to everyone that believeth; to the Jew first, and also to the Greek. (Romans 1:16, KJV). Paul boldly declared that he was not ashamed of the gospel of Christ. Neither should we be ashamed of the gospel nor anything associated with it such as holiness. You are commanded to be holy. Be ye holy, for I am holy (1 Peter 1:16, KJV).

The next time someone calls you a holy roller or accuses you of being holier-than-thou, just shout Halleluiah! Do you know what this means? This means that they recognize you as holy. Thank the person for giving you such a compliment. You are not being called such a wonderful name for no reason, you are being called such a wonderful name because your lifestyle is screaming, 'I am a Christian!' Your lifestyle clearly shows that you are living out the scriptures. Continue to keep up the good work and welcome all the holy titles.

You Have So Much More

Psalm 37:1
Do not fret because of those who are evil or be envious of those who do wrong.

Satan is always making things look good. He does this so that we can be tempted to sin. If we would simply stay mindful of this, we won't worry about the unjust gain of unbelievers.

You are a Christian. You strive day-in and day-out to live a lifestyle pleasing to Jesus Christ. You go to church every time the doors open and you are always out ministering or passing out scriptures. But despite how well your spiritual life may be, financially you are not okay. The one who always says that I'm blessed and highly favored is beginning to wonder how those unbelievers are always going to the canteen and how they always have something to eat when you don't. You are wondering how every time the prison gives food sales or some other fund raiser, that you are never able to purchase anything and have to look at the unbelievers eating right in front of you.

Pull yourself together. This is only a test. You have a responsibility to not let anything move you (1 Thessalonians 3:3). Don't compromise with these people just for a meal. Moreover, you are provided with three meals a day. It may not be what you want but it will sustain you. If you will just trust in God you will see him turn your situation around. Don't give in to the lust of your eyes. Be determined to wait on God and you will see what he has for you is so much more.

Forsake the Flesh

Romans 13:14
Rather, clothe yourselves with the Lord Jesus Christ, and do not think about how to gratify the desires of the flesh.

We are in a war. The war that we are in is not physical but spiritual. Therefore, we need to continue to feed our spirit man and do whatever it takes not to cater to the flesh.

I recall talking to a lady who was about to be released within the hour. She was really excited about going to live at some Christian place. She went on to say that she always used her body to get men, but she no longer wanted to live this life. In order to walk this out she refused to listen to the devil who was trying to get her to call one of the men she use to date; instead she decided to let the ministry pick her up upon her release. She gave absolutely no provision at all to the flesh. This same woman even expressed to me that she struggled with homosexuality. Because of this struggle she didn't even allow other women to comb her hair. This woman was serious about making no provision for the flesh.

One way I practiced forsaking my flesh was living within my budget. Unlike many inmates, if I knew my family only sent me $100 monthly then I did not allow myself to buy everything I wanted. This way I did not cause my flesh to get used to eating things I could not afford. I resisted purchasing a $4 burger from the Prison's Snack Shack and decided to purchase something cheaper that I can get more of and that would last me longer. This way I wouldn't be tempted to compromise just to provide for my flesh.

Don't allow yourself to walk right into sin. This is what we are doing when we give into our flesh. We must do whatever it takes not to provide for the flesh, as this will cause our spirit to have dominion.

Do You Really Believe?

Romans 10:9
If you declare with your mouth, "Jesus is Lord," and believe in your heart that God raised him from the dead, you will be saved.

Jesus is no longer in the grave. God has raised him from the dead. If we believe this, what we say and do should be evidence of this belief.

Thinking back to my childhood, I can recall how much I loved Christmastime. It always behooved me to be on my best behavior so I would get exactly what I wanted. I believed that my behavior would play an important role in how much I got for Christmas; therefore, my actions were based on what I believed.

All too often we see inmate after inmate respond to the call for salvation by doing what Romans 10:9 says to do. Although no one grows up overnight, everyone should grow up eventually. When a child first learns how to walk, he holds on to things because he does not believe he could walk well enough to do otherwise. Soon this child will get a little older and start believing that he can walk without holding on to things and next thing you know he does just that.

Peter did not believe that the gospel was to be brought to the Gentiles. He acted out his belief by only bringing the good news of Jesus Christ to the Jews. Peter stood on his belief until God showed him through a vision that his Word was for both Jews and Gentiles (Acts 10:9-16). Afterwards, Peter preached in the house of Cornelius, A Roman centurion officer (Acts 10:34, KJV).

It's time for us to start living like we believe in the resurrection of Jesus Christ. If we do, then we shouldn't be holding on to our old thieving ways. If we really believed that God promises to meet our needs (Psalms 23:1), then we wouldn't steal. If we really believed that God fights our battles, then why are we engaging in physical confrontations? Make up in your mind and your heart to start living your life in such a way that people will be able to observe you and know what you really believe.

The Weapon Will Prosper

Isaiah 54:17
No weapon forged against you will prevail, and you will refute every tongue that accuses you. This is the heritage of the servants of the Lord, and this is their vindication from me," declares the Lord.

The Bible is filled with promises from God. Unfortunately, these promises are not for everyone. The promises of God are only for His children and they are based on conditions. In order for the promises to be manifested in our lives, all of the conditions of the promises must be met.

Out of all the promises in the Bible one that is often quoted is Isaiah 54:17. However, it is usually the first part of this scripture that is quoted which reads, "No weapon formed against me shall prosper". What's ironic about this is that it's quoted mostly by unbelievers, when this promise is not for them. Don't take my word, let us check out the verse in its entirety: No weapon that is formed against you shall prosper; and every tongue that shall rise against you in judgment shall be condemned. This is the heritage of the servants of the Lord and their righteousness is of me, said the Lord (Isaiah 54:17, KJV). This promise is for those who are serving the Lord and walking in righteousness. Period!

Servants of the Lord do not practice putting others down and there is nothing righteous about this. Servants of the Lord do not live a lifestyle that consist of stealing. Servants of the Lord do not practice homosexuality because there is nothing right about this. Servants of the Lord do not curse security and start mess everywhere they go, because again, this is not right.

Weapons will form in our lives. If the weapon we are faced with results from any of the above or any other act of sin in our lives then yes, this weapon will prosper. Yet, if you are tired of having all these weapons prosper, then make up your mind to stop forming them.

Suffering for Your Own Sake

Luke 6:22
Blessed are you when people hate you, when they exclude you and insult you and reject your name as evil, because of the Son of Man.

Are you ostracized by others? Do people constantly spread lies about you? If your answer to these questions are yes, God will see you through as long as you are suffering for Jesus' sake.

Stephen was one of the seven chosen to supervise food distribution to the needy in the early church. He was a man of God, full of faith and the Holy Ghost (Acts 6:5). Stephen was a man who performed great wonders and miracles among the people (Acts 6:8, KJV). He spoke with wisdom and by the Spirit (Acts 6:10, KJV). Despite Stephens' excellent reputation, there were certain men of the synagogue of the Libertines, Cyrenians, Alexandrians, Cilicia and of Asia who rose up against him to dispute with him (Acts 6:9, KJV). This was done merely because he was a man of God. As a result, he was stoned for Jesus' sake (Acts 7:59).

Daniel was preferred above the presidents and princes because an excellent spirit was in him (Daniel 6:3, KJV). Daniel was a man of God who faithfully prayed to his God despite the decree (Daniel 6:10, KJV). The presidents and princes looked for an occasion to find fault in Daniel but couldn't because there was no fault in him (Daniel 6:4, KJV). They tried to find fault with Daniel merely because he was a man of God. For this very reason, Daniel was thrown into the lion's den (Daniel 6:16). This was all because of righteousness' sake.

Neither Daniel nor Stephen did anything wrong. Unlike us, who practice gossiping, slandering, condemning others and many other sinful acts. All of this is unrighteousness. If you are suffering because of sin then you are not suffering for Jesus' sake, but for the sake of yourself. You are suffering the consequences you caused.

Suffering is not easy and is very difficult to go through. However, when it's done for Jesus' sake, he will see you through (Daniel 6:22 and Acts 7:55). If you find yourself suffering and it is not for Jesus' sake, then you are getting what is due you.

Reaping the Dirt You Sowed

Galatians 6:7
Do not be deceived: God cannot be mocked. A man reaps what he sows.

Mistreatment of inmates by other inmates take place frequently in prisons. Treating people badly is wrong; no one has the right to do so. However, though one never has a right sometimes they may have a reason.

I can recall praying for an inmate who was being tormented by her roommates. The roommates she had were long-timers and they had both been in prison for a very long time. I didn't know the lady but when I found out who she was, I went to her and spoke some words of encouragement. It was very clear to see that this lady was not at peace. Not too long afterwards, this lady was moved to another building into a room with a little old lady who was serving a life sentence. The old lady had many health problems. This woman treated the old lady very badly. I watched the old lady cry out for help. Later I remembered that this woman, who was being mistreated in the other building, was now mistreating someone herself. This woman had been in a room with people who were very dominating. Then, when moved into a room with someone who was weak and feeble, she dominated that person. I began to see the reason she went through what she went through. She went through it all because God can't lie. His word says we will reap what we sow. This woman was being mistreated because she mistreated others. She was reaping the mistreatment she sowed.

Some say what goes around comes around. God says you will reap what you sow. Don't think you will get away with the evil you do to others, God sees it all and he will allow what you dish out to come back to you, so make sure you check what you are serving on your plate.

God Has the Key

Revelation 3:7

To the angel of the Church in Philadelphia write: These are the words of him who is holy and true, who holds the key of David. What he opens no one can shut, and what he shuts no one can open.

If Jesus is Lord of your life, like He is of mine, then He should have complete control over your affairs. Once you realize this and allow Him to have his way then you can rest. You can rest because whatever is going to happen will happen but He must allow it.

Are there some closed doors in your life that you want opened? Are there some open doors in your life that you want closed? Then go to the one who has the power to open and shut doors. You do not have to tell me. I already know that you have been praying and asking God to open the prison doors. If it is His will the doors will open. He has the power to open them. The earth is the Lord's and the fullness thereof; the world, and they that dwell therein (Psalm 24:1, KJV). It doesn't matter to God that you are in prison. The prison belongs to him also. The security guards who work at the prison are His, along with everything and everyone on this earth.

Peter was thrown in prison by King Herod (Acts 12:4). He was sleeping between two soldiers, bound with two chains: and the keepers before the door kept the prison (Acts 12:6, KJV). Peter was bound and heavily guarded. Yet, God sent his angel to release Peter from prison (Acts 12:7, KJV). Not only did God open prison doors to let Peter out, but He even allowed the iron gates of the city to open by themselves (Acts 12:10, KJV).

Don't spend your time in prison being anxious. You are to be anxious for nothing, but in all things, with prayer and supplication with thanksgiving let your request be made known unto God (Philippians 4:6, KJV). Go ahead and make your request known and stop stressing about going home. The Lord of your life knows what He's doing. God has the keys and will open the door in his timing.

The Unclean Deserve Respect, Too

Leviticus 19:32
Stand up in the presence of the aged, show respect for the elderly and revere your God. I am the Lord.

There is so much that God has commanded us to do. One of his many commands is to honor elderly people. Yes, this means that we must honor that elderly roommate of ours who has a smell that turns your stomach. She is not exempt from being honored.

God strengthened me to deal with my roommate, who among many things was a hoarder. God has to have a sense of humor as He placed me, a very clean person, into a room with someone who was just the opposite. I am not just talking about dirty clothes here and there, but very unsanitary conditions.

I will probably never forget moving to room C-19-B. As soon as I approached the door, the smell of urine smacked me dead in the face. The room smelled so bad it made me sick to my stomach. I did not know how I was going to live in that room. Then I remembered, my grace is sufficient for thee: for my strength is made perfect in weakness. Most gladly therefore will I rather glory in my infirmities, that the power of Christ may rest upon me (2 Corinthians 12:9, KJV). It was not easy living with the roommate God put me with but because of God's grace and after a lot of bleach and all-purpose cleaner, I was able to endure.

We should respect elderly people. We should never argue with them, curse at them, call them out their name or disrespect them in any way. It does not matter if they reek of urine, pack stuff everywhere and rarely take a shower, we still have to respect them. The respect that is due the elderly is not based on whether they respect us. We are to respect them because God has commanded us to do so.

Dealing with Your Mountains

Mark 11:23
Truly I tell you, if anyone says to this mountain, 'Go, throw yourself into the sea,' and does not doubt in their heart but believes that what they say will happen, it will be done for them.

At some point, we all have to deal with mountains in our lives, such as sickness, death, discouragement, anger, unforgiveness, and rejection, are just a few. These may or may not be your mountains, but whatever yours are you have to speak to them.

We must practice obeying the word of God. Not just the parts that we like or that makes sense to us, but all of it. When the children of Israel complained to Moses about having a lack of water, God told Moses to hit the rock and water would come out of it, so Moses did as God said and smote the rock (Exodus 17:7, KJV). Later the children of Israel complained again for water. This time, God commanded Moses to speak to the rock. Moses couldn't see how water could come from a rock by merely speaking to it (Numbers 20:8) so he smote the rock again. (Numbers 20:10, KJV). This act of disobedience caused Moses to not enter the Promised Land.

I don't know what your mountains are, but I know that if you would just obey God and tell that mountain to move, you will have what you say. God did not command us to climb the mountain or to go around the mountain, he simply commands us to speak to our mountains. At times we will be faced with mountains that will require us to act, whether the action be walking away from a bad relationship, forgiving someone, working on our own legal work, or writing a letter to the judge. Still, there will be other times when God will only expect us to speak. If your mountains still linger in your life after you have done everything you know to do, then stop what you are doing and start speaking to your mountains.

What Fruit Are You Bearing?

Luke 6:43

No good tree bears bad fruit, nor does a bad tree bear good fruit.

Apples are not found on an orange tree, neither are oranges found on an apple tree. Apples are found on an apple tree and oranges are found on orange trees. Moreover, bitterness, gossiping, lying and jealousy are just a few of the corrupt fruits found on a corrupt tree and should not exist in the life of a Christian.

When I was a young girl, I loved to pick figs and berries. I never once accidentally mixed up the trees because it was obvious which tree was which by the fruits they bore. I never picked berries off the fig tree, neither did I get figs from the berry tree. These trees produced the fruits that were seen on their branches and there was no mistaking the two

Just like I could look at those trees to tell them apart, people can look at us and tell whether we are Christians. When people see us they should not see someone who is always gossiping, lying, and stealing. They shouldn't see someone who comfortably engages in homosexuality. When people see us they shouldn't see someone who uses profanity or someone who operates in jealousy. If people see any of these things when they look at us then we are not bearing the fruit of a Christian and there is a great chance that we are not.

People will know whether or not we are Christians because a Christian will be known by the life they live. If we are bearing corrupt fruits this disqualifies us, but we can become eligible again if we just start bearing good fruit.

Silent Ministry

Matthew 7:6
Do not give dogs what is sacred; do not throw your pearls to pigs. If you do, they may trample them under their feet, and turn and tear you to pieces.

This scripture came alive in my life just recently. I always thought that I could share the word of God with anyone until I met someone who proved me wrong. I learned through this person that there is even a time to minister the word of God.

One day a new lady was moved into the room with me. This lady had a very beautiful voice and often sang in church. She even ministered to the congregation for a few minutes here and there. Although this lady was always singing in church, outside of church she was one hundred percent heathen. Being that this lady was my roommate, I tried ministering to her every chance I had. Every time I did, she would pretend to receive the word, then afterward, I would be called to the control only to have security tell me my roommate reported that she and I had an argument which was so far from the truth. This girl was offended by the word of God because it is quick, powerful, and sharper than any two-edged sword, piercing even to the dividing asunder of soul and spirit, and of the joints and marrow, and is a discerner of the thoughts and intents of the heart (Hebrew 4:12, KJV).

Unfortunately, I had to stop ministering to my roommate with words because every time I did, she reported me to security, accusing me of 'picking on her'. Too many complaints like this could have landed us both in lockdown, so I refrained from telling her anything. I was not able to verbally minister the words of God to my roommate because every single word I spoke offended her, therefore I decided to close my big mouth and instead speak to her through the Christian lifestyle I lived.

The Perfect One Was Called Names, Too

Matthew 10:25
It is enough for students to be like their teachers, and servants like their masters. If the head of the house has been called Beelzebub, how much more the members of his household!

Jesus is the only perfect one who ever walked on this earth. He healed the sick raised the dead and caused the blind to see. Despite how perfect Jesus was and all the miracles he performed, the religious leaders still called him Beelzebub.

In prison we are stripped of so many things. Privacy is one of them. Everyone sees everything. Everyone knows the character of the people they live around. If you are a Christian, then you are really going to be watched closely. Once people see you, many of them will know that you are who you say you are by the way you live. They will know you practice what you preach. They will know that you do not engage in arguments. They know that you love going to church. They see you out witnessing. Regardless of all this, people will still call you out of your name. They will call you the devil. They will call you a hypocrite. These people who are calling you those names know good and well that these names do not describe your true character. All they know is that your righteousness is an affront to them and making up names to call you makes them feel better about themselves. Remember Jesus walked perfectly, and he was accused falsely. As a follower of Jesus, you have to be willing to face what he faced, and then prepare yourself to be called all the things you are not.

You Must Fellowship

Hebrews 10:25

Not giving up meeting together, as some are in the habit of doing, but encouraging one another and all the more as you see the Day approaching.

We are to study to show ourselves approved (2 Timothy 2:15, KJV). To study is going to require some reading. Although reading and studying our Bibles daily is essential, not even these things are to be used as a substitute for worshipping and fellowship with other believers.

Hypocrites are not only found inside the prison chapel; they are also found inside of every church in the world. I hope this does not come as a surprise to you, because it certainly isn't a surprise to God. God knew from the beginning of time that hypocrites would fill the churches and despite this, He still does not want us to forsake the assembling of ourselves together with other believers. We can't allow hypocrites to keep us from fellowshipping. There are some real believers in the church. If you are real you will know who these people are. When you find out who they are you must continuously stay in fellowship with them. We need to follow the example of the first church; they continued steadfastly in the apostle's doctrine and fellowship and in the breaking of bread, and in prayers (Acts 2:42, KJV). When we join in fellowship we can build up one another. But exhort one another daily, while it is called today; lest any of you be hardened through the deceitfulness of sin (Hebrews 3:13, KJV).

You should not allow anyone or anything to keep you from going to church. You see for yourself that the word of God requires us to fellowship. Therefore, stop using hypocrites as an excuse to stay away from the church and make sure you are not one yourself.

You Will Be Held Accountable

Hebrews 10:26-27
If we deliberately keep on sinning after we have received the knowledge of the truth, no sacrifice for sins is left, but only a fearful expectation of judgment and of raging fire that will consume the enemies of God.

We must stop fooling ourselves: God will do what He said He will do. The word of God shows us that God wants us to go to church. Not forsaking the assembling of ourselves together… (Hebrews 10:25, KJV). God does not just want us to go to church, He wants us to hear the Word. He wants us to not leave church in the poor condition we went. Once we come to church and are exposed to the Word we have no excuse to go back to our dormitories to practice ungodliness. You may think that you are going to church just to get out of the building or for whatever other reason but once you hear the Word you are no longer ignorant and you will be held accountable for your disobedience. But the soul that do ought presumptuously, whether he be born in the land, or a stranger, the same reproaches the Lord; and that soul shall be cut off from among his people (Numbers 15:30, KJV).

You must understand that your soul is at stake. Once you know, you will be responsible. For if after they have escaped the pollutions of the world through the knowledge of the Lord and Savior Jesus Christ, they are again entangled therein, and overcome, the latter end is worst with them than the beginning (2 Peter 2:20, KJV).

Now that you know better, God wants you to do better because you will be held accountable. You still have a chance to make it right. You have been exposed to the truth, now it is time for you to live like it.

Slow to Speak

Proverbs 15:28
The heart of the righteous weighs its answers, but the mouth of the wicked gushes evil.

Studying requires going over something repeatedly. If you have a problem with the way you respond to people, then you will have to start practicing answering positively. It takes diligence and calls for constant effort. To do this we must continuously study great acts of humility in the Bible and then apply what we learned.

When the Jews accused Jesus of having a devil, Jesus answered, I have not a devil; but I honor my Father, and ye do dishonor me. (John 8:48-49, KJV). In the book of Mark, the scribes who came down from Jerusalem said, he hath Beelzebub, and by the prince of the devils casteth he out devils. And Jesus called them unto him, and said unto them in parables, how can Satan cast out Satan? (Mark 3:22-23, KJV). Jesus was called names and he chose to respond wisely and we must follow his example.

I don't know about you but I have never seen a one-man argument. This is because it takes two to argue and usually responding negatively to foolishness is what starts most arguments. I don't want to leave prison the same person I was when I arrived. I don't want to keep allowing people to control me. However, whenever someone can say something to me that causes me to give an ugly response, I am giving that person control. It is time for each one of us to stop responding to others quickly when they call us bad names or say bad things to us,. Instead, take a few seconds to study how to answer so we can respond like Jesus would.

In God Alone

Proverbs 3:5
Trust in the Lord with all your heart and lean not on your own understanding.

Abraham understood that he was 100 years old and that Sarah his wife was 90 years old and there was no way he and his wife could conceive a child at their age (Genesis 17:17). Yet, Abraham did not lean on his own understanding. Instead he trusted in the Lord and he and his wife conceived (Genesis 21:1).

When we lean on our own understanding, things often look hopeless. When we lean on our own understanding, the life sentence man sentenced you to means that you will never get out of prison, but when we trust in God and give Him the care of that life sentence, He has the power to overturn it. When we lean on our own understanding we begin to get nervous and start stressing when it is almost time for us to be released because we do not know how we are going to make it but when we trust in the Lord with all our heart we can be assured that He has already made a way for us, and that we will make it. When we lean on our own understanding we spend all our time worrying about the children we left behind but when we trust in God with all our heart we will turn the care of our children over to God.

It is far better to trust in God because depending on our own understanding is not wise, so don't you dare lean on your own understanding ever again.

Temple Maintenance

1 Corinthians 3:16-17
Don't you know that you yourselves are God's temple and that God's Spirit dwells in your midst? If anyone destroys God's temple, God will destroy that person; for God's temple is sacred, and you together are that temple.

We need to spend quality time taking care of our bodies. Our bodies are the temple of Almighty God. Therefore, the way we maintain our bodies are of extreme importance.

Solomon began the construction of the temple in the fourth year of his reign (2 Chronicles 3:2, KJV). It took Solomon seven years to finish this task (1 Kings 6:38). The temple construction was such a major project for Solomon that it required over 150,000 men be involved in its construction (2 Chronicles 2:2). I'll be the first to admit I have often wondered why God gave so much detail regarding his temple. Then I was reminded of the temple being the place the Jews went to worship God; this made every detail of extreme importance.

Today a building is no longer needed for the Spirit of God. Our bodies are the temple and the Spirit of God dwells inside of us (1 Corinthians 3:16). This should be a good enough reason for us to take good care of our physical bodies. God made sure that every single detail regarding the construction of the temple was recorded in the Bible (2 Chronicles 2-4). You may be tempted to skip over 2 Chronicles chapters 2-4, but I encourage you to read these chapters so that you can see how much concern God took in making sure the temple was properly constructed.

Regardless of how immaculate the temple was, it was a building. Yet, God cared about the maintenance of this building. Today our bodies are the temple and God dwells within us, therefore we should be even more concerned with maintaining our fleshy temples.

Hunger Does Not Make Wrong Right

Proverbs 24:24-25
Whoever says to the guilty, "You are innocent," will be cursed by peoples and denounced by nations. But it will go well with those who convict the guilty, and rich blessing will come on them.

As a state prisoner, we are no longer able to take care of ourselves the way we did before our incarceration. Now that we are in the custody of the state, the state is obligated to meet all our needs. However, our needs are not met the way we think they should, but according to how the state chooses to meet them.

I am sure you were sentenced to do hard labor just like I was. I am also sure that the judge ordered you to serve time in prison and not in some fancy hotel. If this is so, then we have no right to any more than our portion.

Inmates are always sneaking through the cafeteria line more than once just to get extra food, claiming they do this because of hunger. Still, this is not an excuse. I have experienced going to the cafeteria, eating my food, and not being full thereafter. I was not hungry; I was just not as full as I wanted to be. Regardless, I refused to do what the other inmates were doing. I was just grateful that God had provided sustenance at that meal. Most inmates uphold this wrongdoing, expressing their belief that it is the right thing to do. It is not the right thing to do, neither does it make it right merely because you weren't full. Sneaking an extra tray is stealing, and stealing is never a righteous act, no matter what. When you see someone doing this don't condone them because this is the wrong thing to do. The state does not owe us anything, it's us who owe a debt to the state for breaking the law. The state is presently facing a deficit. If the nearly 1,200 inmates would decide to sneak an extra tray this would soon cause a serious food shortage and would be an even bigger problem for the state.

If your situation is like mine, then you are incarcerated because you wanted what you wanted so badly you decided to commit the crime you committed in order to get it. Now you are stealing trays because the state is not giving you what you believe you should have. If you are doing this, you have not changed. This is the same mentality that caused you to land in prison and if you don't stop, it will be the same mentality that will bring you back.

Regretting What You Once Desired

Psalms 78:29
They ate 'till they were gorged- he had given them what they craved.

Be careful of what you desire in your heart. God wants to give you your desires so make sure they are pure. Even if your desires are not pure, God is still faithful to give them to you.

Delight thyself also in the Lord; and he shall give thee the desires of thine heart (Psalm 37:4). Those desires God promises to give us in this verse are good desires. I know this because these desires come by delighting yourself in the Lord. When we do this, our God-pleasing desires will come to pass. God says in His word that He will fulfill the desire of them that fear him (Psalms 145:19, KJV). Continue to revere God and your pure desires will come to pass. Even if you don't revere God you had better believe he still will give you your desires regardless to how bad they may be.

The children of Israel desired to have a king over them so that they would be like other nations (1 Samuel 8:5). God told them they would regret desiring to have a king (1 Samuel 8:18, KJV). Yet, the Lord told Samuel to listen to the children of Israel and make them a king (1Samuel 8:22). God gave them the desires of their heart. Their desires caused them to be ruled by many evil kings, such as: King Ahab the son of Omri who did evil in the sight of the Lord above all that were before him (1Kings 16:30, KJV). King Ahaziah the son of Ahab did evil in the sight of the Lord, (1 Kings 22:51-52, KJV). King Jehoahaz reigned over Israel for seventeen years and he did that which was evil in the sight of the Lord. Israel desired to have a king. God allowed them to have 19 kings over a period of time and every last one of them were evil.

Only you and God knows what you desire in your heart. God wants to give you your heart's desires, so make sure they are good. If not, just like the children of Israel, you will regret them.

Who's Your Hope In

Zechariah 4:6

So he said to me, "This is the word of the Lord to Zerubbabel: 'Not by might nor by power, but by my Spirit,' says the Lord Almighty

There will be times when the strength of man may suffice. It's good to have someone strong and powerful around. However, the strength of man will not always be sufficient. Someone can have might as Samson or power like the President of the United States of America, yet it is only by the spirit of God will our mountains be moved.

Prisons all over this world are filled with prisoners who want more than anything to be set free. They sit, waiting and hoping that a new judge takes the bench so that he or she can give them another chance at freedom. Some are hoping and praying that the right law maker or governor is elected so that some law can be passed that will result in their release. Some go as far as writing U.S. Representatives and Senators, or even the President of the United States of America. The reason many inmates put their hope in such people is because of the political power all these people have. However, these people can't do anything for you unless God allows it. This is why our hope and trust should be in God alone. There is no might or power greater than the spirit of God. When Ethiopia's mighty army came up against King Asa's army they were overthrown and could not recover themselves (2 Chronicles 14:11-13, KJV). Although the huge army from Ethiopia was mightier and more powerful, it was the spirit of God that caused them to be overtaken.

Happy is he that hath the God of Jacob for his help, whose hope is in the Lord his God (Psalms 146:5, KJV). If you have been placing your hope and trust in the power of man, it is time that you redirect your hope. Trust in the one and only true God who can handle any situation you're facing by his spirit alone.

Be Content No Matter What

Philippians 4:11
I am not saying this because I am in need, for I have learned to be content whatever the circumstances.

Today is Sunday May 9, 2010 and it is Mother's Day. I find myself sitting on the top bunk in the room I'm assigned to here at the Louisiana Correctional Institute for Women. Just like you, I don't want to be here, but I must say I am content.

My daughter, who is 18 years old and happens to be my only child, did not bother to send me a Mother's Day card. Receiving a card from my daughter would have truly been a blessing to me but I didn't allow myself to be affected spiritually by not receiving one. I didn't join in with all the ladies who didn't get a Mother's Day card from their children, and begin to complain about how wrong they were, or about how we could get even with them by not sending them a card for their birthdays. None of the above was my attitude. Instead, I prayed for my daughter. I continued to send her cards and love letters. I realized that I didn't get a card from my daughter because she was still angry with me for the bad choice I made that resulted in my incarceration. She believed that I would be hurt by not receiving a card from her, for you see, she was hurting. Before I became the person I am today I probably would have allowed this to cause me to be depressed, but I didn't. Yes, I was hurt, but I was not moved. I did not allow the hurt to affect me in a way that it would move me out of my position in Christ. I was still able to praise God for all he has freely given me. Paul said in the word of God that godliness with contentment is great gain (1 Timothy 6:6, KJV). Therefore, I chose to be content.

I love my daughter very much, and I know without a doubt that she loves me. Although a Mother's Day card from her would have made my day, I didn't allow not getting one to destroy it. This just allowed me to see that even with this, I could be content and you can too.

New Things for a New Man

Isaiah 43:18-19

Forget the former things; do not dwell on the past. See, I am doing a new thing! Now it springs up; do you not perceive it? I am making a way in the wilderness and streams in the wasteland.

Many of us were forced to part with possessions that we left behind, such as a fully-furnished home. When I first came to prison, thinking about all the material things I lost made me sick. That big screen television, that beautiful bedroom set, the brand new car and all those material possessions we had before coming to prison are long gone. So stop dwelling on the old, and get with the new.

Starting all over from nothing is a scary thought for a prisoner soon to be released. After all, it probably took years to gather the belongings you had. I know this is a situation that many of you are faced with because I am faced with it right now. However, I am not going to sit down and stress about my tomorrows. Jesus tells us in the word of God not to take thought for our life, what we shall eat, or what we shall drink; nor yet for our body, what we shall put on. Is not the life more than meat, and the body than raiment (Matthew 6:25, KJV). I know it is hard not to think about those things we need. However, we don't have to worry about these things because God will perfect everything that concerns us (Psalms 138:8, KJV). Just stop putting your trust in people and began to trust God with your future. Put your trust in the God who provided for the children of Israel while they were in the wilderness (Deuteronomy 8:15, KJV). He is no respecter of person (Acts 10:34, KJV). What he did for them he will do for you because he is the same God yesterday, today, and forever (Hebrews 13:8, KJV).

You are no longer the old person you were. You are a new creature in Christ Jesus (2 Corinthians 5:17, KJV). So forget about all the old stuff you left behind and get ready for all the new things God has for the new you.

Hindering Yourself from Receiving Mercy

Matthew 5:7
Blessed are the merciful, for they will be shown mercy.

All too often we cry out to God for him to be merciful to us. God is such a good God that He grants our requests and extends us his loving mercy. Yet, we find it difficult to extend this same mercy to others.

Prisoners are constantly bombarding their judge with letters, wanting him to show them mercy by either reducing their time or giving them some other alternative to prison. Many complain how the pardon and parole boards are not merciful and some are even looking to receive mercy from their victim's family. Nothing is wrong with wanting someone to show you mercy, but it is when you can't even show it to others.

A certain king ordered that his servant, who owed him 10,000 talents, be sold along with his wife, children and all that he had as payment for his debt. The servant then fell to his master's feet asking him to forgive him of the debt and the king did so. Afterwards this same servant went out and found one of his fellow servants who owed him 100 pence; he laid hands on him, and took him by the throat, saying, 'pay me what you owe me'. His fellow servant then fell down at his feet asking for mercy, but instead of extending to this man the same mercy that the king extended to him, he had the man thrown in prison until he was able to pay the debt.

Today, make a decision to show someone mercy. Whether it be that person on your dorm, a coworker, or maybe even the prison guard. I know they may have done you wrong but remember that the crime we committed was wrong, too, and we still expect others to show us some mercy regarding it, so make up in your mind to do the same.

Choose Church Regardless

Psalm 31:23c
...but the proud he pays back in full

We are all called to be faithful. God chooses to work through those who demonstrate faithfulness. Faithfulness is a lifestyle, so don't fail to walk in it for a moment of pleasure.

And I will raise me up a faithful priest that shall do according to that which is in mine heart and in my mind: and I will build him a sure house: and he shall walk before mine anointed forever (1 Samuel 2:35, KJV). Eli and his sons were not faithful, so God chose someone who was. The person God chose was Saul.

There are some good church services at the Louisiana Correctional Institute for Women. I faithfully attended the services at least five to six days a week throughout my incarceration. Of course, I was not the only one in these services, there were many others who attended also. However, the majority of them did not attend faithfully. Whenever another function conflicted with church there were only a faithful few in attendance. If a talent show, a dance, or some other worldly activity was taking place, the majority forgot all about church.

God is looking for faithful people. He does not want us serving him only when there is nothing else for us to do. He wants us to forsake all and choose to serve Him no matter what is going on. He wants us to choose him above everything else.

Don't Go Back to Your Mess

John 5:14
Later Jesus found him at the temple and said to him, "See, you are well again. Stop sinning or something worse may happen to you."

God loves us all and He wants the best for us. He has never turned his back on me and He will never turn his back on you; we are the ones who turn away from him. Turning our back on the Lord Jesus Christ after we have accepted Him as our Savior is a very dangerous thing to do, and the consequences are serious.

It is common to see inmates go to church regularly and confess that they no longer want anything to do with their old life. Yet, as soon as these people see something pleasing to them they are back in their mess -- it's like they don't even remember what they said.

I recall a time when two girls ran to the evening chapel services after getting out of a homosexual relationship. I was very proud of these ladies for the decision they had made. They got involved in praise and worship, alter calls, prayer lines, and more. Unfortunately, this did not last. Pretty soon, both girls were back in their mess, subsequently, they suffered the consequences. One of the ladies ended up being forced to move out of the honor dorm and demoted to a less desirable job. The other lady ended up going to lockdown which caused her to lose the trustee status she had earned. Both of these ladies chose to return to their mess and they lost many comforts because of their decision.

When these ladies came into the chapel and cried out to the Lord, He heard their cry. God accepted them back in but once again these ladies turned back to the world; therefore, the consequences they suffered were even worse.

If you are having hard times now, turning away won't make it any easier. Please just hang in there. If you turn back you will only make matters worse.

Misjudging Good Deeds

John 7:24
Stop judging by mere appearances, but instead judge correctly.

Every single one of us make judgments each and every day. Sadly, most of the time we make these judgments without any knowledge of the facts. In a court of law the judge does not make a judgement before hearing all the facts and neither should we.

For righteousness sake, my name was constantly slandered. Currently, I am classified to the chapel and my coworkers are determined to cause me to lose my job. They went as far as asking people to write lies to my supervisor stating that I was stealing from my job. This made me very angry; there was not any truth to it, and my exemplary character did not stop me from being upset.

Before I started working in the chapel, I would always give away the deodorant and toothpaste that came in the monthly warehouse bags given to indigent inmates. I couldn't use the deodorant and I always had extra toothpaste, so I would just bless someone with these items. However, when my coworkers began to lie and say I was stealing from work I stopped this practice because it no longer looked right. People heard the rumors my co-workers were spreading, so for me to be seen giving away personal items would have drawn the suspicions of others. After several weeks I decided not to worry about what people may have thought; I cleaned out my locker and blessed some folks with deodorant and toothpaste. I didn't hide because I knew my actions were innocent. Moreover, God knew my actions were righteous.

Just because you are suspicious of someone's actions does not automatically make their actions wrong. It is wrong to make a judgment without having all the facts. Don't judge a situation because of how something appears because things are not always how they seem.

The Message Will Change When You Change

2 Timothy 1:16
May the Lord show mercy to the household of Onesiphorus, because he often refreshed me and was not ashamed of my chains.

We have every right to oppose the teachings of any preacher under which we sit. In fact, we should make it our business to do so if what is being preached is not biblical. However, if the teaching is biblical then we don't have a case.

Paul asked Timothy to salute Aquila and Priscilla and the household of Onesiphorus (2 Timothy 4:19, KJV). Onesiphorus took a stand for the truth by supporting Paul's ministry when it was opposed by Phygellus and Hermogenes (2 Timothy 1:15-16, KJV). We need to do the same when someone opposes a man or woman of God. We don't have to argue the Word of God, but if the Pastor is preaching the truth we need to support him and make it known.

Often, I witnessed inmates go to church and then leave a few minutes later. After the service, I would hear these inmates say they left because the preacher was preaching about homosexuality and would say that this particular preacher focuses on this subject too much. These inmates would be so angry they would begin slandering the preacher. If what the preacher is speaking about is coming from the Bible, then your anger is directed toward the wrong person. We need to be angry with God instead.

There are no big or small sins. Sin is sin. However, homosexuality is a sin that is more prevalent in a prison setting, which is why some preachers may see the need to touch on this subject more than others. If you are caught up in homosexuality or any other sin, don't get angry with the man or woman of God because they constantly preach about the sins you are practicing. God loves you, and he is using these people to get your attention while you still have time to change.

Stick with What's Right

Deuteronomy 6:18
Do what is right and good in the Lord's sight, so that it may go well with you and you may go in and take over the good land the Lord promised on oath to your ancestors,

We should always take a stand for that which is right; in order to do this, we must use a righteous standard. As you may know, the world has its own definition of right and therefore we shouldn't use a worldly standard. The standard you should use is the only righteous standard there is: The Word of God.

A statement often spoken in prison is, "Inmates need to learn how to stick together". Whenever someone would direct such a foolish statement to me, I always agitated those inmates in my presence by responding, "I don't stick with inmates but with what is right". If the inmates were in the right I didn't have a problem sticking with them. In fact, I am obligated to stick with what's right.

Blacks want to stick with blacks. Whites want to stick with whites. People from Uptown want to stick with people from Uptown. People from downtown want to stick with people from downtown. This is all foolishness. You should never base your reason for taking sides with someone on the fact that you are all the same race or because you all are inmates or share some other commonality. This should not enter into your decision making.

While in prison you have time to get yourself ready to re-enter society. It is difficult to do this if you are upholding people in their wrongdoing because of the commonalities you share. Don't support someone because they are inmates or of a certain race, but for whomever is right.

World in Word Out

Mark 4:19
But the worries of this life, the deceitfulness of wealth and the desires for other things come in and choke the word, making it unfruitful.

We all have problems. Believers and unbelievers both will have problems in this world. Christians are not exempt. However, we can prevent most of the problems we have if we just stop allowing things to enter our lives.

In Matthew 4:1-11 you will find that Satan tempted Jesus in the wilderness. In verse 3, Satan tempted Jesus by telling him to command the stones to become bread. This had to sound good to Jesus, who had fasted 40 days and nights and was hungry and weak. It is not a sin to be tempted but it is a sin to give in to the temptation. Fortunately, Jesus did not. He did not accept the bread Satan offered him, even though he was hungry. I'm sure that Jesus' flesh wanted the bread, however Jesus did not allow this to enter in His spirit. If he would have, this would have caused a problem.

It is very important that we do everything in our power to remain fruitful. The cares of the world will make their way to us. The lust to have other things will make its way to us but the good news is, we don't have to let them enter in, because when we do, we cause ourselves problems.

Christians, stop allowing your cares about freedom and your lust for everything to choke the word. It is easy to start worrying about our children but when we do, we cause ourselves problems. Unfortunately, we will have enough problems in our lives, we don't need to add to them by causing more on our own.

You Can't Make It If You Fake It

Revelation 3:15-16
I know your deeds, that you are neither cold nor hot. I wish you were either one or the other! So, because you are lukewarm -- neither hot nor cold -- I am about to spit you out of my mouth.

There is no such thing as a lukewarm Christian. Perhaps there are lukewarm people who may call themselves Christians. To be a Christian means to be Christ-like, and you can't be Christ-like if you are lukewarm.

I am a Christian and I don't have to go around telling everyone because my lifestyle makes it evident. I thank God that my Christianity is obvious, and that my light shines automatically.

My roommate and I share the same room because of this she and I can observe one another carefully. From observing me she knows that I spend hours in the Word of God. She knows I do this throughout the day, starting early in the morning. She knows I praise him continuously with my life. Simply by watching me, my roommate knows without a doubt that I am a Christian. Whenever my roommate is in my presence she is constantly talking about Jesus, singing gospel songs, and praying out loud. However, when she thinks I'm not around she lives like a heathen. God is not pleased with this kind of behavior.

We shouldn't try to fake Christianity when we are in the presence of Christians. No Christian has a heaven or hell to put you in and needs a Savior just like you do. God knows your heart and he sees everything you are doing.

You know in your heart that you are not ready to be a Christian. My prayer is that you get ready, but until you do it would behoove you to be hot or cold. A mixture of both makes you lukewarm and a candidate for God to spit you out of his mouth.

Show Love

Romans 12:9
Love must be sincere. Hate what is evil; cling to what is good

Christians are often referred to as hypocrites. This is because it is very common for those in the church to not practice what they preach. They say 'I love you' with their mouths and 'I hate you' with their actions.

All the junk I hear spoken in the hall on which I temporarily reside makes me clearly understand why people call so-called Christians hypocrites. The inmates I live with proclaim to be Christians; they frequently profess, "I love you" to others and the minute these people leave their sight they are being talked about and stabbed in the back by the same ones who told them they loved them.

Jonathan and David were best friends. Jonathan loved David very much. In fact, he loved David like he loved his own soul (1 Samuel 20:17, KJV) Jonathan's love for David was not merely words. Jonathan spoke up for David, speaking good of him to his father (1 Samuel 19:4, KJV). Jonathan even told David to abide in a secret place and to hide himself so that Saul won't find him and kill him (1 Samuel 19:2, KJV). Jonathan's actions proved his love for David.

I love you are very strong words. People today use these words too loosely. They are no more than a trite expression. It is okay to tell others you love them but you must mean what you say. You don't mean it if you are saying ugly things behind the back of the one you claim to love.

Until you can practice love, it will be best if you don't utter these words. Keep your professions of love to yourself until you can back it up with your actions; to do otherwise is hypocrisy.

Unexpected End

2 Timothy 1:7
For the Spirit God gave us does not make us timid, but gives us power, love and self-discipline

Death is one of those things in this life that are inevitable, it is the end of life on this earth. Although death is something we all must face, no one wants to face it while in prison.

Unfortunately, I know too many people who died while serving time in prison. This is a topic I have tried to avoid but the Holy Spirit would not allow it, so here it is.

Death is no respecter of persons, neither is it a respecter of places. Death will visit whomever, wherever. Yes, it will come to you even in prison. I know you don't want to think about such things but it has been the fate of many inmates. I think many would agree that they would rather their final moments on this earth be spent with loved ones.

I can recall one inmate who had stressed that she did not want to die in prison. This was a fear of hers. Once she saw this was God's will, the fear left her and she had such a peace about herself. She accepted the fact that she was going to die in prison and about one year after our talk, this woman went home to be with the Lord.

God told Moses he was going to die and that he would not bring the children of Israel into the Promised Land (Numbers 20:12, KJV). Even after this, Moses continued to serve God. Moses knew he was going to die in the wilderness but did not simply sit and wait for death to come; Moses continued to live his life.

If you are walking in fear because there is a possibility your life may end in prison, pray and ask God to allow you to accept whatever His will is for your life. After you pray, start resting in God's peace and then do as Moses did -- continue to live.

The Secret Giver

Matthew 6:1
Be careful not to practice your righteousness in front of others to be seen by them. If you do, you will have no reward from your Father in heaven.

God loves to bless His people. He doesn't leave His throne to come bless His children, neither does he have to. Many times, God does this through others, so be careful how you allow Him to bless through you.

Prison life is so open it's almost impossible not to know what the next person is doing. I say almost because it is possible to do some things without everyone knowing. Yes, if you really want to you can be discreet, even in prison.

At the Louisiana Correctional Institute for Women there is a 'no transaction' rule, however this is not the case at other jails and prisons. If you are housed in a facility that allows transactions, know that there is a way to do this. You don't give someone something to eat or anything else in front of others just for show as the Bible teaches us that we should give in private. Does it hurt you to put something on someone's bunk without letting them know that it was you who did it? If this bothers you then you do have a problem giving in secret, but it does not have to remain a problem if you simply practice giving to others privately. Before you know it, you will have developed a good habit.

The next time you want to give something to someone, do so in private. No one should have to know that you are the giver, just make sure you give from your heart.

Put the Devil in His Place

Ephesians 4:27
And do not give the devil a foothold.

Believers are not powerless over the devil. Therefore, we have no business giving place to him. If the devil has a place in our lives, this is because we gave it to him.

James said submit yourselves therefore to God. Resist the devil, and he will flee from you (James 4:7, KJV). We are not told to bind the devil, Satan will be bound at the proper time and we will not be the ones to do it (Revelation 20:2, KJV). We are not commanded to rebuke the devil but we are clearly commanded to resist the devil, but first we must submit to God before we can do so.

First, let us get something straight: your roommate is not the devil. Your Bunkie is not the devil. That person on your dorm who gets on your nerves is not the devil. Neither the security guards nor the warden is the devil. This may take you by surprise, but the judge who sentenced you isn't the devil, either. The devil uses people and may very well be using some of them. If you are submitting to God, you will know exactly how to apply the Word to resist the attacks of the enemy. When you do this, you are not giving place to the devil.

Satan tempted Jesus with bread at a time he was physically weak due from a fast that lasted for 40 days and nights. However, Jesus did not give in to the temptation and gave no place to the devil by accepting the bread (Matthew 4:1-4, KJV). We must do the same and not give in to temptation.

We must follow the example of Jesus Christ and practice resisting Satan by using the word of God. If Jesus had to do this, then we need to do the same. Remember that Satan has absolutely no place in your life unless it is under your feet.

Be on Constant Watch

Matthew 26:41
Watch and pray so that you will not fall into temptation.
The spirit is willing, but the flesh is weak.

Security guards have a responsibility to watch prisoners. This watch is constant. We have to be watched 24 hours a day, seven days a week. Just as security guards have to watch inmates, we too as Christians should be on watch.

I can recall one of the ministers at a revival at the prison preach from Matthew 26:41. She said we should watch (W-A-T-C-H) our words, attitude, thoughts, choices, and hearts. If we do this, we won't give in to temptation.

As Christians, we should watch to ensure our words are edifying (Ephesians 4:29, KJV). This way we won't tear anyone down. We should watch our attitudes and make sure they are filled with love, joy, peace, longsuffering, gentleness, goodness, faith, meekness, and temperance (Galatians 5:22-23, KJV). We should watch our thoughts to assure they are true, honest, lovely, and of good report (Philippians 4:8, KJV). We should watch our choices and make sure that we always choose to serve the Lord. Finally, we should watch our hearts because it is in the abundance thereof that the mouth speaks (Luke 6:45, KJV).

There is a great deal of negativity inmates can get involved with in prison. If we don't stay on watch, we will find ourselves caught up when temptation comes. Don't stop watching for even a second; if you do, it could cost you your life so do yourself a favor and remain on constant watch.

The Place of No Return

2 Peter 2:21-22
It would have been better for them not to have known the way of righteousness, than to have known it and then to turn their backs on the sacred command that was passed on to them. Of them the proverbs are true: 'A dog returns to its vomit', and 'A sow that is washed returns to her wallowing in the mud'.

Living a lifestyle filled with sin was all I knew once. Of course, this was before I accepted Jesus Christ as my Lord and Savior. Now that I am a Christian, I have no desire to return to the sinful lifestyle I once lived.

Over and over again, minister after minister, preacher after preacher came to the prison to tell us not to go back around the same people, the same places or doing the same things. This was a typical message from many pastors. I believe it's because these pastors knew that many of us got ourselves into the predicament we are in because of the people we hung around and the places we went. These pastors know if we go back to these places it could possibly cost us our lives. When the righteous turn away from his righteousness and commits iniquity, and doeth according to all the abominations that the wicked man doeth, shall he live? All his righteousness that he hath done shall not be mentioned: in his trespass that he hath trespassed, and in his sin that he hath sinned, in them shall he die (Ezekiel 18:24, KJV).

No matter what type of lifestyle you are living behind prison walls, I encourage you to attend church. You do not have to be righteous to go to church. The church is not simply a place for Christians to fellowship but it is also for those who are not living right to get right. By chance you are not ready to live a life pleasing to God, but even if you aren't you can still go to church. Don't respond to the call for salvation when you know in your heart you have not reached the place of no return.

They Said

2 Timothy 2:16
Avoid godless chatter, because those who indulge in it will become more and more ungodly.

As Christians we have to choose the conversations we have. We shouldn't hesitate to excuse ourselves from conversations we shouldn't be a part of. We must be mindful of the ones we may engage in, and of the ones we need to avoid.

Personally, I don't believe in using the word 'they' unless it can be related back to some previously mentioned names. By mentioning names, it makes it obvious who you are speaking of when you use the word 'they' afterwards. Unfortunately, this is usually not the case. I've had numerous people approach me and attempt to tell me what 'they said'. My response would always be, who is 'they'? And just like I figured these people were never able to identify who 'they' were; therefore, I didn't bother to entertain these people, at least not on the level they expected. Instead, this was my opportunity to minister to them. I would ask them how it would make them feel for someone to slander their name or to spread embarrassing stories about them. Once they tell me they wouldn't like someone to do this to them, I then tell them that the Word of God says we are to do unto others as we would have them to do unto us (Matthew 7:12, KJV), and that we reap what we sow (Genesis 8:22, KJV). One thing about a response like this, I never have to worry about this person coming to me with foolishness again.

When someone comes to you telling you what 'they said', do not entertain them. This person is obviously a mess-maker and anything they have to say is not worth hearing.

Different, Not Better

Titus 2:14
Who gave himself for us to redeem us from all wickedness and to purify for himself a people that are his very own, eager to do what is good.

When I got saved and started reading the Word of God, I was determined to apply the Holy Scriptures to my life. I had a strong desire to do that which was right. I wanted so desperately to be a woman with integrity and live up to who God called me to be.

Every one of the ladies at LCIW I associate with knows I love sweets. Because of this, I was often put in situations that challenged my integrity. One day my roommate came into our assigned room, excitedly telling me she had some pecan candy for me. I thanked her for the offer then told her I couldn't accept it. Confused, she asked why. This was a perfect opportunity for me to minister and is exactly what I did. I explained to her I couldn't accept the pecan candy because we can't purchase any of the ingredients to make pecan candy from the canteen. I then told her that I can only assume she obtained the candy through unjust means and for me to eat some would be partaking in a wrongful act. My roommate could not believe someone who loved sweets as much as I did was turning them down. This was strange to her; even more so because it was something I might not have been able to enjoy until I went home and still, I chose to pass up the opportunity.

Unbelievers often look at Christians as strange because our way of doing things goes against the common way of worldly people -- this is because we are called to be peculiar (Deuteronomy 14:2, KJV). This doesn't make us better, only different. You, too are meant to live like you are different by not giving into the ways of the world, even if they have what you love.

Praise God with Your Body

Romans 12:1-2

Therefore, I urge you, brothers and sisters, in view of God's mercy, to offer your bodies as a living sacrifice, holy and pleasing to God - this is your true and proper worship. Do not conform to the pattern of this world, but be transformed by the renewing of your mind. Then you will be able to test and approve what God's will is-his good, pleasing and perfect will.

Your body is the temple of God (1 Corinthians 3:16, KJV). You are not your own. You have been bought with a price (1 Corinthians 6:20, KJV). Jesus Christ our Lord and Savior purchased us with His precious blood. There is absolutely nothing we could do to pay the debt we owe, but the least we could do is present our bodies as a living sacrifice. We can't do this when we get involved in ungodliness.

As Christians, we should not be taking part in worldly talent shows. A talent show may appear to be harmless but it's not when the talents consist of ungodly music and dancing. I am not speaking about all music, only if the lyrics make light of sin. Don't yield your members as instruments of unrighteousness unto sin: but yield yourselves unto God, as those that are alive from the dead, and your members as instruments of righteousness unto God (Romans 6:13, KJV). If you still desire to engage in unclean dance, and to sing music that is not pleasing to God, then you need to pray and ask God to renew you in the spirit of your mind (Ephesians 4:23, KJV). Once this happens you will find yourself doing those things with your body that is holy, and acceptable unto God; anything else is unacceptable.

Being Kind to Difficult People

Ephesians 4:31-32
Get rid of all bitterness, rage and anger, brawling and slander, along with every form of malice. Be kind and compassionate to one another, forgiving each other, just as in Christ God forgave you.

There are people in this world who are difficult to get along with, people who would harm you both verbally and physically. Unfortunately, in prison we are forced to live with some of them.

As a child I could remember saying 'sticks and stones may break my bones but words will never hurt me'. This was not true at all. In fact, this was a lie. Words do hurt, especially when someone falsely attacks your character. I realize people who are not incarcerated also have to deal with difficult people. I know they have to deal with being persecuted, lied on, slandered, and more. However, it's another story when you're forced to live with these people 24 hours a day, seven days a week. I am talking about those people who won't think twice before stabbing someone, spitting on someone or committing some other violent act. You, too may be living around people like this and know how easy it is to be bitter with these people. I wanted to be more than just angry with these people, I wanted to retaliate. Instead I confessed to God how I felt and asked Him to help me not be bitter. I told Him I could not be kind to these people and asked Him to please be kind to these people through me. I had to pray about this over and over again and I continue to pray about this today. I had to practice being kind to these people. This was hard for me, but I decided to do it anyway because I desperately wanted to please God, so I forced myself to be kind for Christ's sake.

If it was up to me, I would only live around people who are easy to get along with. God knows this, and this is why he didn't leave it up to me. Besides, if we don't live around difficult people then who will set their example. Let's make up in our minds to show those difficult people the love of Jesus Christ regardless of how difficult that may be.

Sneaking Food from the Party

Matthew 5:16
In the same way, let your light shine before others, that they may see your good deeds and glorify your Father in heaven.

No matter where you are people will watch you, especially if they know you claim to be a Christian. For this reason alone, we should be sure to glorify God at all times.

The women housed at the Louisiana Correctional Institute for Women is blessed with many volunteers coming in to teach and preach the Word of God. Some of these volunteers host annual parties, and those inmates who faithfully attend the services are invited. At these parties we are allowed to eat all we can but the facility has a rule that we can't take anything from the party back to our dorms. This is not an unjust rule and should be followed, however this rule is only followed by a few. Time and time again inmates break this rule. Remember I did say that most of the party attendees are church goers? Yes, this means it's the church folks taking the food.

As a Christian you should not be taking anything from these parties. Dare to glorify God. Don't worry about being called a holy roller or whatever else. Take a stand and don't do what all the other so-called Christians are doing. Don't take a thing. This will cause your light to shine brightly and others will begin to give God the glory that is due only to Him.

Don't Take the Bishop at His Word

Acts 17:11
Now the Berean Jews were of more noble character than those in Thessalonica, for they received the message with great eagerness and examined the Scriptures every day to see if what Paul said was true.

Inmates are blessed to have volunteers come in on a regular basis to preach the Word of God. There is someone visiting the grounds every day to minister and yet, we still need to ensure what's coming from these ministers is biblical.

Prisons in this great country are obligated to allow inmates to practice their religious beliefs, which means that inmates are exposed to many different religions. However, we should not get caught up in religion and we must be diligent in making sure what we hear is true. We need to practice being like the Bereans. These were more noble than those in Thessalonica, in that they received the word with all readiness of mind, and searched the scriptures daily, whether those things were so (Acts 17:11, KJV). Do not get caught up into thinking someone who comes in under the title Bishop has all the answers or that it's safe to take this person at his word, because it is not. We have to make sure what they are preaching is in line with the Holy Scriptures. If something doesn't sit right with you, write it down then refer to the Word of God. If you have a question regarding what you wrote, then you need to go to that person and ask them to give you some scriptures on what they preached. If they can't back themselves up biblically, then you make it known to them that is the reason you don't agree with them. Your openness may very well cause them to make sure they preach nothing but the truth.

Be Content, Even in the Field

Hebrews 13:5
Keep your lives free from the love of money and be content with what you have, because God has said, "Never will I leave you; never will I forsake you."

Prison life has taught me how to be content. Regardless of what I had or did not have and wherever I found myself, I always found great comfort in taking Paul's advice.

When I worked in the field, I believe I was the only one out of about 100 people who did not complain about working. I took advantage of my time in the field by mowing the grass. I was okay with it because this was my way of killing two birds with one stone. While I was working, I was also exercising and therefore I didn't have to exercise once I got off work. Most of the time I would just enjoy reading my pocket Bible whenever work was slow. I was adamant about finding ways to make my time in the field more useful.

In the summertime, the field was extremely hot and, in the winter, it was very cold. I believe I was able to deal with the weather because of my obedience to God and because I didn't murmur and complain about my job. Don't get me wrong, I do not like to be cold, but still I was okay with working in the field and I found myself not reacting to the job the way my other co-workers chose to. This was my opportunity to show the other ladies that I know how to be content even when working in the field.

Witness Wisely

Romans 14:16
Therefore do not let what you know is good be spoken of as evil.

We are all called to be witnesses for God. This means if we are believers, we should be out witnessing to others. Even when we are witnessing, we must do so wisely so that our witnessing won't be misconstrued.

One afternoon while standing in the cafeteria line waiting to be served, the Lord allowed me to overhear an unbeliever discussing one of my sisters-in-Christ, who had been witnessing to her, with someone else. This lady said she goes to church because my sister invites her and when she goes, she gets to sit close to my sister. My sister is very attractive and shapely. This lady's only reason for allowing my sister to witness to her was to try to lure her into a homosexual relationship. Moreover, she was telling others that my sister-in-Christ had the same motive. I ended up telling my sister what I had overheard and asked her if she was yielding to homosexuality. She told me she wasn't and that she would make sure to be on watch. I told her in everything she needs to be as wise as a serpent and harmless as a dove (Matthew 10:16, KJV).

By all means, if you know that you are strong in the Lord and his Word is hidden in your heart, please don't stop witnessing to someone just because they are trying to lure you into a homosexual relationship. Continue to minister to this person and remember that it takes two. If the person you are witnessing to attempts to bring up an ungodly conversation with you, kindly tell the person you are a Christian and can't partake in such a conversation. It won't be easy to stay in your company for long. In fact, that person will not be able to get away from you fast enough.

Witnessing to others is very important. We must make sure we are being led by the Holy Spirit when we witness to others. We can't stop people from accusing us of witnessing for ungodly reasons, but we can make sure that their accusations are wrong by witnessing wisely.

If You're Holy and You Know It...

1 Peter 1:16
For it is written: "Be holy, because I am holy."

We should all want to be pure. We should all want to be faithful. Everything that God is, we should want to be also; this is why we should strive to be holy.

Before my incarceration I can remember being called some very ugly names. Sadly, I must admit some of the names I was called went right along with my character. Regardless of the reason for me being called these names, I should have been ashamed, but I don't ever think I was. Now that I am saved and applying the scriptures to my life, I am still called some names and these names still better identify my character: holier than-thou, holy roller, Mother Theresa and more. Some Christians are ashamed to be identified with holiness, but I am not ashamed -- I rejoice that I am identified as holy.

When I was a little girl I remember singing a nursery rhyme that went like this:

> If you're happy and you know it, clap your hands.
> If you're happy and you know it, clap your hands.
> If you're happy and you know it,
> and you really want to show it,
> if you're happy and you know it clap your hands

Now let me change these words just a little:

> If you're Holy and you know it, don't be ashame.
> If your Holy and you know it, don't look for fame.
> If your Holy and you know it and you really want to show it,
> If your Holy and you know it, don't live the same.

Why Do Men Speak Well About You?

Luke 6:26
Woe to you when everyone speaks well of you, for that is how their ancestors treated the false prophets.

You have a reason to be suspicious of a Christian who is always praised by others, especially when you are a Christian too, yet the same people hate you. When I observed this, it was obvious to me something was wrong. It didn't take long before I saw these so-called 'Christians' were being praised simply because they were people-pleasers.

Whenever I was in the company of other believers, I noticed that unbelievers would pass and speak to them by name, not bothering to speak to me. Some of them would even ask these people for advice or suggestions regarding something they are dealing with. This was somewhat strange to me because I knew these people were aware these so-called 'believers' walked contrary to the Word and that I was one to obey it. I am not saying this to boast; this is the truth and I'm only trying to get my point across. I was baffled as to why they did not come to me. Then I was quickly reminded of all the false prophets who told the people what they wanted to hear instead of what they needed to hear (2 Chronicles 18:5, KJV). These people would not have dared come to me because they knew I would have told them something they did not want to hear: the truth.

These inmates were known for mincing the Word, for helping inmates by condoning their wrongdoing; and some were even partakers in their illegal schemes. This is why so many people spoke well of them. Please don't get me wrong, it is okay if someone is speaking well of you but when you know you're not living right it would behoove you to ask yourself, 'why do men speak well of me'?

Lying Is Never Necessary

Revelation 21:8
But the cowardly, the unbelieving, the vile, the murderers, the sexually immoral, those who practice magic arts, the idolaters and all liars - they will be consigned to the fiery lake of burning sulfur. This is the second death."

People practice the sin of lying without giving it any thought. Lying is a sin that is commonly practiced. I find that most people lie to spare themselves from being embarrassed. Sparing yourself from embarrassment may be a good reason to lie, but regardless of the reason we should not practice lying.

When I first entered prison, I often put myself in situations that would have caused me to lie. Two of the girls I associated with lived in a different dormitory, which meant they ate with another group. Oftentimes, I would violate by eating outside my group just to eat with these two girls. Randomly, security would ask inmates when entering the cafeteria, "What dorm do you live in?" I found myself in a position where I had to make a choice: I could have lied about the dorm to which I was assigned to escape receiving a disciplinary report and avoid being put out of the cafeteria, or I could have responded truthfully and suffered the consequences.

It is quite common for inmates to lie on a witness statement to help a so-called friend. Sometimes these inmates witness what their friends did and twist the story around. Other times, these inmates are clearly in the blind and still fill out a witness statement claiming to know the facts, as an attempt to keep their friends from experiencing their punishment.

Lying is very serious. It is so serious that God's Word says liars have their way in the lake of fire (Revelation 21:8, KJV). Do not treat lying like it's nothing because it is something, something you don't ever need to do. In Ecclesiastes 3, we see there are times for various things, but it does not say there is a time to lie, because lying is never necessary.

Never Lie About Fasting

Matthew 6:16
When you fast, do not look somber as the hypocrites do, for they disfigure their faces to show others they are fasting. Truly I tell you, they have received their reward in full.

Fasting used to be very difficult for me to practice; not because of the process of denying the flesh of physical food but because of the people I would encounter during my fast.

Many times I was asked if I were going to the cafeteria and I would say no, then I was asked why, and I always said because, "I'm not hungry" or "I don't feel like it". Well, neither of these answers were true. In fact, I was very hungry and did feel like going to the cafeteria but I didn't because I was fasting, and I didn't believe I could tell others because it was my understanding that people were not supposed to know I was fasting. My understanding of fasting was so misconstrued I thought I would be struck down if others knew. Then the spirit quickened me and revealed to me that I shouldn't set out to let others know of my fast as if I'm some super Christian; however, it is okay to let someone know why I wasn't eating if they asked

We should not be a billboard or intentionally place ourselves in situations to tell people we are fasting. However, if someone asks why you are not eating it is okay to say, 'I would love to eat something but I'm fasting'. This is harmless. It is okay to tell someone you are fasting under certain circumstances, but do not ever simply volunteer this information and never lie to hide your fast.

Mere Giving is not Tithing

Malachi 3:8
**Will a mere mortal rob God? Yet you rob me.
But you ask, 'How are we robbing you?' In tithes and offerings.**

For many years I robbed God. Fortunately, I did not know any better. Now that I know better, I no longer rob Him. I know that we are all incarcerated but that still does not give us the right to hold back from God. You may think you do not have to give to God merely because you are not earning a paycheck, but you do not have to earn a paycheck to give tithes and offerings. The Bible does not teach us to just tithe from earnings, we are told to tithe from all our increase (Deuteronomy 14:22, KJV). Any money you receive from loved ones, etc. is considered an increase and it is your responsibility to tithe from it.

One of the inmates had mentioned to me she was going to tithe with a bank that was picking up funds for one of the ladies who used to be in prison with us. This lady had lost several family members in a tragic car accident. Although this was a very nice thing to do for this family, not even this should be considered tithing because this money would go to that family and benefit them alone. If every member in a particular church decided to do that, what would happen to the church? I am not saying we should not help others, but we shouldn't neglect our tithes in order to do so. It is okay to give to others, but it should be in addition to our tithes, not as a substitute.

Then contended I with the rulers, and said, why is the house of God forsaken (Nehemiah 13:11, KJV)? The house of God is forsaken due to a lack of tithes and offerings. If you have not been tithing start doing so, so you won't be in the class who forsake the house of God.

You Must Overcome

Revelation 21:7
Those who are victorious will inherit all this, and I will be their God and they will be my children.

Ignorance is no excuse for us to send ourselves to hell. The Lord is using volunteers to come into the facility to share the gospel with us, but more than that we have the Word of God. Once we are exposed to it, we are no longer considered ignorant.

We cannot live our lives displeasing God and thinking we will inherit everlasting life. This is not so. Neither is it biblical. But he that shall endure unto the end, the same shall be saved (Matthew 24:13, KJV). I am not saying you can be saved in the beginning and not at the end, but the Word of God says just that. Therefore, we must overcome everything we face.

And if children, then heirs, heirs of God, and joint heirs with Christ, if so be that we suffer with him, that we may be also glorified together (Romans 8:17, KJV). To live for Christ we must suffer, yet we must still overcome our sufferings. But the fearful, and unbelieving, and the abominable, and murderers, and sorcerers and idolaters, and all liars, shall have their part in the lake which burns with fire and brimstone: which is the second death (Revelation 21:8, KJV). If these sins are a part of your past, then you do not have a thing to worry about but if you are still practicing sin when you take your last breath then this will be your fate. Now that you see exactly what can cause you to be cast into the lake of fire you need to overcome these things. Nothing is worth being separated from God for eternity. Fight to keep this from happening by being an overcomer.

Push to Keep Doing Good

Galatians 6:9
Let us not become weary in doing good, for at the proper time we will reap a harvest if we do not give up.

Tests and trials are part of life; most of our tests come through the people Satan uses. Satan will use people to rub us the wrong way. Regardless of which way these people rub us, we must still do well by them and not get tired.

I can remember allowing myself to give in to the attacks of the enemy. While singing praises to God, in the room I was assigned to, my neighbor across the hall decided to tell me that she was going to come into the room and shut me up if I didn't stop singing. This lady was not saved. She was only saying what the enemy told her to say. What's ironic is I know all this, but I still decided to respond to this lady which lead to an argument. Just that quick I allowed myself to give place to the devil (Ephesians 4:27, KJV). I allowed this lady to get me angry and on top of that I sinned (Ephesians 4:26).

You see, I messed up because I allowed myself to get tired of being Christ-like with those who called me out of my name. I got tired of turning the other cheek. In other words, I got tired of doing well to the point that I fainted. But God does not want us to get so tired that we faint. We are to endure to the end (Matthew 24:13, KJV). Therefore, I got back up, repented of my sins and asked God to forgive me.

People will say or do things to us that will hurt. Remember, the devil is using those people so do not get on their level. Instead, fight to keep doing good.

Moved by Nothing

Philippians 4:11
I am not saying this because I am in need,
for I have learned to be content whatever the circumstances.

Paul did not say he was content when he was not in prison. Paul did not say he was content only when he had the foods he liked. Paul said that he was content no matter what and we should be also. Contentment should not be based on the job you have, the car you drive, or the people you live around, it should be based on you.

We used to get jelly with our breakfast to put on our biscuits. However, due to the budget cuts the state no longer provided us with it. I really love jelly. I did not eat biscuits for a while because I did not have the jelly to put on them. Although my breakfast was not the same anymore and I did not enjoy it as much, I did not murmur and complain about it and very soon I learned how to be content without jelly.

Prison life constantly brings about changes. For whatever reason, at any time you can be called to move to another room, another building or even another facility. Remember, we are incarcerated and should not get complacent in any situation. If we do, it will be difficult for us to adjust to the change.

Whatever God is doing in your life, be content with it. Whatever you have or do not have, be content. Along with contentment live godly, because godliness with contentment is great gain (1Timothy 6:6, KJV).

We must stop reacting to situations the same way as unbelievers. We are unlike them. People are watching us to see how well we handle situations that arise. The way we choose to respond could very well win a soul to the Kingdom. Do not allow the changes that occur to move you. Be content regardless!

Jailhouse Tattoos

Leviticus 19:28
Do not cut your bodies for the dead or put tattoo marks on yourselves. I am the LORD.

Getting a tattoo is common in prison. If you want to be a part of the so-called cool crowd then getting a tattoo is the thing to do. If you want to show your lover you love him or her, then tattoo their name on your body. Besides, this is like the ultimate expression of love, right? Wrong! The God who knows what is best for us has commanded us not to mark up our bodies; therefore, you do not have a reason or a right to do so.

Solomon spent much time making plans for the building of the temple (2 Chronicles 2). In the second and third chapters of 2 Chronicles we see how Solomon constructed the temple. This temple was being built for the Spirit of God to dwell. It was just a building, but God cared so much about the appearance of it that he gave specific instructions as to how everything should be done. God no longer dwells in a building. He still dwells in a temple, but our bodies are the temple of God and his Spirit dwells in us (1 Corinthians 3:16, KJV). If God cared about the appearance of a building, then how much more do you think he cares about how our bodies look that were made in his image?

God does not want us to mark up our bodies with tattoos. If any man defiles the temple of God, him shall God destroy; for the temple of God is holy, which temple you are (1 Corinthians 3:17, KJV). God is a good God and he only wants what is best for us. If God wanted you to have a tattoo then he would have created you with one. Instead, he created you in his image and he did not make any mistakes so stop acting like he did by marking up your body.

A Time to Hate

Ecclesiastes 3:8
A time to love and a time to hate, a time for war and a time for peace.

When I first came across Ecclesiastes 3:8 I thought it was an odd verse because my perspective was very narrow. As it began to broaden I was able to see things from God's point of view. Soon I came to the realization that it is okay for me to hate. In fact, my prayer to God was for him to help me love what He loves and to hate what He hates. Gradually, I began to notice how much I hated to hear someone slander another.

God is not pleased when we murmur and complain (Philippians 2:14, KJV) and out of nowhere I found myself hating this very thing. I no longer desired to gossip or tear people down. I no longer desired to violate the rights of another by stealing from them. These practices were all wrong and day by day I was beginning to hate them all.

Ask God to help you hate **what** he hates. Notice I did not say **who**, but **what**. God doesn't hate people, but He does hate the bad things people do and we should, too. We should hate stealing, we should hate lying, we should hate gossip; we should hate sin, period. If you are still caught up in your mess and want to get out, cry out to God and ask him to help you hate the sin you're in.

You Will Pay for Living an Ungodly Life

Ecclesiastes 8:11
When the sentence for a crime is not quickly carried out, people's hearts are filled with schemes to do wrong.

Don't think you will not be punished for your sins merely because you haven't been punished yet. Eventually, they will catch up with you. It may look like we are getting away with our mess, but we won't for long.

God is a good God. He is a loving God. He is a God that gives us grace and mercy every day. Although God is all these things and much, much, more, this still doesn't mean he won't punish us. Neither should this give us a green light to continue in our sins. What shall we say then? Shall we continue in sin, that grace may abound? God forbid! How shall we, that are dead to sin, live any longer therein? (Romans 6:1-2, KJV)

If we don't stop our evil works, God will allow the punishment for our consequences to fall on us. We may think we are invincible because we have been practicing evil for so long without getting caught. We will get caught! For evil doers shall be cut off, but those that wait upon the Lord, they shall inherit the earth (Psalms 37:9, KJV).

When are you going to learn? Your ungodly ways led you to prison. Now that you are in prison, you continue to practice evil works. Just as you are being punished for what you've done, you will be punished for what you are doing. It may not happen right away but sooner rather than later you will pay for living ungodly.

Giving to Invest

Proverbs 16:2
All a person's ways seem pure to them, but motives are weighed by the LORD.

It is always good to give to others. In fact, the Bible states that it is more blessed to give than to receive (Acts 20:35, KJV). Although giving is good, we can make it bad when we do so expecting something back in return.

Many people give for the wrong reasons. Instead of giving to bless, they give to invest. If you give to your church, or to your supervisor don't do it because you are hoping it helps you to be placed in a certain position. If you give to a friend or to a neighbor do it with a pure heart and not because you want something. If your giving is based on receiving, this is mere selfishness.

In the book of Acts we see a beautiful example of giving. The believers shared all their possessions without having a motive for doing so but they did have a reason -- they loved God and had giving hearts (Acts 4:32-37, KJV). Let this also be your only reason for giving so you can practice giving to bless and not to invest.

The Real Killer

John 7:24
Stop judging by mere appearances, but instead judge correctly

Prisons are filled with all types of people. Some are in prison for crimes as petty as theft and others are incarcerated for crimes as serious as murder. Unfortunately, some inmates are imprisoned for allowing the enemy to deceive them into killing their own children. Many of these people have been tried and sentenced in accordance with our laws. Although these people have been accused and are serving time for committing such a horrible act, the real killer remains on the loose.

Throughout my incarceration I encountered many people who were serving time for killing their own children. I can recall looking at these people and wondering how could they do something so awful. Then, after spending time around some of them, I saw that they were beautiful people. One lady in particular had a very sweet spirit and was a very nice lady. I had never seen her get in any trouble or be involved in any altercations. The person I saw could not have possibly killed her children. This convinced me that the enemy is real. Satan is the one who deceived these people into committing such a horrible act. He is still as subtle today as he was when he deceived Adam and Eve in the Garden of Eden (Genesis 3). It is very easy to point fingers at people. It is hard for us to hold someone else responsible for the acts of people. However, someone else is responsible. The devil is the guilty party. He is the one who comes to kill, steal, and destroy (John 10:10, KJV). Remember, the enemy is a spirit, so he has to use a body; this is why it is important for us to put on the whole armour of God (Ephesians 6, KJV). When we don't wear the armour of God, the enemy deceives us into abusing drugs, prostitution, stealing, and even murdering our own children.

The enemy has been using people to kill for a very long time. He deceived Herod into having all the male children two years and under killed (Matthew 2:16). He deceived parents into sacrificing their children (Leviticus 20:1-3, KJV). Unfortunately, he is still using people to kill today.

If you are one to judge those who are serving time for killing their children, please stop. God is the only one who may judge them. I am not trying to justify the actions of others because murder is wrong, just like every other sin. The same devil that took over my mind and deceived me into stealing also takes over the minds of others, causing them to murder. These poor individuals were deceived into committing a horrible act, but the devil is the real killer.

Relationships Tested by Time

Song of Solomon 3:1
All night long on my bed I looked for the one my heart loves; I looked for him but did not find him.

Many of us were in relationships before our incarceration. Some of us may have been married or had a boyfriend or girlfriend. However, as the months and years go by the whereabouts of these people are no longer known; usually this is because they have moved on with their lives and do not desire to be found.

Unfortunately, I am unable to speak from a wife's point of view because I have never been married. But at the time of my arrest I did have a companion who I loved dearly. I considered him to be the love of my life and the very thought of being separated from him made me sick. It is very painful being away from our companions. Yet this is a pain we must learn to deal with until time alleviates it.

I must say that I am very grateful to God for my incarceration. It was here in prison I learned that the love of my life didn't really love me. I reached this conclusion because my companion never visited me and communication through the mail was very limited. My companion did a disappearing act but every time I sought the Lord he was right there.

Don't waste precious time trying to find your spouse or companion. If you have to look for them it's because they don't want to be found. You may not know the whereabouts of your spouse/boyfriend but they know exactly where you are and if what you had is meant to be, he or she will reach out to you. In the meanwhile, commit yourself to building an intimate relationship with the one who didn't stop until He found you.

Be Grateful for the Little You Have

Zechariah 4:10
Who dares despise the day of small things.

Everything does not come in big packages -- some things come in small packages. Most of us want it big, but first we must be okay with starting small.

All too often I've seen inmates outright refuse to go to the canteen because they only had a few dollars on their books and they didn't want to go to the store to pick up a small bag. I used to be the very same way until I came across a scripture that said for who hath despised the day of small things (Zechariah 4:10, KJV). And then I remembered that all things work together for good to them that love God to them who are the called according to his purpose (Romans 8:28, KJV). You see this could have very well been a test from God to see if I was going to be grateful. At first I was not grateful; I was embarrassed to go to the store with $2 and $3 when others were spending $100. Then he showed me those people who never get anything and how I had enough to bless them. Immediately, I had to repent for being ungrateful.

We serve a big God who can bless us with big things. Maybe God has not already done so because he knows we have not been walking in gratefulness for the small things we already have. Begin to thank God for the little he's given you, then the bigger things will follow.

No Reason to Overeat

Proverbs 23:2
And put a knife to your throat if you are given to gluttony.

I miss being able to eat what I want whenever I want. Unfortunately, prison life does not allow us to eat the foods we desire. However, sometimes volunteers are approved to bring food in for annual parties. If you are blessed to be a part of such an event don't allow yourself to be a glutton, the fact that you are being served food that you can only get annually is not an excuse to sin.

Self-control is usually a term people relate to controlling one's anger, however it shouldn't be limited to this. Self-control is just what it says, controlling one's self. This even goes for your eating habits.

The food that is served to inmates in the cafeteria is usually the same thing from one week to the next: grits or oatmeal for breakfast; beans and rice, beef stew, jambalaya and a few other starchy foods for lunch and dinner. Being that the food in the prison cafeteria is not what we are used to, inmates look forward to the various annual dinners. This is an opportunity for us to eat some good food that we don't get in the cafeteria. We even get to eat fresh fruits and vegetables. Sadly, some of us don't just eat, but we overeat. We give in to the sin of gluttony. We give in to selfishness. There is no need to do this. God is not pleased with this behavior. Regardless of whether we get this type of food or not, we shouldn't give in to our appetite.

It is okay to go and enjoy yourself when you are invited to one of these dinners. However, you don't have to overeat in order to do so. Besides, everything we do must be done in moderation, and this goes for eating, too.

Don't Put Your Freedom before God

Matthew 6:33
But seek first his kingdom and his righteousness, and all these things will be given to you as well.

Inmates spend countless hours doing legal work. We all are on a mission to obtain our freedom, and nothing is wrong with this. Although physical freedom may be the top priority of most who are incarcerated, this still should not be the first thing we seek.

Reading law books, researching case law for hours a day and preparing motions to send to your judge are all good things to do and shows diligence on behalf of an inmate trying to obtain his or her freedom. Regardless of how good these things are, not even this should come before God. God will not settle for any other place but first.

We are commanded to seek first the kingdom of God, which is not meat and drink, but righteousness and peace, and joy in the Holy Ghost (Romans 14:17, KJV). Now that you know that you should first be seeking the kingdom of God, put down that law book and pick up your Bible. Take a break from researching law and start searching the scriptures. Put down that motion you are sending to your judge and began to communicate with the ultimate Judge.

God wants to give you everything that He has promised. Yet, you stop Him from doing so when you seek everything else first but Him. I know how badly you want your freedom, but you have to make up in your mind to first seek the only one who can set you free.

Provoke Others to Love

Hebrews 10:24
And let us consider how we may spur one another on toward love and good deeds.

Provoking others happens a lot in a prison setting. There are those who provoke others to argue and those who provoke others to fight. Yet, it is not often you see people provoke others to love.

Jesus is the most perfect example of love. Jesus is love. If we would just follow the acts of Jesus Christ, we could very well provoke others unto love. We can follow Jesus' example by sitting down to eat with sinners (Matthew 9:10). We can provide food for the hungry. We can offer to comb our roommates' hair if they can't do it themselves. We can get someone's laundry, fold it, and take it to them. You can openly forgive your enemies just like Jesus did (Luke 23:34, KJV).

Volunteers are also excellent examples of love. These people sacrifice their time to come and minister to inmates. Some of them take money out of their own pockets to purchase Bibles to distribute and to send inmates cards for birthdays and holidays. I must admit that their examples have provoked me to love others the way they love us.

There are many things we can do to show love to others. However, there are not many who are willing to do these things. I encourage you to start practicing acts of love so that you can provoke others to do the same.

Who's Really Scared?

Proverbs 28:1
The wicked flee though no one pursues, but the righteous are as bold as a lion.

Don't allow others to persuade you into doing what they want you to do by using their weak psychology; we must stop being so easily influenced. The world wants us to believe that we are scared and weak when we refuse to do wrong, but the word of God says we are bold as a lion.

When I worked in the kitchen, one of my co-workers asked me to fill up her bowl with sugar. Immediately, without thought, I boldly said no. She then told me to stay out of jail if I am scared. From this lady's perspective she viewed my actions as being scared, but I knew without a doubt that my actions exemplified boldness. I noticed that whenever one inmate asked another inmate to violate the rules for them, the inmate who refused is the one labeled as scared.

You will find in the Word of God that the lion is the strongest among beasts (Proverbs 30:30, KJV). Furthermore, God considers those who are righteous and take no part in wrongdoing as bold a lion. Why is this? This is because those who choose to do the right thing will suffer for it; when we choose to suffer by doing what's right, we are strong. It takes strength to walk in righteousness. On the other hand, those who are doing wrong are the ones who are really scared.

You are not scared because you are not giving people extra food from the line. You are smart. Moreover, you are bold. You know that when you refuse to violate the rules for another inmate you will be ridiculed by that person and their so-called friends, yet you do the right thing anyway. There is absolutely nothing scary about your actions. You are called to be bold and this is exactly what you are doing when you don't give into their selfish demands of you.

Don't Plan to Fornicate

1 Corinthians 6:18
Flee from sexual immorality. All other sins a person commits are outside the body, but whoever sins sexually, sins against their own body.

Unless you are married, sex should not be on your agenda upon release. Sexual intercourse is supposed to be experienced between a man and woman after marriage. Sex outside of marriage is fornication, and fornication is a sin. Therefore, if you are single this should not be a part of your plans.

Being intimate with my boyfriend was a part of my lifestyle before I came to prison. I'm not sure if I thought this was wrong or not. I most certainly had no idea what the Bible said about sex outside of marriage. However, I was determined to learn what the Word of God said and clean up all the areas of my life that were contrary to it. I knew that I would be released one day, and I didn't want to disobey God when I got out.

In reading the Bible I came across two words that drew my attention; those two words were flee fornication (1 Corinthians 6:18). I had to start working on this part of my life. I didn't want God to give me up to uncleanness through the lusts of my own heart (Romans 1:24, KJV). I learned that it is the will of God, even our sanctification, that we should abstain from fornication. That every one of us should know how to possess his vessel in sanctification and honor (1 Thessalonians 4:3-4, KJV).

Now that we know what the Word of God says about fornication, we need to hide these scriptures in our heart so we won't sin against God (Psalms 119:11, KJV). God has big plans for our lives, we can't mess them up by giving ourselves over to sin. If this is something that you are anticipating I hope that now you have a change of plans.

Murdered, but Not a Murderer

Acts 13:22
After removing Saul, he made David their king. God testified concerning him: 'I have found David son of Jesse, a man after my own heart; he will do everything I want him to do.'

We are no longer what we were before we came to Jesus Christ. The seed you allowed to uproot in your heart that resulted in you murdering someone does not have to remain. Regardless of the crime you committed you, too, can be recognized as a person after God's own heart.

King David had everything a man could want, but it was not enough. King David committed adultery with Uriah's wife, Bathsheba. As a result of this adulterous act, Bathsheba conceived a child (2 Samuel 11:5). To cover up this terrible thing, David wrote a letter to Joab telling him to set Uriah in the forefront of the hottest battle and then retire from him so that he would be killed. Joab did exactly as he was ordered, and Uriah the Hittite died in battle (2 Samuel 14-17, KJV).

King David was an adulterer and a murderer, but even after this he was known as a man after God's own heart. David didn't deny what he did instead he confessed his sin. (2 Samuel 12:13). We too must follow David's example and confess our sins unto God.

You can tell everyone your version of what happened that day when your actions claimed someone's life. Telling others can't help you; people would even use your own words to hurt you. God is the one you need to pour your heart out to; sure he already knows what you've done but he still wants you to confess. The quicker you admit this to yourself and to God the quicker you can walk in freedom.

People are cruel and they say and do cruel things. Don't be moved when someone call you a murderer, the word of God says that you were these things (1 Corinthians 6:9-11, KJV). Besides if you have sincerely repented as David did, soon others will be able to look at your lifestyle and see that you are someone after God's own heart, too.

Let the Lord Lead You

2 Samuel 5:19
So, David inquired of the Lord, "Shall I go and attack the Philistines? Will you deliver them into my hands?"

We say we trust God and that we are leaning and depending on Him, yet we fail to go to Him for guidance. Before we do anything we must seek the Lord first. After all, he's the only one who knows the end of a thing at the beginning (Isaiah 46:10, KJV).

King David didn't go up against the Philistines before inquiring of the Lord (2 Samuel 5:19, KJV). David understood that he didn't have control over his own life and was careful to consult the one who did. The Philistines came up yet again, but David didn't make a move until he inquired of the Lord, and this time the Lord told David not to go up (2 Samuel 5:23, KJV). And David did as the Lord commanded him (2 Samuel 5:25, KJV).

Throughout my incarceration I made many moves without inquiring of the Lord. I said with my mouth that Jesus Christ was Lord of my life, yet I was calling all the shots. I spent many days and nights working on my case, only to be denied by the courts. If only I would have gone to God first to ask what I should do regarding my legal matter, then he could have pointed me in the right direction and I would have been spared much heartache and wasted time.

If Jesus Christ is truly Lord of your life then start living like it and don't make another move unless He tells you to. God wants to be involved in our lives because He knows all about us. It is wise to allow the one who knows it all to make all the decisions.

No Right to Sin

Matthew 5:48
Be perfect, therefore, as your heavenly Father is perfect.

Jesus Christ was the only perfect man who ever walked on this earth. As Christians, we are called to be like Him. To do this we must stop using the fact that we are not perfect as a reason to sin and start striving for perfection.

Jesus said for us to be perfect even as our Father which is in heaven is perfect (5:48, KJV). Jesus did not say this just to say it, He said it because he knew that in Him, we can be perfect. We can live our life without practicing sin. Paul said they preach warning every man and teaching every man in all wisdom; that we may present every man perfect in Christ Jesus (Colossians 1:28, KJV). It is possible for us to live a perfect life as long as we are in Jesus Christ our Lord and Savior.

People are watching you. They are listening to you. They see you when you steal. They see you when you engage in homosexuality. They see you when you strong-arm others. They hear you when you use profanity, when you gossip, and when you tell lies. They also see that you attend church regularly. The problem you have is that you know these people are aware of how you live and your way to justify your lifestyle is to say, 'I am not perfect'. This is absolutely no excuse to sin.

If you are someone who regularly attends church services, yet practices sin daily, I encourage you to continue to go to church, but don't deceive yourself into thinking that you are sinning because you are not perfect. You do not have to be perfect to refrain from stealing and lying or any other sin. Look at those around you, those who live lives pleasing to God; this does not make them perfect, but they are willing to strive for perfection.

Look for Ways to Do Good

Proverbs 3:27
Do not withhold good from those to whom it is due, when it is in your power to act.

We are blessed to be a blessing. Don't allow an opportunity to do good for someone to pass by you. Everyone we encounter is due our love. We owe everyone love. Love goes beyond lip service; it is a verb and requires action.

Don't take it lightly that you have the use of your limbs, for this is a blessing. Not all of us are blessed in this way. Many inmates are confined to wheelchairs; some have to use walkers or canes. If you are not in need of any of these things, this is a blessing but you can do good for those who are in need of them. It is not easy for someone who has to use a walker or cane to carry their canteen bags. You can do good by volunteering to carry their bags for them without expecting anything in return. This means your motives for helping these people should be pure.

I can only assume that wheeling yourself around all day must be tiresome, yet someone who is confined to a wheelchair has no other choice. Since you are so blessed to have your health and strength, go ahead and ask the next person you see in a wheelchair if they need a push. Do unto others as you would have them do unto you (Luke 6:31, KJV). Wouldn't you want someone to give you a break if you were the one in the wheelchair? It is in your power so don't withhold this act of love that is due others.

Another Chance to Choose Life

Deuteronomy 30:19
This day I call the heavens and the earth as witnesses against you that I have set before you life and death, blessings and curses. Now choose life, so that you and your children may live.

It is obvious that we all took our freedom for granted. When we were blessed to have it we decided to give it up by not choosing life. Now that we are placed in this controlled environment, don't rebel or run from this blessing; instead let it teach you how to make the right choices.

Whenever the prison gets overcrowded, the decision is made to ship some inmates to other facilities. One day one of the ladies heard from one of the girls who had been shipped. The girl had written to tell her to also request a transfer because there are no rules to follow, you don't have to work and you can do whatever you want. News flash! Before we came to prison we were free to do whatever we wanted and with that freedom we chose to break the law. We did not choose life. Thus, we were removed from society in order to get our acts together.

The last place you need to be is in a facility with no rules. Until you surrender all over to the Lord Jesus Christ you need to be in a strictly controlled environment. Don't look at this as a bad thing, because it is not. This is truly a blessing. You need to be in a place that will help you by making decisions for you until you are wise enough to make them for yourself.

God wants to bless you. He wants you to live. So, utilize the time you have in prison to study the word of God so that you can learn how to choose life. Besides, if you can't obey the rules of the prison, you will not obey the laws of the land.

Don't You Dare Ask for A Job Change

Jonah 1:3
But Jonah ran away from the Lord and headed for Tarshish. He went down to Joppa, where he found a ship bound for that port. After paying the fare, he went aboard and sailed for Tarshish to flee from the Lord.

Use your time in prison to learn job skills. I know that you may not like the job that you have, but you don't have to like it to do the job. Strive to do your best and be a model worker.

Wherever you find yourself in this life, stability is extremely important. We must even show stability on the job that we are assigned to in prison. Remember you are not working for man. Whatsoever ye do, do it heartily, as to the Lord, and not unto men: knowing that of the Lord ye shall receive the reward of the inheritance: for ye serve the Lord Christ (Colossians 3:23-24, KJV). Now that you know who you are working for, quit being so quick to request a job change. It doesn't matter that your supervisor screams at you all day. It doesn't matter if your coworkers dislike you as long as you are doing the right thing and being obedient to the Lord. He is all that matters. God knows who your supervisor is and what kind of work you're doing. He has you where you are for a reason. If you continue to change jobs every time something doesn't go your way, this means you lack stability. You have to learn to deal with these problems, so that you will be prepared to work in the free world.

God told Jonah to go to Nineveh, but Jonah went to Tarshish instead because he didn't like the task God had told him to do (Jonah 1:1-3, KJV). Don't let the light afflictions you are faced with on your job keep you from doing the task God has equipped you to do. Stop running from the task you have been given and allow God to use it to prepare you for the task that awaits you.

A Just Portion

Proverbs 11:1
The Lord detests dishonest scales, but accurate weights find favor with him.

Some inmates are responsible for serving other inmates their meals in the cafeteria. Don't think that this means you are in control or that you are running things because you are not. The inmates you serve do not owe you anything. This is the job you have been assigned to do and you are expected to do it justly.

Don't give someone you don't quite care for less food because you can. They deserve an equal share. The word of God says thou shall not have in thy bag divers weights, a great and a small. Thou shall not have in thine house divers measures, a great and a small. But thou shall have a perfect and just weight a perfect and just measure shall thou have: that thy days may be lengthened in the land which the Lord thy God giveth thee (Deuteronomy 25:13-15, KJV). God does not only want you to be fair when weighing things, he wants you to be honest in all things. If you would practice this, God promises to increase your days on this earth.

If you have been placed in a position to supply others with goods of some sort, do so honestly. Don't fail to give someone their fair share just because you don't like them. This is wrong and it is an abomination to the Lord. Make up in your mind to put the foolishness aside and start giving everyone who comes through the line a just portion.

Leave Vengeance to God

Romans 12:19
Do not take revenge, my dear friends, but leave room for God's wrath, for it is written: "It is mine to avenge; I will repay," says the Lord.

It is human nature to want to hurt those who hurt us. We humans always feel the need to do unto others as they did unto us. We need to do away with this mentality and leave vengeance to God.

When I came to prison I was determined to get it right. I was determined to not only quote the Word but live it. I was sold out and my mind was made up. My determination to shun evil and stand up for the right caused me to have many enemies.

There were those who hated the Jesus in me so much that they would lie on me. One of my co-workers wanted me to fail so badly that she asked other inmates to write my supervisor and tell him that I was stealing from my workplace. When I found out about this plot, the first thing that came to my mind was revenge, but because of my relationship with Christ I quickly decided against it.

The Lord allowed me to find out some things about my co-worker that could have caused her to lose her job. I said that the Lord allowed, because He was testing me to see if I was going to take what I knew about my coworker and use it to expose her or if I was going to let Him handle the matter. It was very hard for me not to take matters in my own hands, but I didn't. Instead I turned the matter over to God since vengeance is His anyway.

Faced with Fears

Proverbs 10:24
What the wicked dread will overtake them; what the righteous desire will be granted.

Before my incarceration my life was a mess. The mess I had made of my life often caused me to walk in fear. Sadly, I didn't fear God because I didn't have enough sense to fear Him. The thing I feared the most was getting caught and going to prison.

Law-abiding citizens couldn't care less if the police are driving alongside them. In fact, most people feel safe when the police are around. They don't get nervous because the police pull them over to ask for their identification. When you are doing the right thing, being stopped by the police is no big deal.

I walked in fear every day before I went to jail. I feared most of the people in the mall because I was on a mission to shoplift. In my mind, everyone in the mall were plain clothed cops. Sin had me bound with fear, yet I didn't allow my fears to stop me from sinning. As a result, I was sentenced to 20 years for shoplifting. Finally, my sins had caught up with me and I found myself faced with the one thing I feared.

I know many of you can identify with me. Your crime may not have been shoplifting but whatever it was I'm sure we shared the same fears of getting caught. Now that the getting caught part is all over, we no longer have to walk in fear. Getting caught and being forced to face my fears brought me so much relief. I didn't want to go to prison, but unbeknownst to me I was in prison way before I got caught.

Let's stop fooling ourselves: the life we chose to live was miserable. No one in their right mind should ever want to go back to a life of sin. In fact, living a life of sin is no life at all. God did every one of us a favor, and we need to thank Him every day for allowing us to be faced with our fears and freed from the sin we were in.

Prison Over Parole

2 Corinthians 5:17
Therefore, if anyone is in Christ, the new creation has come: The old has gone, the new is here!

Parole is a blessing extended to some inmates. Sadly, some of these inmates reject this blessing. These inmates want to go home but they don't want to be paroled out. Someone who is serious about walking with the Lord and desperately wants to do the right thing should not have a problem with being released on parole.

It touched me whenever I heard a fellow inmate say that they were not going to be able to do anything when they go home until they get off parole. This always bothered me because the things that a parolee are not allowed to do are things that a Christian should not be doing anyway. If we claim to be Christians, then the prohibitions of parole should not move us. Yet, some inmates are so nervous about being released on parole that they refuse it and decide to do the rest of their time in prison instead.

One day the conversation came up about how in the near future law makers were contemplating passing a bill that will allow lifers, who meet certain criteria, to be released on parole for the rest of their lives. If I had a life sentence this would have sounded like music to my ears. However, I heard one lifer say that she would rather stay in prison than to be placed on parole for the rest of her life. I couldn't believe what I was hearing.

If you have sincerely changed and have it in your heart to do the will of God, then it should not matter to you if a parole officer lived in your house or was assigned to follow you everywhere you went. It is time to get rid of the old and walk in the new. If you are really changed from the inside out, then you would be able to live your life as a productive citizen in society. I believe if you would do this, God would cause your parole officer to recommend that your parole be terminated. He will do this because your new lifestyle will be so exemplary that it would cause your parole officer to see that supervising you would be a waste of time and money.

An All the Time Friend

Proverbs 17:17
A friend loves at all times, and a brother is born for a time of adversity.

Good friends are hard to find. When we think we have a friend, sooner, rather than later, we discover the person is not a friend at all. Most people consider a friend to be someone who tells them what they want to hear, instead of what they need to hear. People like this can't be trusted and most definitely shouldn't be considered a friend.

Are you a friend who loves at all times? When you are an all the time friend, you will love your friend when she tells you that you are wrong. An all-the time friend will love you when you tell them that you are not buying them cigarettes because they are harming their temple. An at-all-times friend will love you even when the two of you disagree.

Don't be so desperate to have a friend that you compromise to keep them. It is best that you tell them the truth, so you know if your friend is really a friend at all. If they don't stick around no matter what, then it is best you don't consider that person a friend. Especially if he or she are not one at all times.

Wrongful Gain Will Not Remain

Proverbs 13:22
A good person leaves an inheritance for their children's children, but a sinner's wealth is stored up for the righteous.

Evil doers obtain many material things through their sinful lifestyles. However, there is no need for us to fret over what they have because it is not for them. Little do they know everything they have obtained unjustly will be taken from them and given to the righteous.

When I entered prison and came across Proverbs 13:22, I could hardly believe what I was reading. I couldn't believe this scripture had manifested in my life. You see, I had many nice things in my house. I had a brand-new stove that I barely used. I had a big screen television and several smaller ones. I had a computer, fax machine, and brand-new furniture throughout my home. However, all this stuff was obtained illegally, and it all fell into the hands of my brother's mother-in-law, who happened to be an older Christian woman who didn't have much. Yes, my unjust gain was given to the just.

In prison I still see this scripture come to pass. Several times I've seen security confiscate a store bag from an inmate who obtained it through some illegal scheme. Many times the officer would take the bag and distribute it to indigent inmates.

It is wrong to accumulate anything by means of illegal activity. We shouldn't want anything so badly that we resort to criminal behavior. You may get away with doing so for a while but right when you least expect it, your wealth will be taken away and given to the righteous.

Walk in Your Authority

Mark 1:27
The people were all so amazed that they asked each other, "What is this? A new teaching and with authority! He even gives orders to impure spirits and they obey him."

Homosexuality is a sin that is commonly practiced, especially in prisons. Most of the people who practice this sin do not respect themselves, neither do they care who they disrespect. However, you don't have to tolerate this lifestyle being forced on you.

If you call yourself a Christian, start acting like one. Don't get Christianity twisted and think this means you have to be a doormat. Don't think that Christianity means you must be exposed to ungodliness. I'm telling you, you don't have to, and you need to utilize the authority you have in Jesus Christ to take a stand against it.

The shower area is for inmates to shower. The janitor closet is an area used to store cleaning supplies. You are free to access these areas. You do not have to avoid these areas merely because a homosexual couple insist on using them for their ungodly activities. If you approach one of these areas and you find someone using them for sexual activities, don't you dare wait for them to get out. Instead, with the authority you have in Jesus Christ, you command them to come out so that you can do what you need to do. You don't have to be ugly. You can do this in love, but you must speak with authority. If they refuse to leave the area you have every right to report them to security. Who cares if the world sees you as a "rat"? Your concern should be that Christ sees you as a Christian who is bold enough to take a stand against unrighteousness.

Are You Really Being Led?

John 14:6
Jesus answered, I am the way and the truth and the life.
No one comes to the Father except through me.

Before Christ, believers were led by a pillar of cloud by day, and a pillar of fire by night (Exodus 13:21, KJV). Although Christians today are no longer led by these things, we still are being led but must understand the Spirit's leading. You will never be led to do something that is contrary to the Word of God.

I've noticed that when a believer doesn't want to do or say something, to avoid whatever they don't want to do or say they use the Holy Spirit as an excuse. They say that the Holy Spirit has not led them. We should not make a move without the Spirit's leading, but first we need to know if it's really the Holy Spirit leading us.

One Sunday morning, myself and some other inmates were leaving a church service. Shortly thereafter we were approached by a security officer who was clearly abusing the authority she had over us. She screamed at us and rudely ordered us in the direction she wanted us to take. I noticed that this security had recently come in with one of the churches and sung on the praise and worship team. Remembering this, I sarcastically responded, "Yes ma'am, Ms. Christian." I'll be the first to admit I was wrong for responding this way, but my flesh won me over. This security became so upset that she snatched my ID from my shirt and later I received a disciplinary report. I would have been okay if the security had written me up for what I said, but instead she lied. The girl who witnessed the incident claimed to be very angry because of this. Yet, when it was time for her to tell the truth about what happened she said the Spirit told her not to get involved. I don't doubt that this girl was told this by a spirit but it certainly wasn't the Holy Spirit leading her to withhold truth.

People are called to be witnesses to testify to the truth. If you are ever called to be a witness, you are obligated to do the same. We must stop claiming we are being led by the Spirit when we are not. Besides, Jesus Himself is truth, and He will never lead you to withhold it.

Don't Look Back

Genesis 19:26

But Lot's wife looked back, and she became a pillar of salt.

Everything God has in store for us is in our future and not in our past. The old lifestyle we once lived is behind us. God has delivered us from it so don't you dare look back.

Abraham's nephew Lot and his family lived in the City of Sodom. The people of Sodom were very wicked people. They were so evil that God decided He was going to destroy the entire city (Genesis 19:13). Yet before doing so, God gave Lot and his family an opportunity to leave. Lot warned his sons, but they did not take him seriously and they stayed in Sodom. As Lot's wife was leaving the city she looked back and was turned into a pillar of salt (Genesis 19:26).

What has God delivered you from? Drugs, lying, stealing, perhaps gossiping. Whatever it is, God has delivered you and it is up to you to stay delivered. You can't do this by looking back. When you look back you'll be tempted to go back. There is absolutely nothing in your past but heartache and pain. Remember, it was your past that caused you to be where you are today. This is nothing you want to experience again, so take advantage of your deliverance and whatever you do, please don't look back.

Prison Is a Blessing in Disguise

Romans 8:28
And we know that in all things God works for the good of those who love him, who have been called according to his purpose.

The God we serve is an awesome God. He can take our time in prison and cause it to work out for our good. I couldn't see this happening when I first read the scripture above. My thoughts were, 'what's good about prison', but He didn't say that the thing was good, only that He will cause it to work together for our ultimate good.

Don't look at your prison experience as a bad thing. If you try to broaden your perspectives, prison wouldn't look so bad. Stop focusing only on being set free, then you will be able to see the benefits of prison.

I've seen countless women arrive at prison looking their worst. This was because drugs had taken a toll on their physical appearance. However, after spending years in prison I saw these women transform. Their hair was healthier, they no longer looked anorexic, missing teeth were replaced by the state; I mean, a complete makeover.

You see women and men who are sent to prison lacking a high school diploma but leave with their GED and a college education. You see those who discover how creative they are and go on to spend their time making beautiful crocheted items, furniture, cards, clothing, and so much more. More importantly, they become involved in church services and Bible studies that lead them toward building a strong relationship with our Lord and Savior Jesus Christ. They find themselves witnessing to others, telling them about the good news. They are reading the Bible daily, something they never did before.

Take a few moments to think about the condition you were in when you came to prison and look at yourself now. Think about all you've accomplished that you wouldn't have on the outside. Now thank God for allowing your time in prison to work together for your good.

Picked Out to Be Picked On

Job 1:8
Then the Lord said to Satan, "Have you considered my servant Job? There is no one on earth like him; he is blameless and upright, a man who fears God and shuns evil."

We are all called to walk uprightly. If you are doing so, I want you to know God is pleased with your walk. The Lord is so pleased that He has allowed Satan to use people to slander your name, lie on you, plot against you and commit all other types of light affliction against you.

Jesus Christ the same yesterday and today and forever (Hebrews 13:8). The same God who asked Satan 'have you considered my servant Job?', is asking Satan 'has he considered you?'.

No one said your Christian walk was going to be easy. In fact, many are the afflictions of the righteous: but the Lord delivers him out of them all (Psalm 34:19, KJV).

There are many people in this world who are self-destructive and couldn't care less about righteous living. This attitude is expressed even more in the prisons. Trying to live life as a Christian is difficult, but I am a witness that it can be done. You just have to be mindful that God considers you faithful and because of your strong faith you will be tested even more. To whom much is given much is required (Luke 12:48, KJV).

God has given you so much and you are boldly operating in those gifts, for this reason alone Satan is angry. He will continue to use everyone who will submit to him, to come up against you. God knows you have what it takes to withstand all the attacks, which is why God has allowed you to be picked out to be picked on.

Resist Rejoicing

Proverbs 24:17-18
Do not gloat when your enemy falls; when they stumble, do not let your heart rejoice, or the Lord will see and disapprove and turn his wrath away from them.

Every day on this earth we need to strive to please God. In order to do this, we can't give in to the temptation to please the flesh, and it pleases the flesh when we see our enemies fall. This is why we don't live to please the flesh, because when we do, we displease God.

When our enemies do whatever they can to hurt us, whether it be physically or mentally, we want to see them get what we think they deserve. Forgetting all the many times we crucified our Lord and Savior Jesus Christ and didn't get what we deserved. Instead we received his grace and mercy. We should never be glad to see bad things happen to people, not even an enemy. David experienced this very thing, he said in mine adversity they rejoiced, and gathered themselves together: yea, the abjects gathered themselves together against me, and I know it not, they did tear me, and ceased not (Psalm 35:15, KJV).

The Jews were God's chosen people. Yet the Jews refused to accept Jesus as their Lord and Savior. Because of this the gentiles were able to come in through adoption. Still, Paul warned gentile Christians not to rejoice because they were grafted in and the Jews on the other hand were rejected.

Somebody may tell a lie about you that sends you to lockdown, and some may go as far as trying to physically harm us. Regardless of what is done to us, we cannot allow their actions to cause us to want to see harm fall upon them. These people will face the consequences of their actions eventually, but when they do, set your mind on pleasing God by not rejoicing.

Saving for Release

Luke 16:10
Whoever can be trusted with very little can also be trusted with much, and whoever is dishonest with very little will also be dishonest with much.

Unlike many of the inmates with whom I served time, I did not have a family who was able to send me plenty of money. Don't get me wrong, my family sent me money, but most of the time it was not much. I was grateful for the little they sent me and made sure to spend it wisely.

Eating junk food is something I love to do. I purchased snacks whenever I had the funds to do so, but I made sure to purchase the things I needed first. Also, I didn't just purchase things I could use in prison; wisdom caused me to look past prison and began preparing for my release.

If you are in an institution that allows you to make some outside purchases, take advantage of this opportunity by purchasing things you will need when you get home. I purchased an iron and I bought bras and panties. I stacked up on socks and sleepwear. Even if you cannot make outside purchases you can still purchase what you can from the canteen. You can stock up on soap, deodorant, lotion, and other personal items you will need upon your release. This is a wise way to spend your money, especially if you won't have much help once you are discharged.

There are some inmates who get so much money from their families that if they would just save a portion of it they would have enough to purchase a brand-new car when the time comes. Yet they waste their money instead. I didn't have enough to save for a new car, but I made sure I bought what I could afford. This was my way of eliminating a few of the expenses I would be faced with upon release.

You see, my family could not afford to help me financially when I got out of prison. This is why I chose to be a good steward over the little money my family sent me. When we do our best with the little we have, God will faithfully bless us with much more.

Don't Scheme to Get Money

1 Timothy 6:10
For the love of money is a root of all kinds of evil. Some people, eager for money, have wandered from the faith and pierced themselves with many griefs.

I'm sure each one of us could use more money. Having enough money makes life so much easier, though we should never rely on deceitfulness just to obtain it.

Most of the people I've encountered in prison complained about everything. This always baffled me because inmates already have everything they need. No, we are not living luxuriously, nor should we, but we do have it made. Inmates do not have to pay bills, we don't have to pay for necessities, neither do we have to pay for groceries even though we eat every day. We are provided with minimal healthcare for little to no cost, yet inmates are always looking for ways to scheme money out of the prison system.

One day while eating in the cafeteria I witnessed an inmate slip on water. There was a wet floor sign, but I can only assume the lady did not see it. She was not hurt so she got right up. A few inmates who saw the incident began shouting at the girl, saying she was stupid and if it had been them, they would have faked an injury just to file a lawsuit.

You may think you are hurting the employees at the prison, but you are not. You are hurting yourself because you have to deal with God. You will suffer the consequences of your actions. Just in case you don't know, taxpayers pay to house prisoners. Yes, they are being made to take care of us for our wrongdoing. Don't take more money from the taxpayers with your deceit. It is okay to wish you had more money. However, don't allow your desires to cause you to start thinking about deceitful ways to get it. Start thinking about those things that are true, honest, just, pure, lovely and of good report (Philippians 4:8, KJV) and you won't have time to imagine deceit.

Don't Say a Word in Your Defense

Ecclesiastes 3:7
A time to be silent and a time to speak.

When people accuse us falsely, we don't need to respond. People who respond usually do so when they're trying to prove a point to others. This is a sign of weakness. We need to learn how to practice being silent; silence is an excellent way to handle accusations, lies, and anything else the enemy brings our way.

After Jesus was arrested, He was led away to Caiaphas the high priest, where the scribes and the elders were assembled. At this hearing, Jesus was falsely accused. Out of all the false witnesses who came up against Jesus, He did not see the need to defend Himself in word or deed; He remained silent (Matthew 26:57-63).

There are going to be times when people will openly and falsely accuse us, slander our name, lie about us, and much more. Unfortunately, we face these times more often in a prison setting. However, regardless of what people may say to us or about us, we don't have to say a word. This is the perfect time to keep silent (Ecclesiastes 3:7).

Silence is not a sign of weakness; it is a sign of strength. It takes strong self-control to remain silent while you are being falsely accused. It is natural to want to defend yourself, but you don't have to. Instead you can follow the example of our Lord and Savior Jesus Christ and not say a word in your defense.

You Can Find Grace in Prison

Genesis 39:4

Joseph found favor in his eyes and became his attendant. Potiphar put him in charge of his household, and he entrusted to his care everything he owned.

God is always ready to bless us with His grace. Grace is not available only to those who are physically free but is extended to everyone, even prisoners. No matter where we are, God's grace can find us.

Joseph, who was sold into slavery by his jealous brothers (Genesis 37:11-27), ended up being taken down to Egypt where he was thrown in jail. Joseph found grace in the sight of Pharaoh, who placed Joseph over his house. Pharaoh told Joseph that all the people would be ruled by his word, and that he would be the only one greater than Joseph. The same grace that Joseph found with Pharaoh can be found with the prison officials who have authority over us. At the Louisiana Correctional Institute for Women inmates are often given the opportunity to purchase food. The food that could be purchased was food that we couldn't get from the cafeteria, such as: bacon cheeseburgers, fried chicken, and chef salads. However, to purchase this food, there must be money in their accounts, or family could purchase it through visitation. Unfortunately, I wasn't getting money often and I only had about five visits in eight years, so there was no way I would have been able to purchase some good food.

One day I was called and told I would be working the food sale. I was very grateful for such an opportunity. This meant that the food all the other inmates had to purchase was given to me for free and in abundance. This was truly the grace of God. I couldn't afford to purchase this food for myself, but after finding grace in the sight of God, he moved on the heart of man to place me in a position where I was able to earn the food I couldn't afford to buy.

Church Behavior

Ecclesiastes 5:1
Guard your steps when you go to the house of God. Go near to listen rather than to offer the sacrifice of fools, who do not know that they do wrong.

Confirmation! This was a word I yelled out during church services all too often. After doing so for a long time I was convicted. The Lord showed me that I wanted everyone to know that I was on one accord with the preacher, and that I could say confirmation because in this area of my life I had it all together. As if because of this, I'm so much holier than everyone else in church. Please don't get me wrong -- there is nothing wrong with the Lord using someone to confirm something in our lives. However, it is out of order when you have to disrupt the church by letting everyone know that He did. Our relationship with God is personal, and God knows when something was confirmed for us, no one else needs to know.

If the preacher begins to quote a scripture, let him finish it without your help. It is a good thing if you have memorized scripture, but no one has to know. God already knows how well you know the Bible, no one else should matter.

The next time you go to church, go ready to hear and not to be heard. You don't have to blurt out confirmation or quote scriptures for the preacher. No one else needs to know how much scripture you know, just let them see how much scripture you can live.

Beware of Making Promises to God

Ecclesiastes 5:4
When you make a vow to God, do not delay to fulfill it. He has no pleasure in fools; fulfill your vow.

We have all made promises to people at some time or another. Sometimes we make promises to God, but usually this is done when we are in trouble. Nothing is wrong with making promises to God, but when we do, we better make sure we keep them.

In the word of God, we find where promises were made to God. The writer of Psalm 66 wrote: I will go into thy house with burnt offerings: I will pay thee my vows, which my lips have uttered and my mouth hath spoken, when I was in trouble (Psalm 66:13-14, KJV). As you can see, the Psalmist made a vow in time of trouble, and he was faithful to pay that vow.

One of the volunteers who came to the prison was an inmate many years ago. This woman was given an 18-year sentence. In the first year of her sentence she made a vow to God that if He would get her out of prison, she would serve him for the rest of her life. Not long afterwards, God turned this woman's 18-year sentence into 18 months. This woman remembered the vow she made to the Lord and fulfilled it by returning to the prison as a volunteer to teach the Word of God.

When thou shalt vow a vow unto the Lord thy God, thou shalt not slack to pay it; for the Lord thy God will surely require it of thee; and it would be sin in thee (Deuteronomy 23:21, KJV). As inmates, we make many vows to the Lord. The vows of inmates are made from a place of desperation. Regardless of how desperate we are when we vow a vow unto the Lord, we are expected to keep our word and there will be no reconsideration (Proverbs 20:25, KJV).

Until Prison Do Us Part

Exodus 20:14
You shall not commit adultery.

Remember the vow you made to your spouse? That you will be faithful and remain together until prison do you part. I know you said death and not prison, yet you have allowed prison to part you from your spouse.

If you are fortunate enough to have your spouse by your side during your incarceration, this is a blessing. Some spouses are faithful enough to stick around. Usually wives support their incarcerated husbands to the end, but this is seldom the case with husbands.

Inmates who are married tend to enter prison and begin to engage in relationships with other inmates. We all know there are no co-ed prisons here in America, so these relationships are obviously between the same sex, which means you are not only committing adultery but are also engaging in homosexuality. You may be deceived into thinking that your spouse is also being unfaithful. Whether this is true or not, it should not be the basis of your faithfulness. You are to be faithful regardless. If your spouse is unfaithful, give it to God and let Him deal with it. Even if your spouse admits to you that he or she is being unfaithful, that still does not give you the right to do the same.

If you are committing adultery it will behoove you to end the relationship right now. Confess your sins to God and repent. You are married and should do everything in your power to prevent your incarceration from ending it. You made a promise to be with your spouse until death, so stop allowing prison to tear you two apart.

Father Knows Best

Ecclesiastes 6:12
For who knows what is good for a person in life, during the few and meaningless days they pass through like a shadow? Who can tell them what will happen under the sun after they are gone?

Only God knows the end of a thing from the beginning (Isaiah 46:10, KJV). He knows what's good for us and we don't, so we need to let Him lead us. Besides, the fact we are all incarcerated is evidence we don't know how to lead ourselves.

Abram and Lot's herdsmen had strife between them over having too many possessions and not enough land. To settle this conflict, Abram asked Lot to choose any part of the land and he would take what was left. And Lot lifted up his eyes, and behold all the plains of Jordan, that it was well watered everywhere, before the Lord destroyed Sodom and Gomorrah, even as the garden of the Lord, like the land of Egypt, as thou come unto Zoar (Genesis 13:10, KJV). Lot chose the land that looked good to the eyes and thought he had gotten the better part of the deal. What he didn't know was that because of his choice he would lose his possessions, his wife, and his daughters. What Lot thought was good really turned out to be bad; he should have sought God first and allowed God to lead him.

The bottom line is, we don't know what's good. What looks good today could very well prove to be deadly tomorrow. I'm sure that going home sounds good to all of us, but though it may sound good it may not be good for us to go at this time. We are anxious to get home but God, who knows best, may very well be keeping the doors closed for our good.

Nothing Is Crazy About Telling the Truth

John 8:32

Then you will know the truth, and the truth will set you free.

Lying always made me feel horrible. It made me feel untrustworthy and dishonest and rightfully so. This is something I don't ever want to practice again. Regardless of what type of bad situation we may find ourselves in, lying should never be an option.

One day an inmate approached me and told me she had been in violation of the no smoking indoors rule. She further said she was smoking in her room the other night and right after she finished the Major passed and said she smelled smoke, then asked her if she had been smoking. She said that she responded by saying yes. The major told her she was not going to give her a disciplinary report because of her honesty, but also stated that she would get one if it happened again. When the other inmates found out that she told the truth, they all thought she was stupid, which caused her to question herself.

After David had Uriah killed, God sent Nathan to him to confront him with his sin. To confront David, Nathan used a parable about a rich man and a poor man. As soon as David heard the parable he knew immediately that he was the rich man; David did not lie about his actions, instead he admitted that he had sinned against the Lord (2 Samuel 12:1-13, KJV).

Tell the truth at all times, even if the truth means a potential disciplinary report. Of course, carnal minded people are going to think you are crazy and that you've lost your mind, but when you develop the mind of Christ you will see there is nothing crazy about telling the truth.

Money Can't, but Jesus Can

Ecclesiastes 10:19
A feast is made for laughter, wine makes life merry, and money is the answer for everything.

Money is used in every part of the world. It may not be called money everywhere we go, but it is used for the same reasons. People use money to buy food, pay bills and so much more. Regardless of how important it is to have money, it still isn't the answer to all things.

I believe all inmates have the same thing in mind upon entering the parish jail at the time of arrest: get on the phone to find someone with the money to bail us out. There are times the bond we have is so high we simply can't afford to pay it. Then there are times we pay our bonds and discover we still can't get out because the probation or parole officer has placed a hold on us. Then there are those isolated cases where no bond is set at all.

Money is not the answer to all our problems. In fact, money is not the answer to any of our problems. Yes, we use money to get ourselves out of some binds, but it still isn't the answer. Jesus is the answer. Jesus is the only one who can touch the heart of the probation or parole officer and cause them to lift the hold. Jesus is the only one who can enable whomever to work and earn money so they have the means to post our bonds.

A certain lame man was carried daily and laid at the gate of the temple which is called Beautiful. This man asked people for money as they entered the temple. One day as Peter and John were about to go into the temple, this lame man asked them for money. Peter said, 'Silver and gold have I none; but such as I have give thee: In the name of Jesus Christ of Nazareth rise up and walk'. Immediately his feet and ankle bones received strength (Acts 3:1-7, KJV). This man was expecting money, but he got something far greater than money could buy.

As you can see, money is not the answer to any of our problems. Sure, we can all benefit from having money and it can certainly help us to an extent, but it still isn't the answer. Jesus Christ is the answer to any situation that arises, so give Him a try and stop wasting your money

Dealing with Rejection

John 1:11
He came to that which was his own, but his own did not receive him.

Rejection is a painful thing to experience. Unfortunately, we will all face it at some point in our lives. The question is, how will you deal with it when it comes your way?

The thing that hath been, it is that which shall be; and that which is done is that which shall be done: and there is no new thing under the sun (Ecclesiastes 1:9, KJV). There is nothing new about rejection. If you just look through the Bible you will see exactly what I'm talking about.

Jeremiah was rejected, not only by the people but also by members of his own family (Jeremiah 12:5-6). Cain's offering was rejected by God (Genesis 4:3-5, KJV). Jesus himself was rejected by the people of his hometown of Nazareth (Matthew 13:55, KJV), and by the religious leaders (Matthew 21:42, KJV). Rejection has always been and will always be.

Prisons are filled with men and women who refuse to tolerate rejection. Some of these people are serving time in prison for taking the lives of their spouses or companions because they couldn't accept being rejected by them. These same people come to prison, get involved in a homosexual relationship and, once they are rejected, they result to violence. I've heard inmates say 'hurt people, hurt people'. I say this only happens when hurt people lack self-control.

There are millions of people who have been hurt due to rejection and didn't choose to turn to violence. I am one of those people. When Jesus sent out the 12 disciples he told them to shake the dust off their feet when they leave the house or city of those who receive them not (Matthew 10:14, KJV). The disciples did not result to violence; they took Jesus's advice and moved on.

Many of us are planning to go before the parole or pardon board, yet how do we expect a favorable hearing if we have a pattern of violence in our prison files, due to rejection. Jesus said He will never leave or forsake us (Hebrews 13:5, KJV), but we must face the fact that others will. We don't have the right to take a life because someone doesn't want us anymore, or resort to any other form of violence. Cry out and ask Jesus to help you walk in self-control. Then the next time you are rejected you'll be able to shake it off and move on.

Invading Privacy with Your Eyes

1 Corinthians 13:5
It does not dishonor others, it is not self-seeking, it is not easily angered, it keeps no record of wrongs.

Prisoners do not have much privacy and the little we do have is usually violated by the stares of other inmates. Privacy is unheard of in a prison setting. However, if you would do your part it doesn't have to be.

I know God gave you eyes to see and you use them to look at whomever or whatever you choose. I agree with you if this is your position. However, we don't have to use our eyes to stare at people, especially when they are trying to get dressed or perhaps take a shower. You can make these people feel a little better by forgetting they exist in these moments.

Whenever I see someone is getting ready to get dressed or undressed, I do whatever I can to respect the little privacy they have. To do this I may have to turn and face the wall or just put the covers over my head. Whenever I was in a facility where the showers were in an open area, I made it my business not to look in that direction unless I was headed to the showers myself. If I was in fact on my way to the shower, I was determined not to face the others in the shower. I was adamant about respecting everyone in whatever way I could.

Believe it or not, it is very rude to stare at people. If you are being rude then you are not walking in love in this area because love is not rude (1 Corinthians 13:5). As inmates, we have put ourselves in a position that has stripped us of most of our privacy -- don't allow your staring to take away the little privacy we have by invading it with your eyes.

Watch Out for the Small Foxes

Song of Solomon 2:15
Catch for us the foxes, the little foxes that ruin the vineyards, our vineyards that are in bloom.

Relationships of all kinds are often torn apart. Most relationships end because of some small matter. The same small foxes that Satan used to try to destroy the relationship between Solomon and his love will destroy yours too, if you don't watch out.

Throughout our lifetime, we will encounter many different relationships. We have relationships with our parents, children, siblings, and other family members. We also have relationships with our spouses and friends. For any of these relationships to succeed, we must work at them and never act on assumptions.

I see relationships between inmates come and go all the time. I'm talking about relationships between believers broken over foolishness. The devil comes to kill, steal, and destroy (John 10:10). If we let him, he will destroy our relationships and most of the time he uses small foxes.

The devil wants to bring division any way he can. He knows he can't come with something big because we would see it coming and wouldn't give in to it. He waits until we are told no after asking someone for something, then he comes into our mind and say things like what kind of Christian is she/he telling you no, or she has more than enough, how dare she not give to you, or she didn't tell the other person no. None of this is our business. The fact is you were told no, so don't allow this to ruin the relationship you have with others. Therefore, be on the lookout if you want your relationships to last by watching out for the small foxes.

Nice for A Reason

Proverbs 19:4
Wealth attracts many friends, but even the closest friend of the poor person deserts them.

As Christians, what we do is of extreme importance. People are watching us and they see what we are doing, how nice and kind we are to certain people. Above all God sees us too, he sees everything we do, but he is more concern about why we do what we do.

We are told in the word of God that it is a sin to have respect of persons (James 2:9, KJV). When we have respect of persons we are being deceitful. In prison, it is common to see one result to this as a means of survival.

Unfortunately, there are many pregnant women in prison. I can recall one girl who was placed in the room with me. She was very naïve, which is not a good thing to be in prison. This girl was blessed financially and, because of this, had many so-called friends. My roommate didn't have to make her bed because someone did it for her. She didn't have to concern herself with washing clothes because her so-called friends took care of this, too. She even had someone run her bath water for her. On the surface there was nothing wrong with this, but I had to question their actions because there was another far less well-to-do pregnant girl on the same dorm with us who made her own bed, washed her own clothes and ran her own bath water. This woman did these things herself because no one volunteered to do them for her.

I can't stress enough how wrong it is to take advantage of people because of what they have and what you might get. If you are one of those people who caters to others for these reasons you are a deceiver. Don't give in to the temptation to misuse others just to get what you want; practice helping others simply because it's the right thing to do.

Rebuilding Hindered by Wars

1 Kings 5:3
You know that because of the wars waged against my father David from all sides, he could not build a temple for the Name of the Lord his God until the Lord put his enemies under his feet.

At this point in our lives we should all focus on starting anew. However, it's almost impossible to start fresh when we are constantly at war with people. The wars must first cease before we can proceed with rebuilding our lives.

When David offered to build the Temple, God told him, through the prophet Nathan, that he wasn't going to be the one to build it (2 Samuel 7:1-17). David was a mighty warrior; a man who was always at war, who had shed much blood. Therefore, God did not choose him for this task. God wanted the temple to be built during a period of peace (1 Chronicles 28:2-3), but David couldn't possibly take on this assignment because he was constantly at war.

Our incarceration doesn't have to be the end. In fact, it could mark the beginning of a wonderful life. However, we can't do what it takes to rebuild our lives if we are always at war with others, making choices that cause us to go back and forth to lockdown. We must not spend our time wastefully. Learn how to read and write if you don't know how. Get your GED if you don't have a high school diploma. If you don't have a trade, take the necessary college courses to get one. More importantly, if you don't know the Lord Jesus Christ as your personal Lord and Savior, find a Christian and tell them you want them to lead you in the prayer of salvation. These are just a few steps toward rebuilding your life.

We can't afford to wait until we get home to start taking care of business. Time is of the essence. Therefore, we can't spend it bickering and warring with people. Haven't you heard that the battle is not yours but the Lords (1 Samuel 17:47, KJV)? Now that you know this, stop fighting with people and start rebuilding your life.

In Prison I Received My Sight

Psalms 146:8
But Jesus said, "Someone touched me; I know that power has gone out from me."

Being blind is bad but is much worse when you don't even realize it. The blind do not see anything wrong with fornication; after all, who does it hurt? The blind do not see anything wrong with shoplifting, as they think the merchants won't even miss the stolen items. The blind do not see anything wrong with drinking and partying. We only have one life to live and we live our life how we choose, right? Boy, was I deceived.

When I started serving my prison sentence, I also started reading the Word of God and immediately my blind eyes were opened. I realized that those areas of my life in which I sinned, were the areas in which I failed to trust God. When the Lord opened my eyes, He showed me that fornication was a sin (1 Corinthians 6:18, KJV) and that I didn't trust Him to keep me in that area. He clearly revealed to me all the harm I was doing when I was stealing from merchants and caused me to despise the very act of theft. Moreover, He told me I stole because I didn't trust Him to supply my needs. The Lord also showed me that I had no right to live my life the way I wanted because my life is not my own -- I was bought with a price (1 Corinthians 7:23, KJV).

The life you are living should be one that is in line with the Word of God. If it isn't, then you are blind. Yet, you don't have to remain that way if you would just allow the Lord to use your prison experience to open your eyes.

What Makes You Think You're Ready?

Jeremiah 12:5
If you have raced with men on foot and they have worn you out, how can you compete with horses? If you stumble in a safe country, how will you manage in the thickets by the Jordan?

As long as we live in this world we must deal with some type of authority. Many of us are where we are because we had a problem obeying authority when we were at home. If we still have a problem with authority, it will behoove us to practice submitting while in prison.

Jeremiah was one of God's faithful prophets. He was obedient to God and he loved God, yet life was still not peaches and cream for him. Things appeared to be so bad for Jeremiah that he began to complain to God (Jeremiah 12:1-5). God told Jeremiah that if he could not handle what he was presently facing he could not possibly handle what he would face next (paraphrased).

It is all too common to hear inmates complain about being in prison. Some complain about the unjust guards as though unjust police don't exist. Some complain about the small medical fee we are charged to see the doctor, when thousands of dollars are charged in the free world for the same service. Many complain about all the rules we have to follow, as if though we will be free from them upon release.

I do not want to be in prison. Whether I want to be here or not, here I am. While I am here I will not waste time complaining but will use this time by allowing God to show me how to live victoriously in prison so I may do the same once I am discharged. Don't fool yourself into thinking you will suddenly change upon release, when there is no change in you now. If you cannot handle your present situation and have a problem with the rules, you will not be able to handle what awaits you.

You Should Be Ashamed

Luke 15:17
When he came to his senses he said,
How many of my father's hired servants have food to spare, and here I am starving to death!

Paul said that he is not ashamed of the gospel of Christ (Romans 1:16) and we shouldn't be, either. We should, however, be ashamed to still be in our mess. If we are living in sin, we have a reason to be ashamed.

I will never forget how embarrassing it was to get caught shoplifting, to be walked through a department store in handcuffs escorted by the police. This happened to me and it brought me much shame; today it doesn't because I'm no longer bound and I can tell my story to help set someone else free.

Looking out the window one day, I saw someone who professed to be a believer, digging in the ash trays collecting cigarette butts. This lady was obviously a cigarette smoker and was willing to go as low as digging through ashes for butts. This is a perfect time to be shameful. The Prodigal son had enough sense to be ashamed of his lifestyle to the point he could no longer live the way he was (Luke 15:16-21).

You should never be ashamed to tell others about Jesus. You should never be ashamed to pray over your food or gather to pray but I dare you not to be ashamed of stooping so low as picking up butts from the trash because you are better than that. I dare you not to be ashamed of getting caught stealing and you are already in prison. I dare you not to be ashamed of being in an intimate relationship with someone who is not your spouse. If you are practicing any sin whatsoever, I pray you have enough sense to be ashamed.

Tired but Still Going to Church

Hebrews 10:25
Not giving up meeting together, as some are in the habit of doing, but encouraging one another and all the more as you see the Day approaching.

Laying down in the bed always feels so much better when it's time to go to Church. We must push pass the sleepiness, tiredness, and anything else that may stop us from going to church and go anyway. If we don't push pass all the stuff that gets in our way, we will not do it when we get home, either.

Unfortunately, much foolishness goes on behind prison walls, however there are also positive activities such as church, which is where I spent much of my time. There were times I didn't want to go, after working out in the field all day in extreme humidity or being too tired from cutting grass all morning. Regardless of what type of hard job I had to do I didn't use it as an excuse not to go to church and neither should you. There are many scriptures in the Bible, but I have never come across one that said this Christian walk will be easy -- it will require serving God even when you're tired from working all day. You are not to forsake the assembly of yourself with other Saints (Hebrews 10:25, KJV). I'm not saying you can't miss at all but it shouldn't be often and you should have a good reason for doing so. Keep in mind, going to church can keep you from a lot of foolishness.

The next time you are so tired from working hard, and that flesh of yours tells you not to go to church, go anyway. Your body will fight against you, but you must push. Once you are assembled with the other Saints you will be glad you pushed past your tiredness. I'm sure when you get there the message will be just for you.

Nothing Decent to Wear

2 Thessalonians 3:13
And as for you, brothers and sisters, never tire of doing what is good.

Don't complain about not having any decent clothes to wear to visitation or to court when you haven't done all you can to ensure you do. Washing your clothes along with the dorm may cause them to become dingy. If you don't want this to happen to your clothes, try washing them by hand.

I always made sure I had a decent state outfit to wear in case of unexpected events, such as visitation or court trips. In preparation of this, I often washed most of my clothes by hand. I know you may not feel like doing extra work, but you must if you want your clothes to stay in good condition.

It's ironic how some inmates refuse to wash at least one outfit by hand so they can have something presentable to wear when needed, yet these same inmates complain they don't have anything decent to wear. Then, whenever they get an unexpected visitor, they can be found running around trying to borrow a decent shirt. Anytime someone would ask to borrow one of my shirts because theirs were in poor condition, I saw this as a perfect opportunity to minister on diligence.

Prison is a controlled environment, but we never know when we will be called to go somewhere unexpectedly. Therefore, we should always keep a decent state outfit available. For this to happen, you must stop being lazy and do what the other inmates do: wash it by hand. Having decent clothes to wear is a good thing, and you should never get too tired to do good.

God Favors the Obedient

Leviticus 26:9
I will look on you with favor and make you fruitful and increase your numbers, and I will keep my covenant with you.

The scripture, God is no respecter of person is often taken out of context by those who blatantly refuse to obey God. This is usually confused with the favor of God. Yes, God is so gracious that He rains on the just and the unjust (Matthew 5:45, KJV) but He favors only His children.

To have respect of persons is not good: for for a piece of bread that man will transgress (Proverbs 28:21, KJV). This scripture is telling us not to favor someone because of who they are or what they can do for us. We shouldn't treat the rich better than the poor. We shouldn't treat inmates on our dorm who have a lot of money better than those with few resources. This scripture is set in place so that we will treat everyone the same.

Peter perceived of a truth that God is no respecter of persons (Acts 10:34, KJV). Initially, Peter believed he was only to bring the gospel to the Jews and not to the gentiles until God showed him a vision that this was not true (Acts 11:5). When it comes to spreading the gospel, we should not have respect unto whom we share it with. Whatever the person's background: Muslim, or Jehovah witness, or Mormon, rich or poor, we are to minister the Word of God. We should be willing and ready to share the Word of God with whomever wants to hear it.

God does have respect unto a certain class of people: those who are obedient to His word (Leviticus 26:3-13, KJV). When security or other inmates lie about you and slander your name, when they continuously attack your character and your integrity, don't give in to the temptation to fight back in the flesh. Remember, the battle is not yours but the Lord's (2 Chronicles 20:15, KJV). Instead, walk in His statutes, keep His commandments, and do them (Leviticus 26:3, KJV) and you will see how God will show respect unto you just as He has done for me.

Going to Church is Not Enough

Hebrews 10:25
Not giving up meeting together, as some are in the habit of doing, but encouraging one another - and all the more as you see the Day approaching.

Do you know of people who go to church every time the door opens? I'm talking about the ones accused of knocking everybody else down to get through the door. I'm sure you know several, and I was often told I was one of these people, too. Whether I was or not was irrelevant to me, as long as I made it to church. After all, the Word of God teaches that we are to go to church and not to give this up. Yet, there is still more to it.

I spent much of my time attending different church services. I attended church more than anything else. There were several other ladies who went to church just about as much as I did, which is very good, but not good enough -- it takes more than just going to church.

The Pharisees were no strangers to going to church; in fact, they were religious leaders, teachers of religious law. Yet, Jesus called them hypocrites! He further stated they were like whitewashed tombs -- beautiful on the outside but filled on the inside with dead people's bones and all sorts of impurity. Outwardly the Pharisees looked like righteous people, but inwardly their hearts were filled with hypocrisy and lawlessness. (Matthew 23:27-28). My God! The Pharisees were terribly involved with the church, but it was only on the surface.

We can all go to church and praise and worship God, listen to the message being preached and then go on our way until the next day. All this is very easy to do. The hard part is living scripture when we are not at church. What type of jokes are we laughing at? What are we listening to? What are we reading? The answer to these questions will determine who we really are. You must understand that you are not fooling anyone. You are being watched. Believe me when I tell you, everyone knows who the Christians are, and who they are not. You're not fooling anyone just because you go to church.

Broke for God's Glory

John 9:3
"Neither this man nor his parents sinned," said Jesus, but this happened so that the works of God might be displayed in him.

We have to know the Word of God for ourselves. When we don't, we will give in to how others interpret it. Don't allow anyone to cause you to believe that lack of finances, physical ailments or even death is the result of sin. If you are experiencing any of these things, it may be for the Glory of God.

Jesus' disciples assumed that either the man born blind or his parents had sinned, causing the affliction. Jesus had to tell them the man's blindness was not a result of sin but so that God can get the glory (John 9:1-3, KJV). Jesus knew once the people saw Him heal the man who was born blind that they would glorify His Father in heaven.

When Lazarus became sick and died, it was not a result of him sinning but so that God might be glorified (John 11:4, KJV). After being in the grave for four days, Jesus raised Lazarus from the dead (John 11:17, 43-44). This was so anyone who heard of this miracle could give glory to God.

Unfortunately, I experienced much financial lack throughout my incarceration. Inmates often took my lack as a result of sin -- they assumed I wasn't doing something right, but what they didn't understand is that I was experiencing a financial lack so people would see that I continue to remain faithful and give glory to my Father in heaven. People who are incarcerated know exactly who gets money and who doesn't. They knew I didn't have the funds to purchase many things from the store like other inmates. However, I didn't allow my lack to cause me to steal from other inmates or from my job. I didn't allow my lack to cause me to compromise at all. I remained faithful to God and gratefully ate whatever was served in the cafeteria without complaining.

On top of this, I was able to minister to others who always allowed themselves to be moved because they didn't get money from home. In fact, God placed me in this situation to show others they don't have to resort to sin just because they don't have much. No matter what it is you experience, remember that people are looking at you. Your response to what you are going through can cause others to glorify your Father in heaven.

Distinguishing Trash from Garbage

1 Peter 3:11
They must turn from evil and do good; they must seek peace and pursue it.

Do you know the difference between a trash can and a garbage can? Well let me tell you. A trash can is for trash, such as paper, water bottles, deodorant containers and any other small items that don't draw ants or flies. A garbage can is for soiled items, empty food or soda containers and the like. Now you know the difference, so stop piling garbage in trash cans.

Today, make the decision to keep the peace in your dorm, cell, or room. If you are used to tossing empty soda cans, empty Vienna sausage cans, or anything else that can draw ants into the trash can, you need to stop. If you don't you will cause problems with your roommate or the people on your dorm.

Ladies, dispose of your sanitary napkins properly. Don't throw them in the trash can in your cell/room. Wrap your sanitary napkins in paper and put them in the garbage can. You will soon see that this practice will keep you from many verbal attacks, and your time in prison will go a little smoother.

The Word of God teaches us to eschew evil, and do good; let him seek peace, and ensue it (1 Peter 3:11, KJV). The more you study the Word of God, the more you'll grow closer to Him. You'll become more sensitive to His will and His ways, then you'll be able to see the problems your actions may cause.

You and I both know how much trouble can arise from keeping empty food containers, soiled items, etc. in your cell/room. People will start calling you dirty and lazy and this will certainly lead to an argument. However, it doesn't have to if you would distinguish trash from garbage and then dispose of yours properly.

Get on the Lord's Side

Exodus 32:26
**So he stood at the entrance to the camp and said,
Whoever is for the Lord, come to me. And all the Levites rallied to him.**

It is easy to get involved in mess and confusion. Regardless of all the confusion going on around you or who is causing it, it will behoove you to get on the Lord's side and stay there. If you don't, you may find yourself in a world of trouble.

After filing a racism complaint against an employee at the facility in which I was incarcerated, this same person ended up being my supervisor shortly afterward. Most of the inmates knew my history with this employee; as a result, my coworkers used this to their advantage. They immediately sided with this person and continuously came up against me. This employee worked with my coworkers and several other inmates, causing me to lose my job. There were many times when other inmates wouldn't speak to me because they wanted to please this employee. The more these people came up against me, the more I fasted and prayed. I so desperately wanted to give in to temptation and try to handle the situation with my own strength, but instead I kept my peace and allowed God to intervene.

Over and over again, as a result of my complaint, I was mistreated on my job, and was even falsely accused of making derogatory statements about this employee. I continued to trust God and allowed Him to fight the battle for me (2 Chronicles 20:15). Then, right when I thought I couldn't take anymore, this employee was transferred to another facility.

No matter where we are people and events will come up against us, but it doesn't have to be the end. We will have victory over whatever it is, as long as we are on the Lord's side.

Is the Churchgoer Different?

2 Corinthians 5:17
Therefore, if anyone is in Christ, the new creation has come: The old has gone, the new is here!

Inmates who spend their time going to church are usually judged a lot. Many choose to judge these people merely because they are incarcerated. They believe the church goers have impure motives for their attendance. I believe there is some truth to this. People in prison go to church for many reasons but if there are some who go because they love Jesus and want to live for Him, you will know them because they will be different.

I was one of many inmates who went to church almost every time there was a service. Often, I would hear people comment that no one has to go to church every day. I must say I agree with this statement. However, I did not see how staying out of church was working for anyone. Usually, if one was not in church they were hanging out in the yard, watching television, playing cards or dominoes, or maybe on their assigned bunk reading a novel. I am not boasting, but I believe I was the most changed inmate in prison. I was serious about my relationship with Jesus. I didn't bow down, but neither did I compromise my convictions. Maybe my stand can be contributed to going to church nearly every day.

It takes a lot to push past all the distractions and all the mess and go to church. Stop picking on the inmate who's strong enough to walk away from all the foolishness and get to church. Not everyone who's in church is faking, those who are real will stand out because they will be different from the rest.

Self-Promoted

1 Kings 1:5
Now Adonijah, whose mother was Haggith, put himself forward and said, "I will be king." So he got chariots and horses ready, with fifty men to run ahead of him.

Even behind prison walls, inmates work toward getting better jobs. Sometimes, through acts of dishonesty, these inmates are cheated out of these jobs. Someone may presently be in a position that is rightfully yours; if so, don't allow this to move you, because what God has for you is for you.

Because of righteousness sake I was denied a position to work in the chapel despite being eligible for the position. Yet, I didn't allow this decision to move me. I continued to walk in obedience and waited on God to do the rest.

Adonijah attempted to place himself in a position that God didn't give him. He tried to seize the throne from Solomon (1 Kings 1:5, KJV). Not only did Adonijah fail at his attempt, but he was also killed (1 Kings 2:24-25) and David made Solomon King (1Kings 1:43). Adonijah tried to block Solomon but he was not successful because it was God's will for Solomon to be king.

Prisons are filled with inmates who try hard to please wardens and security guards, and whomever else. This is usually done either to keep or obtain a certain position, a position that rightfully belongs to someone else. If you are not working to please God, then the position you have will be taken from you and given to someone who rightfully deserves it.

Because of my faithfulness and obedience, God moved the mountain that was blocking me from obtaining a position in the chapel and gave me free reign. Eventually, God removed all of the inmates from the chapel who were against me. I didn't have to result to backbiting or other dishonest acts to make it happen, I just continued to walk in humility and God worked it all out.

The Heart of the Matter

1 Samuel 16:7e
People look at the outward appearance, but the Lord looks at the heart.

Isn't it ironic how those we are forced to live around continue to choose a lifestyle contrary to the Word of God, then so quickly say that God knows their heart? It is correct that God knows the heart of man, this scripture is used by unbelievers frequently to justify their ungodly actions. Yet in the Word of God, this scripture is not applied to those who are doing what's wrong, but to those who are doing what is right.

Although God knows the heart of the unbeliever, he doesn't have to look at their heart because their actions reveal their heart. God doesn't have to look at your heart to see if you are stealing, to see that you cursed out the guards or another inmate, or to see that you are fornicating. Your actions are speaking loudly. It is clear from your actions that you are doing all these things, therefore God does not need to look past them.

Many times believers would take time out to walk the compound handing out scriptures. Some would walk around toting Bibles and quoting the word of God. Others you will see ministering here and there or providing for someone's needs. All of this is good, and we should do these things; however, God looks past all the good we do and look at our heart to see why we are doing them.

God has to look at the heart of the man who draws close to Him with their mouth. God has to look at the heart of the man who honors Him with their words (Matthew 15:8, KJV). God has to look at the heart of those who do good to see if their actions are sincere. He doesn't have to look at the heart of the ones who are doing wrong, because it is clear you are doing so because of the evil in your heart (Luke 6:45, KJV).

The Length We Go for Cigarettes

Romans 12:1
Therefore, I urge you, brothers and sisters, in view of God's mercy, to offer your bodies as a living sacrifice, holy and pleasing to God -- this is your true and proper worship.

Many of us did things on the street to support our habits. Sadly, most women sold their bodies to get a fix. Prostitution may be a lifestyle you lived before coming to prison, but now that God has removed you from that situation don't allow anything to cause you to succumb to this behavior again.

Satan knows the lifestyle you once lived. In fact, he will do whatever it takes to tempt you to go back to where you came from. Satan knows about all the times you sold your body to support your drug habit, and He also knows how far you will go to support your other habits.

Cigarettes have many people in bondage. When I first was arrested and placed in the holding cell at the parish jail, I witnessed women who wanted a cigarette so badly they went as far as revealing their body to the male inmates just to get one. They called this flashing. Whenever I found myself in a holding cell, I always found women in there with me who desperately wanted a cigarette and were willing to degrade themselves to obtain one. These women would stalk the window until they saw one of the male inmates who were willing to give them a cigarette in exchange for a flash of their body. Sadly, these ladies were succumbing to the same mess that had them bound on the outside.

Ladies, this is a trick of the enemy. You fell for his scheme and traded off your body in the past and now you are doing it again. This is totally unacceptable to your creator. Just in case you haven't heard, you are to present your body as a living sacrifice, holy, acceptable unto God which is your reasonable service (Romans 12:1, KJV).

Regardless of what you've done in the past, God has already forgiven you. However, you must not get caught up in your old way of living again. I don't care what lies the enemy tells you, God loves you and wants you to love yourself. God loves you so much that He bought you with a price (1 Corinthians 6:20, KJV), and you are not yours to sell.

Your Actions Prove Your Beliefs

James 2:19
You believe that there is one God. Good!
Even the demons believe that and shudder.

Believing in Jesus is good. Unfortunately, just believing in Jesus is not good enough; more importantly is *what* we believe about Jesus.

There are so many people who will tell you they believe in Jesus -- I do not doubt they do. There are some people who believe Jesus was just a prophet, and there are some who believe He was just a great man. There are some who believe Jesus did not live a sinless life. I can go on and on about what people believe about Jesus, but I'm sure you get my point.

So many times throughout my incarceration I heard people say, "I know I'm in my mess" or, "I know I'm not living right", but, "I still believe in Jesus". Believing in Jesus will not stop us from spending eternity in hell if we are still in our mess or not living right when we die. The Word of God says that the devils believe in Jesus also (James 2:19, KJV), yet, the devil's destiny is hell (Revelation 20:2-3). This is clear evidence that believing is not enough.

When I went to jail, I learned that Jesus Christ was my Lord and Savior. Not only did I learn that He was, I believed it! Moreover, from studying the Word of God daily, I discovered how believers were to live. I discovered that I had the mind of Christ (1 Corinthians 2:16, KJV). Suddenly, I began to notice I had been changed. I noticed I was sensitive to the ways of God. My talk was different. My walk was different. I no longer responded to situations the way I used to. The transformation I experienced was so evident I didn't have to tell anyone I was a believer because my lifestyle clearly supported my beliefs.

A Right to Speak Slander

James 4:11
Brothers and sisters, do not slander one another. Anyone who speaks against a brother or sister or judges them speaks against the law and judges it. When you judge the law, you are not keeping it, but sitting in judgment on it.

People are going to speak evil of you whether it's true or not. They are going to say you are what you are not and that you have what you don't have, but you can't be moved by their folly. People like this are not only found in prison, they are on the outside too. As long as you live on this earth you will encounter them, but you can't let such people affect you.

One day as I stood outside talking with another inmate, we were approached by another girl who was distraught over what people were saying about her. This lady said that she had just left the infirmary and something took place while she was there that caused the inmates to assume this girl had AIDS. She wanted to know what she should do and stressed that she didn't want people to think she had this disease Well, whether she wanted them to think it or not wouldn't stop them, nor stop them from saying what they wanted to say.

I'll be the first to say I know how evil people can be. It is even worse when you can't put distance between yourself and these people because you are incarcerated. It makes no sense to try to defend yourself. Jesus was lied on (Matthew 26:65) and called Beelzebub (Matthew 10:25). Yet he remained cool, calm, and collected. He was not disturbed by the false statements. Jesus was on a mission to save all mankind and if He had allowed all the foolishness people said about him to cause him to be moved, we would all have been doomed.

In the book of James we are commanded not to judge or speak evil of people. He knew this would be a problem that people have. You can't stop people from speaking evil but you can make sure that you are not one of those people yourself. Don't allow the things people say about you to take you by surprise. If you begin to expect these attacks, you won't be moved when they come.

Certificates Don't Change Your State of Mind

Ephesians 4:23
To be made new in the attitude of your minds;

Before I committed the crime I committed I thought about it first -- I planned it all out in my mind. My mind was where it all began, which is why it is so important that our minds are renewed. The certificates we have don't mean anything because a certificate can't change our state of mind. To renew our minds, we must meditate day and night on the Word of God.

There are several programs offered inside of prisons: substance abuse, re-entry, and GED are just a few. I couldn't help but notice the large number of inmates who completed these programs, but completing such programs are not good enough.

It is not a sacrifice to sit through a substance abuse, anger management, or parenting class instead of going to work. In fact, for most inmates it's a blessing to sit in a class that will get us out of work. Obtaining a GED is an excellent achievement but is the least you could do while you are locked away in a controlled environment. Again, I am not knocking the programs offered in prisons, because these programs are needed and very beneficial but there is nothing magical about them. Finishing these programs does not mean that you are changed.

There are too many people trying to complete every program available just so they can present all these certificates to the judge, parole, and/or pardon board. What if your judge decided to talk to a few other inmates, a few officers, or your supervisor with regard to your character and decide whether he will release you based on their reports? What if the judge or members of the board decide to look at your library records to see what type of books interest you, or go through your lockers and read a few of your letters; would their findings cause you to be released or not?

Remember, I am qualified to write this because I am where you are. I have both a parenting and an anger management certificate. Yet, it was through the Word of God where I was taught how to be a good mother and deal with my anger. I know of many inmates who possess an anger management certificate yet still physically and verbally attack others. I am familiar with those who have substance abuse certificates but constantly talk about doing drugs upon release.

It is imperative that you take this time and allow God to change you from the inside out. Don't be deceived into thinking your accumulation of certificates means anything, because they don't. You have to discipline yourself to spend time with God day and night so that He can do for you what only He can.

Give Your Last

1 Kings 17:15
She went away and did as Elijah had told her. So there was food every day for Elijah and for the woman and her family.

Don't allow the little you have to be an excuse not to bless someone. There are always those who have less than the little you have. God blesses others by using people just like you and me. In order for Him to use us, we must step out in faith and trust God.

Whenever I would be down to my last bag of chips or whatever else, I always found myself saying, "I only have one left" when someone would ask me to give them a bag. I didn't take into consideration that this person may not get any money from home and may be hungry. Not only this, but I believe such a response shows a lack of trust. If someone is hungry and we can help them, then we should help them and trust God to provide for us when we are hungry. I'm not saying you have to give everyone your last but if you let the Spirit lead, you will know when to do so.

The widow woman was planning to cook the little flour she had left so she and her son could eat, then die. Elijah asked the woman to give him a morsel of bread out of the little she had, and to give him his portion first. The widow woman trusted God and did just as Elijah said. Miraculously, their food didn't run out (1 Kings 17:11-16). God will do the same for us if we just trust Him.

I know there are inmates who refuse to go to the cafeteria because they don't like what's being served or because they would rather mooch from you; I am not speaking of these inmates. But when that inmate who doesn't have and who faithfully goes to the cafeteria and still is hungry asks you for something to eat, don't respond by saying you only have one. If you are not eating whatever it is that same day, give it to that inmate who is hungry today and trust God to feed you tomorrow.

Be a Good Steward

Luke 16:10
Whoever can be trusted with very little can also be trusted with much, and whoever is dishonest with very little will also be dishonest with much.

As Christians we should be mindful that others are watching us. Knowing this, we should be determined to do the right thing in all that we do. We shouldn't carelessly leave the water running when we are not using it or fail to turn it off all the way, causing water to constantly drip. We shouldn't leave the lights on if we are not using them or slam the door to the microwave. A good steward wouldn't do any of these things.

Many times, I have heard people say, 'I don't care about this' or, 'I don't care about that', 'this is not my house, I'm just passing through'. It may very well be that we are only passing through and that we are fortunate enough to have a release date. However, we should keep in mind there are some who do not have release dates or are serving long sentences and our careless actions could very well affect those we leave behind. More importantly, God sees all we do and if we aren't faithful with what belongs to another man, God will not bless us with our own. Even the little we do have will be misused by others because of our own choice to carelessly deal with the things of others.

Just because we're in prison doesn't give us any reason not to be good stewards over those things in our immediate surroundings. It doesn't matter if we are in an open dorm, a small room, or a jail cell; we are obligated to take good care of what belongs to another. If you stop misusing the comforts you are blessed to have in prison, then others can learn from you how to be a good steward.

Planted to Preach

Romans 1:15
That is why I am so eager to preach the gospel also to you who are in Rome.

The Word of God has to go forth. The gospel must be preached wherever, whenever, and to whomever. We have to be ready at all times. You may very well be where you are today so that God can use you to bring forth His Word to those others can't reach.

Paul said he strived to preach the gospel, not where Christ was named, lest he should build upon another man's foundation: (Romans 15:20, KJV). There are many people in society who have given up on us, yet there are also many volunteers who regularly go to prisons because they believe in us and know there is power and deliverance in the Word of God. These volunteers are willing and ready to reach out. Although these volunteers are ready to come into the prisons, they can't stay. They have to leave, but we are still here when they are gone.

We are in prison for a set time. The volunteers can't do it all. They are limited, but we are not. We are able to preach the gospel throughout the dormitory. We have the freedom to minister to that person who may be contemplating suicide. We have the freedom to minister to the one who is crying in the middle of the night. We are free to preach the gospel to all those inmates who the volunteers can't reach because they don't ever go to church. It is imperative that we don't allow these opportunities to pass us by. Be ready to take every chance you get to preach the Gospel.

Move it or Use It

2 Timothy 2:24
be kind to everyone, able to teach, not resentful.

Placing your towel on the shower is very inconsiderate. I know this seems trivial, but it is not. If this was a trivial matter, then it wouldn't result in so many arguments. If you avoid doing this, you may prevent a senseless dispute.

Many times throughout my incarceration I saw inmates engage in foolish altercations over someone selfishly trying to hold a shower by placing an article of clothing, or some other personal item of theirs, over it. This was done in an attempt to have a shower available right when they were prepared to use it. Holding a shower is a selfish act and can also be a form of pride. When you do this your actions are speaking loud and clear. What are your actions saying? I'm glad you asked. They are saying, "I worked all day and I'm very tired, therefore I shouldn't have to wait to take a shower, so I'll just put something on it until I get prepared. It doesn't matter to me if someone else is prepared, they just have to wait because I want to get right in the shower when I get to it. I know there are nearly 75 women on the dorm, but they will just have to wait." This is selfishness.

I can recall several times someone offering to hold a shower for me or advising me to place something on the shower to hold it; I took this as an opportunity to minister. I explained why this is wrong according to the Word of God. I wanted people to see that I was different. I wanted people to see that no matter how tired I may have been, I was not going to give in to selfishness.

Dreaming Your Thoughts

Jeremiah 29:8
Yes, this is what the Lord Almighty, the God of Israel, says: Do not let the prophets and diviners among you deceive you. Do not listen to the dreams you encourage them to have.

Thoughts of freedom are probably what bombards the minds of prisoners the most. For me, freedom is something I think about on a regular basis. It may even be safe to say that I think about my freedom every day. Sometimes I would just allow my imagination to run wild. I saw myself going to my daughter's high school and waiting until school was out to surprise her. I also saw myself showing up at the shoe store she worked at to surprise her there. Yet, these dreams never came to pass.

I dreamed about going home many times. The dreams I had, felt very real and I believed they were, until I woke up. I also believed that my dreams were from God and that they would come to pass. Time after time it was confirmed that my dreams were not from God. It was obvious that I had caused my own dreams.

I knew I wasn't going to be present for my daughter's high school graduation because she had already graduated. It became apparent that I couldn't take heed to all of my dreams because I was only dreaming about whatever consumed my mind the most.

If you are constantly thinking about something so much that it consumes your thoughts, then you dream this same thing, it would be wise not to take heed to this dream. God does speak to us through our dreams; however, sometimes our dreams aren't from God. It would behoove you to commune with God through prayer so that He can reveal to you which dreams are from Him and which are not.

Leading the Young Astray

Titus 2:3
Likewise, teach the older women to be reverent in the way they live, not to be slanderers or addicted to much wine, but to teach what is good.

There are many inmates who have been in prison for a long time. These inmates know the rules and how to behave. However, some of these inmates don't do what they are supposed to do. As an older offender it should be your desire to lead the younger offenders in the right direction. Sadly, this is seldom the case.

Time and again I've seen the older offenders teach the younger ones illegal ways to survive in prison, although the state provides all offenders with the basic necessities. Furthermore, the Lord promises to provide all believers with all their needs, and He does. However, many offenders fail to trust God, and resort to illegal ways to take care of themselves.

Younger offenders have to deal with older offenders approaching them to inform them that someone is attracted to them. The younger offenders who are already involved in homosexuality can count on many of the older offenders to counsel them on how to stay in their mess. Some of the older women even get into homosexual relationships with these young people themselves.

Young people, if an older person is suggesting that you engage in immoral and/or illegal activities, this person does not care about you. Someone like this does not mean you any good and it would be best to avoid them. If by chance you are one of these older people yourself then you need to stop leading the young ones astray, repent, ask God to forgive you, and start behaving like a positive role model.

Pretending to Be Sick

Jeremiah 17:9
The heart is deceitful above all things and beyond cure. Who can understand it?

You are blessed if you are in good health. Don't pretend like you're not just to avoid working. When you do this you are being deceptive. Deception is wrong and should not be practiced by a believer.

When people are brought to prison, they are handcuffed, shackled, and escorted. This is because none of us are willing to go, as we don't want to be incarcerated. Although the majority of us are because of some crime we committed. This doesn't erase the fact that none of us wants to be here.

Some of the inmates I've encountered can't see themselves working for little or no pay. These inmates are so adamant about not working that they will make up a sickness to avoid doing so. Sadly, the deceitfulness and wickedness that is in the hearts of man comes to the surface even more when we are incarcerated. Some are so deceptive they end up getting a wheelchair assigned to them for the duration of their prison stay. Some go as far as faking seizures. Some inmates would do just about anything to get out of work.

Inmate to inmate, I know exactly how you feel. You don't want to be a slave for anyone. I don't blame you, I didn't want to slave for anyone either, so I decided not to work for people and work for my Lord and Savior Jesus Christ instead. After all, we are supposed to be servants of Jesus Christ. This means He is our master so let us work to serve Him.

Unfortunately, there are many inmates who are sickly and honestly in need of medical care. Don't delay their medical attention by clogging up the system requesting help you do not legitimately need. It is a blessing to be able to work, so do your job and stop pretending to be sick.

An Eye-Opening Experience

Romans 8:28
And we know that in all things God works for the good of those who love him, who have been called according to his purpose.

What's good about going to prison? Absolutely nothing! Remember, if we just allow God to use us according to His purpose, He will turn our situation around and cause our prison experience to be a good one. I know He will because He did it for me.

Before going to prison I was in bondage to fornication, shoplifting, lying, gossiping, and pride. I didn't know it then but I was messed up. The devil had deceived me into thinking that I had it going on, that I was on top, but when I went to prison it was then that I realized I was on top of the bottom.

Going to prison was my Damascus Road experience (Acts 9:1-19). It was in prison that I realized I was lost and in desperate need of a Savior. It was in prison when I made Jesus Christ the Lord over my life. It was in prison where I decided to no longer be a child of the devil (1 John 3:10, KJV) but instead live my life in a way that I would be a threat to his kingdom.

Strive to Keep Your Light On

Matthew 5:16
In the same way, let your light shine before others, that they may see your good deeds and glorify your Father in heaven.

It is not difficult at all to let our light shine when nothing is going on. This is very easy to do. However, we should allow our light to shine at all times, even under pressure and in the hustle and bustle of everyday life.

One of the employees at the prison chose me to work with her to sell snack cakes to inmates. When the time came for us to distribute the cakes, I became agitated; there was no system and for the most part we were very unorganized. This bothered me because I've always had excellent leadership skills and have always been a very organized person. Yet, I found myself in an unorganized work environment and allowed it to move me out of character. I was snapping at others for getting an order wrong or for not doing things the way I thought they should be done. It was clear that my light was no on. I was convicted each time. God showed me that I didn't let my light shine when working under pressure. Immediately, I asked God to forgive me and repented of my ways.

We are commanded to let our light shine and there are no exceptions to this command. This is not just when things are easygoing but even in the midst of a rough day. Once we are released and employed, we can't allow ourselves to explode just because things aren't going smoothly. Let's allow the pressures we face on our job now, prepare us for how to deal with the ones we will face on the job we will have on the outside. When people see that our light continues to shine even under pressure, this will cause them to give glory to our heavenly Father. Therefore, strive to keep your light on.

Jesus Will Keep You If You So Desire

2 Timothy 1:12
That is why I am suffering as I am. Yet this is no cause for shame, because I know whom I have believed, and am convinced that he is able to guard what I have entrusted to him until that day.

Homosexuality is very prevalent in prison and I believe most inmates engage in this sin. Most of the people I have ministered to regarding their lifestyle told me they had never been with a person of the same sex before entering prison -- they couldn't even believe they had chosen it now. Some told me they were only engaging in such a lifestyle because they were incarcerated.

During my incarceration I heard preacher after preacher come into the institution and preach against homosexuality. I know many of you say these people are not in prison with you and therefore they don't know what it's like. You are so right, they don't know what it's like and they are not in here with us, but I know what it's like. I know if you surrender to Jesus and allow Him to be the Lord and Savior of your life that He will keep you. Homosexuality is a sin and God destroyed an entire city because of this sin (Genesis 19:28-29). Don't think that you have to participate in homosexuality because of your situation; if you think this way the devil has lied to you. You can be confined to prison and not engage in homosexuality; I know you can. Jesus kept me because I faithfully committed my life over to Him and if you do the same, He will keep you, too.

Be Known for Having a Word

Genesis 50:5
My father made me swear an oath and said, I am about to die; bury me in the tomb I dug for myself in the land of Canaan. Now let me go up and bury my father; then I will return.

Commitments we make should not be broken. When you carry out what you've promised this establishes trustworthiness and demonstrates that you have a word.

Jacob lived in Egypt but didn't want to be buried there upon his death. To ensure he wasn't, he had to find someone he could trust, someone who would keep their promise. Jacob knew his son Joseph was a trustworthy person and therefore made Joseph promise not to bury him in Egypt, but with his father. Joseph promised to do what Jacob asked of him (Genesis: 29-31) and when Jacob died, he kept his word and carried out his promise.

Many of you have burned a lot of bridges in your life and because of this it may be that members of your family don't want anything more to do with you. They no longer trust you. Now that you are imprisoned, you write home making promises to your loved ones that you will no longer steal from them or disappear for days, weeks, or months at a time without contact. If this is you and you have put your family, and especially your children through hell and now you are promising to never do so again if only they will accept you back home, make sure you mean every word you say. Your children need you but are better off without you if you are not someone they can trust.

Little Matters Still Require Faithfulness

Luke 16:10
Whoever can be trusted with very little can also be trusted with much, and whoever is dishonest with very little will also be dishonest with much.

I remember working on the line serving food shortly after arriving at the Louisiana Correctional Institute for Women. There were a few occasions when one of the two ladies I closely associated with would ask me to give her extra butter. Despite her many requests I only gave her what security said inmates were allowed. After she asked several more times, I began to doubt myself. It's just butter and we are close, I thought. I wanted to do everything right, yet I was beginning to believe that giving her extra butter was a small matter and therefore would be okay.

God knew I was about to be deceived by the enemy who was causing me to think it was okay for me to give away extra butter. God stepped in and led me to read the daily bread which was miraculously titled Two Pats of Butter. To paraphrase a little, this reading was about two men who had lunch together to discuss one of the men hiring the other for a job at his bank. However, as the two men stood in line waiting to pay for their meals, the bank manager saw the other man slip two pats of butter under his tray instead of paying for them. This small dishonest act showed the manager this man could not be trusted in his bank. It blew my mind that God would allow me to come across this reading while I was considering giving out extra butter; more importantly, this showed me that God requires us to be faithful in the little matters, too.

Ask and Don't Order

Matthew 7:7a
Ask and it will be given to you.

It is very rude to order people around. You'll find that if you just ask instead, you may be much more likely to receive. In fact, you are not told to order you are told to ask, so check your approach.

Jesus is in the blessing business. He is willing to give us whatever we ask of Him as long as we are asking him for things in accordance with His word and in line with His will. If we are not receiving, then perhaps we are ordering Jesus instead of simply asking him. It's easy for me to say this because I heard inmates order other inmates every day. Go call someone for me! Give me some chips! I am going to get you to cut my hair later! Instead, try asking, 'will you please call whomever for me?', 'may I have some of your chips please?', 'will you please cut my hair at your convenience?'. Doesn't the latter sound better? It sure does, and therefore you should try asking.

As inmates, we have been stripped of being asked to do things. Usually, we are told what to do in the form of an order. It's enough that we must take orders from security, we shouldn't have to take them from our fellow inmates, too. I know some of you may even be used to this type of communication from the streets and may have even accepted this as normal but if you change your approach you can create a 'new normal'. Don't allow being ordered around, to cause you to start giving orders yourself.

Hindering Heart

Psalms 66:18
If I had cherished sin in my heart, the Lord would not have listened.

Unfortunately, in this life we will encounter people who will wrong us in some way. Sometimes the wrong done to us may come in the form of abuse. There is absolutely no reason to ever wrong someone. Yet, if it happens, we must let it go. Some things may not be as easy to let go as others; still, we must make the effort.

People have a tendency to start praying or pray much more when they are in trouble. This explains why so much praying goes on in prison. Praying is good. In fact, this is the way we communicate with God. We are told to pray without ceasing (1 Thessalonians 5:17). When we pray we believe our prayers are heard, but it is up to us to make sure they are being heard and not hindered.

I have heard many disturbing stories told by other inmates throughout my incarceration. Some inmates testify about being physically abused by a spouse, others about being molested by a family member, there are still others who tell how their family no longer want anything to do with them because of their incarceration. Whatever it is, you cannot hold on to these things. You must let them go.

When people wrong us, it's not easy to get over what they have done. This may come to you as a shock, but it was not easy for Jesus either. Jesus suffered for our sake and then He asked His Father to forgive those who wronged him (Luke 23:34). Jesus didn't hinder His blessings by allowing the wrong done to Him to dwell in His heart. We must do the same.

Perhaps you have been praying to God to get back in court or for some type of early release. If God is ready to open the door for you, you can stop Him if your heart is not right. We cannot hold people in our heart for something they did to us; if we do we are hindering our own prayers. God will not hear us because our heart is filled with iniquity. Stop holding people in your heart so God can stop holding up your blessing.

The Good Suffers for the Bad

Jonah 1:12
Pick me up and throw me into the sea, he replied, and it will become calm. I know that it is my fault that this great storm has come upon you.

Trouble has a way of finding us wherever we are. Regardless of how hard we may try to avoid it, it still ends up finding us. What's worse is when we find ourselves in trouble for someone else's sake.

The mariners were on a ship headed to Tarshish minding their own business. The next thing they knew they were in the middle of a storm. The mariners didn't do anything to cause the storm. They were in it for Jonah's sake (Jonah 1:1-12).

Inmates are often punished for the sake of someone else. There were times I recall working late in the field in the heat until our task was complete, for the sake of one or two inmates who neglected their duties. I can recall another time I was awaken from my sleep and required to spend part of the night in the gym, for the sake of an inmate flooding the dorm. Last but certainly not least, I was made to endure lockdown for the sake of two inmates conspiring together to lie about me. I am all too familiar with suffering for the sake of other people.

Unfortunately, in this world there are people who don't choose to do the right thing. Many of these people are in prison with us and will be the cause of some of our troubles. Unlike the mariners, we cannot stop the trouble by throwing someone off a ship. However, we can ask God what it is He's trying to teach us through the trouble and allow ourselves to be taught during our period of suffering.

Paper Abuse

Luke 16:12
And if you have not been trustworthy with someone else's property, who will give you property of your own?

God loves us so much that He has allowed the Holy Spirit to dwell inside of us to keep us in line. Nothing is too trivial for the Holy Spirit to correct. When the Holy Spirit brings a wrong to our attention it is so we can make it right.

God expects us to be faithful in all our dealings. This means we shouldn't use blank forms of any kind to take score for a game, to add up purchases or anything else outside of its use. When we do this, we are wasting paper and costing the state more money. I know you are probably thinking that this is prison and the state owes you something. This is not true and the wrong attitude to have. The state does not owe any inmate anything; however, they are required to see to our needs and provide a decent place to lay our head. Taxpayers are the ones who pay the cost for us to be housed in prison. If we continue to misuse paper, we can potentially cost the taxpayers more money. Think about it: if approximately 1,100 inmates use one piece of paper everyday to keep score, more than 1,000 sheets of paper are being wasted on a daily basis.

I don't know about you but despite my incarceration I am believing in God for a prosperous future. I believe that one day God will allow me to have a business of my own. I also know that if I want God to bless me with my own business, I need to be faithful in that which is another man's (Luke 16:12). If I don't, then I can expect my employees to abuse my supplies. Yet, I don't have to concern myself with this because I will be sure not to abuse what belongs to someone else, not even paper.

Hated for a Good Cause

Matthew 10:22
You will be hated by everyone because of me, but the one who stands firm to the end will be saved.

Many Christians are scared to obey the word of God because they fear being hated. Hate is a very strong emotion, and no one wants to experience it, especially for doing good.

While standing in the cafeteria line waiting to be served, I noticed one of my sisters asking someone what they did or didn't want on their tray. This particular sister is a very sweet girl who happens to be very sensitive. Immediately, I sensed in my spirit that this girl was trying to be a respect of person, she did not deliberately set out to be disobedient but she was scared to do the right thing. This girl knew that nearly 1,000 inmates came into the cafeteria to eat and she didn't want these inmates to call her names or pick on her every time they saw her. Therefore, she allowed fear to cause her to compromise.

If we call ourselves Christians, we need to learn how to live like one. The Word of God says that we are bold as a lion (Proverbs 28:1). I'm quite sure lions don't get pushed around and you shouldn't either. Face it, you will be hated for the sake of Jesus Christ. Don't allow this to make you scared, let it make you courageous. Go ahead, obey the Word of God and let them hate you. Remember, they hated Jesus first.

Mind Those in Line

2 Timothy 2:24
And the Lord's servant must not be quarrelsome but must be kind to everyone, able to teach, not resentful.

Usually wherever we go in prison we have to stand in a line, which is one thing inmates hate to do. Whether going to the mailroom or to the infirmary, there is most likely a line.

I never really had a problem with standing in lines but would get very upset to see people skip someone who is ahead of me. This puts everyone back even further. So, I decided to start skipping too. Immediately, the Holy Spirit convicted me. I couldn't believe I was being convicted about something that seemed so trivial. I was reminded that I was a Christian and I am obligated to live righteously. Everyone is standing in line for the same reason, who am I to commit such an inconsiderate act? This is no way to represent an Almighty God. Your entire lifestyle should be exemplary. I didn't waste any time taking heed; I got up off the spiritual ground, asked God's forgiveness and decided to utilize the time I spent standing in line reading my pocket Bible or praying for those on my prayer list.

I know you may not think that the Holy Spirit would admonish you about such a matter, but He will, so you won't lose your witness. Besides, you shouldn't want the words 'she's supposed to be a Christian' to have any merit. However, it does when you are selfishly skipping ahead of others.

Prison Is Our Great Fish

Jonah 1:17
Now the Lord provided a huge fish to swallow Jonah, and Jonah was in the belly of the fish three days and three nights.

The same God who prepared a great fish to swallow up Jonah is still preparing things today for the same purpose. The prison we are in may be what he has prepared for us.

Now the Word of the Lord came unto Jonah the son of Amittai saying, Arise, go to Nineveh, that great city, and cry against it; for their wickedness is come up before me (Jonah 1:1-2, KJV). Instead of Jonah taking heed to the voice of the Lord and going to Nineveh, he disobeyed God and boarded a ship going to Tarshish. Jonah's disobedience didn't stop the mission God had for him, it only slowed it down. To get Jonah's attention, God allowed him to be thrown off the ship he boarded and swallowed up by a great fish. (Jonah 1:15, 17).

The Lord tried to get us to fulfill our purpose. However, we chose to disobey God and do what we wanted to do. We wouldn't take heed to wise counseling. We wouldn't attend church or participate in positive things. We know all the other things we wouldn't do, that we should have been doing. Some of us probably never even prayed until we came to prison, just like Jonah who prayed to the Lord out of the belly of the fish (Jonah 2:1).

After the Lord spoke unto the fish, it vomited out Jonah upon dry land (Jonah 3:10, KJV). This time Jonah was ready to go to Nineveh just as the Lord had previously commanded. Make sure you are ready to do thus said the Lord once He opens the prison doors for you; if not, you will be swallowed by another great fish.

No Boundaries

John 8:36
So if the Son sets you free, you will be free indeed.

Prison life hinders us from doing many of the bad things we used to do. It's a good thing we are not able to freely practice some of these bad habits but we must be sure that we are no longer doing those bad things due to deliverance and not boundaries.

Before my incarceration I lived a lifestyle that involved shoplifting and fornication. Due to the boundaries of the prison I am no longer able to go to the mall but despite this fact I believe with all my heart that even if I was able to go I wouldn't steal anything because I am delivered. However, I am not too sure about the fornication. I want to please God. I do not want to hurt God anymore. Yet, I don't believe I'm delivered from fornication or whether I just think I am due to the boundaries that prevent me from being alone with my ex-companion.

While incarcerated I diligently searched the Bible for scriptures regarding fornication. It was important that I knew what God had to say about this sin that I once practiced. It was essential that I get fornication scriptures in my heart. It was essential that I meditate on scriptures dealing with fornication day and night, for I knew this was the only way I would be delivered.

Your entanglement may not have been shoplifting and fornication, but whatever yours are you have to get set free from them. It's not enough to think that we are free, we need to find all the scriptures we can relating to our situation and stand on them until we are delivered. You must be absolutely sure that you would not practice the sin you once lived if there were no boundaries.

Pass Up the Good Meal

Matthew 6:16
When you fast, do not look somber as the hypocrites do, for they disfigure their faces to show others they are fasting. Truly I tell you, they have received their reward in full.

Fasting is not an option. This is why scripture doesn't say **if** you fast, but **when** you fast. Now that you know you have to fast, don't do so based on what's being served in the cafeteria.

Fasting is much more of a sacrifice for someone who is incarcerated than it is for someone who is not. It also requires more self-discipline. Unlike inmates, someone who is free can eat their favorite meals at any time.

God is all-knowing. He knows when we fast and why we are fasting. You shouldn't wait until the menu comes out to see what day they are serving something you don't eat, and then decide that's the day you'll fast. That is not sacrificing. Yes, you are depriving yourself of food, but the food you are depriving yourself of is food you don't like. This is equivalent to offering up to God an animal with a blemish (Leviticus 1:3, KJV). Totally unacceptable! If you are going to look at the menu, see which day they are serving something you like to eat, or what you like the most and choose that day to fast. You can do it. I've done it several times. Unless I was led to fast spontaneously, it was the norm for me to fast on every first Sunday, this way I was committed to fast without any knowledge of what was being served on those days. The discipline comes when you've already committed yourself to fasting on a certain day, then see something you love such as peach cobbler, one of my favorites, on the menu and still stick to your commitment even though this dessert may never be served again.

Remember God knows your circumstances and He knows your likes and dislikes, so stop cheating God and sacrifice your best by passing up the good meal.

Locked Up and Locked Down

Deuteronomy 30:19
This day I call the heavens and the earth as witnesses against you that I have set before you - life and death, blessings and curses. Now choose life, so that you and your children may live.

You would think that lockdown is an understatement, considering we are literally locked up in a prison, but we both know it's not. Being removed from general population and placed in maximum security should not be an option, however many times prisoners decide to take this path; yes, that's what I said! Many times prisoners consciously choose this road.

As prisoners, we know there are rules we must follow. We are well aware of the serious offenses that can send us to lockdown. Therefore, we need to avoid making foolish decisions that will cause us to be sent there. I know there are times when you may be lied on by security and sent to lockdown; it happened to me and I know it can happen to you. We can't stop a person from lying on us, but we can stop making the same kind of choices that caused us to come to prison in the first place. Make up your mind to stop choosing death -- choose life instead, so while you're locked up you won't have to be locked down.

Ignore Your Senses and Obey

1 Kings 17:21
Then he stretched himself out on the boy three times and cried out to the Lord, "Lord my God, let this boy's life return to him!"

When God tells us to do something, we must be obedient even when we think it doesn't make sense. We must not allow our own thoughts or how something seems to prevent us from doing what God tell us to do.

We have to start obeying God no matter how strange what He tells us to do may sound. Not only do we have to obey, but we must do so immediately. This means we can't wait until we feel like it, or when we think it is time to move. We must do it right away.

In 1 Kings Chapter 17, we read that the son of a widow woman had died and how Elijah restored the boy to life by stretching himself on the boy three times and cried unto the Lord (1 Kings 17:17-24 KJV). If the restoration of someone's life depended on me stretching myself on them, this person would still be dead. Unfortunately, I would allow the foolishness of the act to hinder me from being obedient. I would be more concerned about looking foolish even though the Word of God teaches us that God hath chosen the foolish things of the world to confound the wise (1 Corinthians 1:27a, KJV).

One day the Lord put an inmate in my path who He wanted me to lay hands on. This lady was very sick. Her skin had turned dark and she looked very fragile. When I saw this lady, I looked at her until she was out of my sight, without doing what God had asked of me. A few days later I was in the infirmary and the Lord allowed me to see this lady again. She was getting around with a walker. The Lord was giving me another opportunity to pray for this woman, and sadly I disobeyed again. I allowed the sight of this fragile young woman, whose sickness made her look older, to discourage me. I thought it was foolishness to lay hands on someone who looked so lifeless. To me it was hopeless. This was the wrong attitude to take. I had to repent for my lack of faith and disobedience.

We don't know what God wants to do through us. Moreover, we will never know if we don't do as we are told. Regardless of how bad things look we must be quick to obey God and trust Him to do the rest.

Blocking Our Blessings

1 Kings 8:56
Praise be to the Lord, who has given rest to his people Israel just as he promised. Not one word has failed of all the good promises he gave through his servant Moses.

God wants to do great things for you. If you just look for yourself you will see all He has for you. If you are not receiving what God has for you, He is not the reason. You are.

It was God's will that Adam and Eve live in the Garden of Eden. This would have been just like living in heaven. Unfortunately, due to their disobedience they were no longer able to remain in the Garden (Genesis 3:23). God wanted this for them but they were the reason they didn't get to enjoy it. They had blocked their own blessings.

We are just like Adam and Eve; we forsake our blessings by not keeping our part of the deal. God promised to hear from heaven, forgive our sins, and heal our land, but only if we humble ourselves and pray (Chronicles 7:14, KJV). God promised to forgive us all our wrongs, but first we must forgive others (Matthew 6:14). God doing His part is contingent upon us doing ours.

God cannot lie (Titus 1:2). If He said it, He will do it. But He cannot do it unless we do what we have to do. Everything God said will come to pass (Joshua 21:45, KJV). This is because His answer to his promises are yes and amen (2 Corinthians 1:20, KJV).

God wants to bless us all. He made us many promises and He wants to see them manifest in our lives but before this can take place we must first meet the conditions. Once they are met then our blessings will no longer be blocked.

You and God Are the Majority

1 Kings 18:22
Then Elijah said to them, I am the only one of the Lord's prophets left, but Baal has four hundred and fifty prophets.

Martin Luther King Jr. is someone I will always admire. His life inspired me in many ways. This man was faced with injustice and took a stand against the majority as an attempt to bring justice to all. However, he paid for this with his life, and although he didn't live to see it, justice was done. We should never allow the fact that the majority are against us to stop us from taking a stand against injustice.

When I arrived at the Louisiana Correctional Institute for Women it didn't take long before I noticed inmates speaking negatively about a certain employee. The most common complaint I heard from the inmates was that this person was racist against black people. Being the person I am, I didn't allow what I heard to cause me to prejudge this person, neither did I allow this to cause me to form an opinion. Instead I observed this employee for myself; sadly, it didn't take me long at all to come to the conclusion that the others were correct.

I ended up filing a complaint against this employee, followed by several other complaints. Afterward, this employee became my supervisor and although this person claimed to be a Christian, he sought to do everything he could to cause me to lose my job. This employee teamed up with high-ranking officers and many of my coworkers in an effort to get me reclassified to another job. But regardless of how many were against me, the Lord showed me that as long as I was on his side, we were the majority. As a result of standing strong on the Word of God and being unmovable, the Lord uprooted this employee and transferred him to another facility.

Always be willing and ready to take a stand against injustice. Remember when God is for you it doesn't matter how many are against you. Moreover, when God is for you whosoever is against you is in big trouble.

Your Response Matters

Proverbs 15:1
A gentle answer turns away wrath, but a harsh word stirs up anger.

Disagreements between roommates are very common in prison, I'm sure you would agree. Sadly, most of these disagreements stem from someone wanting to be in control.

My remedy to dealing with every situation in which I've found myself was to apply the Word of God. This will never fail. Applying the Word of God to any situation will always turn the situation around for the better.

After living with my roommate for a few days she realized I was not an ordinary roommate. She also realized I would not be under anyone's control. This really disturbed her. One morning I was awakened to the sounds of my roommate beating on my assigned bed. This really startled me. I laid there in silence wondering what was up with this woman. The next thing I know she said, "I hope they call you to control in the morning and inform you that your mother has died." Unbeknownst to her my mother had died many years prior; still, this did not stop her words from cutting me deeply. I laid on the top bunk fighting back tears, wanting so desperately to handle the situation in the flesh. Instead, I forced myself to swallow my pride and very humbly said I guess I would then have to prepare myself for a funeral. I'm confident my response to her cruel words was more of a shock to her than her words were to me. Although my roommate tried many other things to provoke me, responding softly to her many attacks resulted in God turning this situation around.

My roommate began purchasing my favorite snacks and placing them on my locker, she started defending me when people would attack me verbally, and when she ate in the cafeteria she didn't want anyone to prepare her food but me. God worked things out between my roommate and I in a short time. If you respond with love, God will do the same for you. If you think about what you say before you speak you will find that your response matters in determining the outcome of the situations you face.

No Right to Be Angry

Jonah 4:1
But to Jonah this seemed very wrong, and he became angry.

We humans find it very hard to extend mercy to others. I am so grateful that God is not like us. No one or nothing that God has created is in a position to dictate to God, whom He extends his mercy to, neither do we have a right to get angry when He shows mercy to another.

When it comes to God extending His mercy to an individual, He is no respecter of persons. We are not the only one God shows mercy to. God shows mercy to others as well. No one deserves God's mercy. No one can earn God's mercy. God's mercy is a gift, and He gives it to whomever he will.

After the people of Nineveh heard the Word of the Lord from the mouth of Jonah, they repented of their sins. As a result, God decided not to destroy these people, and He showed them mercy instead (Jonah 3:4-10). Jonah was very angry because he didn't want God to be merciful towards the people of Nineveh (Jonah 4:1). Jonah was out of line!

I thank God that today I am sold out for the Lord. However, there was a time when I was not. There was a time when I lived a life that involved fornication and shoplifting. But in the midst of my mess and my evil ways, God showed me mercy because He knew the day would come when I would surrender all and serve Him.

If you are one of those people who gets angry because God shows mercy to the worst person in the prison, you need to check yourself. Obviously, you need to be reminded that you are who you are and God is God. Moreover, if it wasn't for His grace and mercy, that none of us deserves, we wouldn't be who we are today. The next time God shows mercy to someone, remember you have no right to be angry.

Death of a Loved One

Psalm 30:5c
Weeping may stay for the night, but rejoicing comes in the morning.

Serving time in prison can be very hard. However, there are some times that are harder than others, like being told a loved one has died.

I remember finding out that my 17-year-old nephew had been killed. My nephew and I were very close. He was like my own son. I went to my assigned room, climbed into the top bunk and cried as I stared at my nephew's pictures. I cried myself to sleep. Two days later I was lying in the bed, still crying and preparing to be depressed for some time, but God had other plans. In the middle of preparing for my depression, I was led to walk the compound until I found someone to minister to. I obeyed God immediately, although I couldn't believe I did. Not long after being on the yard, a girl ran up to me with her problems and I found myself ministering to her. Immediately after she departed I was comforted, but I didn't realize it until a few days had passed. I didn't understand it. I wanted to spend months lying on the bed crying over my nephew, but because of my obedience to help someone who was hurting while I myself was hurting, God comforted me. God dried my eyes and gave me His joy. You must understand that before my incarceration I had experienced a lot of death in my immediate family and every time I had fallen into a deep depression. Now I lost a loved one while in prison and immediately I was comforted. This was nobody but Jesus.

You may have lost a loved one while serving time in prison; if this is so, you don't have to give in to depression. Know that the same God that comforted me will do the same for you. He is no respecter of persons. If you just allow him to do so, he will comfort you, too.

Show Someone the Way

Hosea 4:6
My people are destroyed from lack of knowledge. Because you have rejected knowledge, I also reject you as my priests; because you have ignored the law of your God, I also will ignore your children.

Don't be so quick to judge those who don't do things the way you do. Don't be so quick to judge those who act inappropriately -- maybe they don't know any better. Maybe God has you where you are to teach them.

The Israelites were destroyed for lack of knowledge (Hosea 4:6, KJV). This is because the religious leaders kept the people from knowing God. They didn't have the knowledge of who God really was.

Knowledge is extremely important, and it is much harder to get through this life without it. I've heard it said many times that knowledge is power, and I definitely agree.

There may be many people who live around you who are clueless about what things that should be common. Their behavior may be wrong to you, but to them it is the norm and is all they know.

I was always against getting my clothes washed with the other inmate's clothes. My main reason for not wanting to do so is because inmates who didn't know any better would throw their underwear into the laundry instead of washing them by hand. This practice was very unsanitary and totally inappropriate. It was obvious the inmates who were doing this didn't know any better. They didn't try to hide or do so secretly because to them they weren't doing anything wrong. To them there was no need to be embarrassed. They couldn't do better because they didn't know a better way.

Don't jump to the conclusion that a person is nasty or lazy because they practice unsanitary practices, for this is not always the case. It may be that the person just doesn't know and needs someone who does to show them. If you witness someone doing something inappropriate, quietly and gently pull them to the side and show them a better way.

Singing Lies

John 4:24
God is spirit, and his worshipers must worship in the Spirit and in truth.

There are many Christians in prison who strive to live by God's Holy Word; these people are not perfect but are committed to striving for perfection. Then, you have those who choose to live a life contrary to the Word of God, join the choir and lie to God through song.

It is not unusual to see inmates live ungodly lifestyles on a daily basis and then join a Christian choir. I am talking about those inmates who are always tearing people down and then go on to sing, "I won't harm you with words from my mouth". I am speaking about those inmates who clearly tell God 'no' with their actions, then sing 'Yes to God's will and His ways' with the choir. It is time-out for playing with God. We should not just practice what we preach but should also practice the gospel songs we sing.

God is not concerned with how beautifully we sing; the beautiful voice we have comes from God. A beautiful voice does not move hearts, the anointing does. It is the anointing that destroys yokes (Isaiah 10:27, KJV). If you are living a lifestyle contrary to the songs you are singing then you are merely lying through song and God hates lying (Proverbs 6:16-17).

Make a choice today to get your act together or leave the choir. We are told to worship God in Spirit and truth; we are not doing this if we are singing lies.

Who Are You Serving?

1 Kings 18:21
Elijah went before the people and said, "How long will you waver between two opinions? If the Lord is God, follow him; but if Baal is God, follow him." But the people said nothing.

God is a jealous God (Exodus 20:5, KJV). He will not settle for us serving him along with someone or something else. We will have to serve one or the other.

We cannot serve both God and mammon, because we will love one and hate the other (Luke 16:13, KJV). I've seen this scripture lived out by people who didn't even realize they were doing so. These people claimed to be Christians, but it was clear they hated the things of God. These people didn't pay tithes because they used their money to purchase more material possessions. These people practiced homosexuality and showed hatred toward anyone who didn't condone their lifestyle. These people hated anyone who was trying to sincerely serve Jesus.

It was wise for Elijah to tell the people to follow God or Baal. He knew that it was best for them to serve one or the other than to try and serve them both. Jesus said that those who are neither cold nor hot are lukewarm, and he will spit them out of his mouth (Revelation 3:15-16).

God is a good God. You've tried everything else and it didn't and couldn't satisfy you. It's time you try God, and God alone. Don't do so thinking this is your way out of prison but do so merely because He is the only way.

Jail House Religion

James 1:26
Those who consider themselves religious and yet do not keep a tight rein on their tongues deceive themselves, and their religion is worthless.

It is very common for an inmate to regularly read their Bible, quote scriptures, and participate in church services and other religious activities once entering the prison system. Most accuse those inmates of having 'jailhouse religion'. Unfortunately, this accusation is often correct.

In a prison it is common for everyone to know one another. Everybody knows how the inmate who went to every service treated their roommate, how they behaved themselves in the dormitory, how they mouthed off at security, and how they stole goods from their job and sold them to other inmates.

If you are going to church for anything other than to praise and worship Jesus Christ, then you need to examine yourself. God is not to be played with. He is not a God that you turn to only when your back is against the wall.

Remember that God is all-knowing. He knows when you are just going through the motions. He knows that you are going to church every night because you don't have anything else to do so you'll just fake it to make it to look holy and righteous before others. You may fool others sometimes, but you can never fool God.

If you have no intention of serving God upon your release, then you have no more than jailhouse religion. Make a decision to put down your jailhouse religion and establish an intimate relationship with God. He is waiting on you.

The Family of Believers

Psalms 68:6a
God sets the lonely in families, he leads out the prisoners with singing; but the rebellious live in a sun-scorched land.

When I first got to prison, I felt all alone. I was away from my family whom I loved, yet after I was saved God was so faithful to bless me with a beautiful new family: a family of believers.

While Jesus was talking to the people, someone informed him that his mother and his brethren desired to speak with him. Jesus responded by asking: Who is my mother? And who are my brethren? Then he answered his own question by saying: For whosoever shall do the will of my Father which is in heaven, the same is my brother, and sister and mother (Matthew 12:46-50, KJV).

Although I was a member of a church, and said the prayer of salvation, I don't believe I was saved until I came to prison. It was in prison that I really understood I was adopted into the family of Jesus Christ and that I now have many sisters and brothers. At first, I was not clear as to how I was to determine who my sisters and brothers were, but after I came across Matthew 12:46-50, I knew it would be those who did the will of my Father in heaven. This meant that those who did not do the will of my Father in heaven were not my sisters and brothers. Instead, they were the children of the devil (1 John 3:10, KJV).

You too may feel very alone being away from your biological family, but you don't have to feel this way. God is ready to welcome you into your new family of believers. All you have to do is get saved and do the will of your Father in heaven. Don't delay because your new family awaits you.

Sin-Free Eating

Philippians 4:11
I am not saying this because I am in need, for I have learned to be content whatever the circumstances.

In prison the items sold in the canteen is what defines most inmates. Having canteen in prison is almost like having money on the outside, and most inmates had no limits to what they would do for canteen.

It was very common for inmates to steal from their job and sell the stolen items for canteen. Sadly, some of the inmates who called themselves Christians were the ones doing the stealing. The ones who were not doing the stealing were doing the buying, taking, or partaking, same difference; one is no better than the other.

I can recall purchasing tuna from the canteen a few times. I would try to make it taste good by adding what little was available through canteen, but no matter what I added it still tasted bland. I would see the other inmates putting all manner of things in their tuna that I wished I had for mine. Many times, I was tempted to buy some stolen seasonings and onions to hook up my tuna, but I never once gave in to the temptation. Instead, I was led not to buy tuna anymore. I didn't want to eat it bland, and the only way to prepare it the way I wanted was to purchase stolen ingredients which was not even an option, especially for a Christian.

As Christians we have to be willing to sacrifice. We can no longer be willing to get what we want at any expense. This attitude is why many of us are in prison and if we don't get it together it will be the reason many of us return.

Truth Haters

1 Kings 22:8
The king of Israel answered Jehoshaphat, "There is still one prophet through whom we can inquire of the Lord, but I hate him because he never prophesies anything good about me, but always bad. He is Micaiah son of Imlah." "The king should not say such a thing," Jehoshaphat replied.

We must strive to walk in truth. For many of us this will take much practice. Unfortunately, there are people who just don't want to hear the truth, especially when the truth is not in their favor. However, we must tell it anyway even though we may be hated for doing so.

And Elijah the Tishbite, who was of the inhabitants of Gilead, said unto Ahab, as the Lord God of Israel liveth, before whom I stand, there shall not be dew nor rain these years, but according to my word. And it came to pass after a while, that the brook dried up, because there had been no rain in the land (1 Kings 17:1, 7, KJV). Afterwards, King Ahab sent for Micaiah, shall we go against Ramoth-gilead to battle, or shall we forbear? And Micaiah said, I saw all Israel scattered upon the hills, as sheep that have not a shepherd: and the Lord said, these have no master, let them return every man to his house in peace (1 Kings 22:15, 17, KJV). This prophecy later came to pass just as Micaiah prophesied (1 Kings 22:36-37). The king of Israel hated Micaiah because he spoke the truth. It didn't even matter that the truth he spoke shortly came to pass.

When ministering to some inmates I often told them their evil lifestyle was going to result in them going to lockdown, but they never wanted to hear what I had to say. Then, sooner than later, I would see these very same people handcuffed and shackled, headed to lockdown. Although what I warned these people about did come to pass, this didn't stop them from hating me, and it won't stop them from hating you. More importantly, the truth did not stop the people from hating Jesus.

Work or Be Cold

Psalms 139:14a
I praise you because I am fearfully and wonderfully made.

During my incarceration I was classified to work in several areas; one area I wish to focus on now is the field. Most inmates dreaded working in the field, but I didn't. Actually, I liked working in the field. The only thing I didn't like about the field was working in the cold.

I can recall working in the field one very cold winter. I, along with some other inmates, just stood there in a huddle trying to get warm. The other inmates began to complain and the Lord told me to minister to them. I didn't know what to say because I was cold too, then immediately the Lord allowed me to recall the time I marched in the parade in high school. I had on very few clothes, but I wasn't cold. Then he reminded me of all the times I've seen construction workers out working in the cold in T-shirts and jeans. Okay God, I get what you're saying, I wasn't cold in the parade because I was marching, and the construction men were not cold because they were working. If I didn't want to be cold, I also needed to start working.

I was out in the field to do a job, and that job was to be done unto the Lord (Colossians 3:23, KJV). I told the ladies that the Lord has blessed us all with a built-in heater that works when we work. We all stopped standing around shaking and started working. Soon we were taking off our jackets and thanking God for our built-in heaters that worked when we did.

God is so good. He created us perfectly. He knew that some people would have jobs that would require them to work in the cold. Therefore, he created us in such a way that working would cause us to be warmed. This is so awesome and just one of many ways we are fearfully and wonderfully made.

Show Kindness to Your Enemies

Proverbs 25:21-22
If your enemy is hungry, give him food to eat; if he is thirsty, give him water to drink. In doing this, you will heap burning coals on his head, and the Lord will reward you.

We are called to be followers of Jesus Christ although living such a lifestyle will cause us to have many enemies. Yet, we should not allow this to bother us. Moreover, we should still do good to people every opportunity we get.

After Elisha captured the Syrian army and led them to Samaria, the King of Israel asked Elisha if he should kill them. And he answered, thou shalt not smite them. Would thou smite those whom thou hast taken captive with thy sword and with thy bow? Set bread and water before them, that they may eat and drink, and go to their master (2 Kings 6:22, KJV). The King of Israel could have done anything he wanted to do to the Syrians, and he decided to take Elisha's advice and show them kindness. The Syrians didn't go into the land of Israel anymore.

Making enemies in prison isn't hard at all. The more we live the Word of God the more we will make enemies. Thank God that He will cause our enemies to be at peace with us (Proverbs 16:7, KJV). However, in order for God to do this we have to walk in the Spirit, so we won't fulfill the lust of the flesh (Galatians 5:16, KJV). We have to walk in the Spirit to ignore the attacks of our enemies; give them something to drink if they are thirsty, and something to eat if they are hungry. People will not understand why you are giving something to eat to that inmate on the dorm who is ugly to you. When people see such behavior this will strengthen our witness and plant seeds that will cause them to show kindness to their enemies too.

Live the Scriptures You Quote

James 1:22
Do not merely listen to the word, and so deceive yourselves. Do what it says.

There is nothing wrong with quoting scriptures. However, there is something wrong if you are just quoting them. We must go further by also living the scriptures we quote.

I find that many times when it is hard for an inmate to practice living the Word of God, they result to quoting the Word of God. When I ask someone how they are doing they usually respond by saying 'blessed' and 'highly-favored', but yet they're walking like they're cursed. Some may say I got the victory, but yet they are walking like they are defeated. It was clear that their talk did not line up with their walk.

If you have to walk around quoting scriptures everywhere you go this may be a sign you are not living them. If you are letting your light so shine before men (Matthew 5:16, KJV), then there is no need to try to impress people with how well you know scripture. The devil knows scripture also, this is why knowing is not enough; we must live them.

Stop walking around quoting scriptures you are not living. It's time for you to get real because you are not impressing anyone. I challenge you to start living the scriptures you quote. Stop going around telling everyone you are blessed and highly favored, and instead start living like it. Soon everyone will know that you are.

Never Seek to Be Honored

Proverbs 25:6-7
Do not exalt yourself in the king's presence, and do not claim a place among his great men; it is better for him to say to you, "Come up here," than for him to humiliate you before his nobles. What you have seen with your eyes.

Nothing is wrong with sitting on the front row unless you are seeking honor, if so, you are on the front row for the wrong reasons. If you are one of those people who love sitting in the front, consider sitting in the back sometimes or else you may be asked to move.

Jesus' parable about seeking honor speaks about not sitting down in the highest room when invited to a wedding. Doing so may possibly cause the host to ask you to move to a lower place so that someone else can have your seat which could be very embarrassing.

One day while attending a big church service, the preacher asked everyone who was seated in the front to move elsewhere so a certain group of ladies, who was being honored, could have the front seats. This caused all those who was sitting in the front to find seats in the back.

I always sat in the front when I was in a church service. Don't get me wrong, there is absolutely nothing wrong with doing so; sometimes you have to sit up front just to get away from those inmates who came to church only to sit in the back and talk. However, sitting in the front may one day cause you to be asked to move so a certain group of people can have the seats.

The next time you go to a church service or any other gathering, don't take it upon yourself to sit in the best seat, as you may be asked to move. Before you get to the chapel prepare yourself to sit anywhere but the front row then you won't have to bother giving up your seat. Unless of course you are being asked to move to the place of honor.

Condemned by Your Own Words

Matthew 12:37
For by your words you will be acquitted, and by your words you will be condemned.

If you are someone who is used to saying the wrong words it may behoove you to think about your words before you speak. This will require you to not speak so quickly. The words we choose should be chosen wisely or else they may come back to hurt us.

During Herod's birthday celebration, Herodias danced for him. Herod was so pleased with her dancing that he promised to give her whatever she wanted. Before she told him what she wanted she first consulted with her mother, who told her to ask for the head of John the Baptist (Matthew 14:5-8, KJV). Herod did not want to kill John and regretted making such an oath. However, he had made this oath in front of many people and therefore he had to have John the Baptist beheaded (Matthew 14:9-10).

Our words may never be the cause of someone being killed, but our words can do damage, and much of the time the damage is done to us. If we are not careful our very words will be our downfall.

Threatening to do someone bodily harm is taken very seriously. Many times, I've seen someone get so angry that they would threaten to hurt another. Usually, the threat is made in front of many witnesses. Once this gets back to security and they begin to investigate the facts, these witnesses will usually say what they heard. As a result, the person's own words are what sends them to lockdown. Things do not have to go this way and they won't if you only make it a practice to choose your words wisely.

Come Back to Your First Love

Revelation 2:4
Yet I hold this against you: You have forsaken the love you had at first.

Many of us grew up going to church. As a child I liked church, but I loved going to Vacation Bible School even more. I believe most children did. Yet, at some point in our lives we stopped loving things dealing with God and started loving everything else instead. This time we have in prison is a perfect time to come back to our first love.

Seldom would I hear someone say that before their incarceration they were involved in ministry. One of the ladies owned a dance studio, where she herself taught dance. However, the ministry these ladies had did not stop them from falling out of love with Jesus and in love with someone or something else.

It is the devil's job to kill, steal, and destroy (John 10:10, KJV). The devil knew how you were on fire for the Lord, he knew you were a servant of his and for this he hated you. This is why he consulted with God and asked God if he could go after you. The devil wasn't going to stop until he had us under his control.

Prison is not the end of the road; in fact, it can be the beginning. It can be the place where we come to realize we made a poor decision when we started loving everything else but God. Now that we have discovered that loving things will gradually pull us away from loving God, we can repent, ask God to forgive us and turn back to our first love.

To God Be the Glory

Proverbs 25:27
It is not good to eat too much honey, nor is it honorable to search out matters that are too deep.

You should not do or say something as a means of obtaining glory. All glory belongs to God. Once we realize this, we won't try to seek it for ourselves.

While at Bible study one day, I heard something that really hit home for me. The lady who was teaching the Bible study said these words, "There is no end to what a man can accomplish if he doesn't care who gets the credit". When she spoke those words, I immediately began to ponder them. The Lord revealed to me that I was someone who couldn't do something unless others knew I'd done it. He showed me I was one of those people who just had to let those around me know that the great idea was mine.

Whenever I would give something to someone I would try to do so in secret (Matthew 6:1, KJV). I didn't want anyone to know that the Lord had used me to bless someone. Although I was adamant about this practice, it evaded me that in several other areas I had to get the credit.

One day an inmate gave a praise report at church. After she did, another inmate continuously said, "I prayed for her". This lady began speaking as if it was because of her prayers alone this woman was healed. No one had to know that she had prayed for this woman. I'm sure many of us had also prayed for this lady, but we were not looking for credit.

If you are praying for someone, especially for an unbeliever, you don't have to let this person know you are praying for them. Just pray. No one has to know that you are, unless you are looking for credit or seeking glory for yourself.

Same Foolish Actions Same Foolish Results

Proverbs 26:11
As a dog returns to its vomit, so fools repeat their folly.

I never heard of a person rescued from drowning, jump back in the water. It is not wise for someone to be rescued from danger then turn back toward the situation. Yet when God delivers us from the mess we put ourselves in, we are foolish enough to go back.

The Lord sent Moses to Pharaoh and told him to tell Pharaoh that the Lord said let my people go (Exodus 7:16, KJV). Moses turned the water into blood as an attempt to get Pharaoh to let the people go. When this didn't work the Lord sent hordes of frogs (Exodus 8:6, KJV). After God took away the frogs, Pharaoh hardened his heart again and continued to be disobedient (Exodus 8:15, KJV). Pharaoh continued in his mess and the plagues got worse. Finally, the Lord killed all the first born in the land of Egypt, from the firstborn of Pharaoh (Exodus 12:29, KJV). For if after they have escaped the pollutions of the world through the knowledge of the Lord and Savior Jesus Christ, they are again entangled therein, and overcome, the latter end is worse with them than the beginning. For it had been better for them not to have known the way of righteousness, than after they have known it, to turn from the holy commandment delivered unto them (2 Peter 2:21, KJV).

We are all inmates. Yet, many of us make serving time harder because we outright disobey the rules and get sent to lockdown. While on lockdown we say we are going to change, then when we get out and do the same thing and find ourselves back on lockdown again.

It's time for you to stop putting yourself in lockdown. If you can't live in the general population without going to lockdown, you won't live in society without returning to prison. You must determine to no longer be a fool returning to his folly.

You Hate the One You Lie On

Proverbs 26:28
A lying tongue hates those it hurts, and a flattering mouth works ruin.

Hatred is a negative emotion. We should not allow feelings of hatred to dwell within our hearts. We are operating in hatred whenever we choose to harm someone by telling lies about them.

Thou shalt not hate thy brother in thine heart (Leviticus 19:17a, KJV) is a commandment that is violated every time we lie about others. The Bible does not contain scriptures that teach us how to hate, because people don't have a problem doing so. However, there are many scriptures in the Bible to show us how to love. Often, 1 Corinthians 13 is related to as the love chapter. If we are doing things that contrast the scriptures in this chapter, we are clearly walking in hate.

We see in the scriptures that love seeketh not her own (1 Corinthians 13:5-6, KJV), yet I often see inmates lie about one another just to obtain something for themselves. Love thinketh no evil (1 Corinthians 13:5, KJV) but hatred does. The lies you tell are first formed in your mind and become your thoughts. Those lying thoughts are not good so they must be evil. Also, if love rejoices in the truth, then hatred must rejoice in lies.

You may have some so-called friends who claim to love you, or you may claim to love them, but this is not the truth if you lie about one another. Lying results in hurt and no one wants to hurt those they love. There is nothing that should cause you to lie about someone to hurt them. If by chance you are lying to hurt someone then this is who you hate.

No More Sorrow

Psalm 126:5
Those who sow with tears will reap with songs of joy.

I was devastated when I first went to prison. I did a great deal of crying my first few years of incarceration and didn't ever think I would ever stop. Then out of nowhere I was filled with joy.

There were many times I allowed my situation to reduce me to tears. I was only 29 years old when the judge sentenced me to 20 years. It made me sick to my stomach to think of my 9-year-old daughter being 29 years old herself when I got out of prison. I constantly thought about this and every time I did, I would cry. However, I thank my Lord and Savior Jesus Christ that the tears did not last, at least not the tears of sorrow. I am now filled with tears of joy. I can't even put a finger on exactly when the exchange took place, all I know is that it did. The tears I cried then can't even be compared to the joy I have now. When you have joy you don't respond to situations the way most would because the joy of the Lord is your strength, (Nehemiah 8:10h, KJV). You don't get angry with your family because they don't visit, you just come to realize that your family didn't put you in prison and then be content with writing them. When the only option for filling your belly is going to the cafeteria to eat food you really don't like, the joy you have will cause you to be so grateful for what the Lord has blessed you with you'll forget you didn't like the food in the first place.

At the writing of this passage, I have not had a visit in a year. I don't have any money in my account. I can't call home regularly because the collect calls are too expensive. Yet, none of this moved me, and I am still filled with joy.

Lying Displeases God

1 Thessalonians 2:4
On the contrary, we speak as those approved by God to be entrusted with the gospel. We are not trying to please people but God, who tests our hearts.

Lying is a sin. Don't get caught up practicing it just to please man. If we live to please God only, we won't find ourselves lying to please man.

The King of Israel gathered the prophets together, about 400 men, and said unto them shall I go against Ramoth-gilead to battle, or shall I forbear? And they said, go up; for the Lord shall deliver it into the hand of the King (1 Kings 22:6, KJV). These 400 men were all false prophets; they were telling the King what he wanted to hear because they wanted to please him. The Lord did not deliver the Syrians into the hands of Israel as prophesied. Instead, King Ahab died in battle and all of Israel were left scattered (1Kings 22:35-37, KJV).

Nothing is wrong with pleasing people. In fact, I often think about ways I would like to please my daughter when I'm released from prison. However, we should not want to please people, to the point that we would lie to do so. And we should never ever please others at the expense of displeasing God.

No one sentenced to serve the rest of their life in prison wants to hear that they may die there, and no one wants to speak such words to someone sentenced to life. However, telling every lifer you encounter that they are going to be released one day is avoiding possible reality. God is a good and he can do anything. A life sentence is nothing for Him to take away, but the fact that lifers die in prison every year shows us that sometimes he don't.

Ministering to others is sometimes difficult, so be sure to do it in love, and ask God to lead and guide you as to what you should say, before you find yourself trying to please someone by saying words that won't come to pass.

Gaining by Any Means Necessary

Revelation 3:17
You say, 'I am rich; I have acquired wealth and do not need a thing.' But you do not realize that you are wretched, pitiful, poor, blind, and naked.

Being wretched, miserable, poor, blind, and naked are all bad characteristics to possess. However, there are many of us who possess them. To possess such characteristics are bad, but it is much worse when you don't even realize you possess them.

Sadly, I have seen so many young people enter the prison system throughout my nine years of incarceration. Many of them arrive with a messed-up mentality. They are only concerned about getting money from loved ones or trying to figure out a way to con fellow inmates out of their money so they can 'live it up' in prison.

If you are allowed to wear civilian clothes at the facility you are in, don't waste time and energy trying to figure out what you can do to obtain a new outfit. Some inmates go as far as engaging in sexual activities just to keep their lockers filled with material things.

If you had money of your own, you wouldn't spend time with the people you are presently hanging out with. Yet, to live the life you choose to live inside prison you have to pretend to be friends with people you don't even like simply for financial support; this is a miserable way to live.

Money and possessions should never be anyone's focus. Our only focus should be Jesus Christ. A focus on material things are why many of us are incarcerated. When we focus on obtaining things, we find ourselves living in misery.

Having things does not define anyone. Don't think you are all that and a bag of chips because you are degrading yourself for stuff. If you think like this you are wretched, miserable, poor, blind, and naked. However, you do not have to remain this way.

Be Understanding

Proverbs 4:7
The beginning of wisdom is this: Get wisdom
Though it cost all you have, get understanding

A person who has understanding will get through life much easier than someone who doesn't. If you have a lack of understanding, pray and ask God to help you understand. It will make your time in prison much better.

It's no big secret that prison is a controlled environment. As inmates, we are not allowed to sleep whenever we want to sleep. We can't shower when we want to shower. When it is time for us to go to work, we go or suffer the consequences.

Many times, I witnessed arguments merely because an inmate walked on a wet floor while someone else was mopping. If we can avoid doing this then we should do so, but if we can't then we have to do what we have to do. The one mopping has to understand that when an inmate has to go to work then they have to go. Being late for work can cause an inmate to get a disciplinary report. Whenever an inmate is called to the infirmary, they have to go at that time. We have been stripped of the freedom to go to the doctor at our convenience. These are things that we just can't control. These are things that you should understand and not cause unnecessary problems because someone walks on the wet floor after you mopped it.

We are all in prison together. We have to learn how to live together yet doing so will be nearly impossible if we lack understanding. If this is you, God is willing to give you understanding if you ask Him. It will benefit you and everyone around you to understand.

Confident Prayers

2 Corinthians 1:20
For all the promises of God in Him are yea, and in Him Amen, unto the Glory of God by us.

Prayer is an extremely powerful weapon. Sometimes we want God to answer yes to our prayers and sometimes we want Him to respond no. Either way, we can be confident of the answer.

When the chief priests and the elders of the people came with swords and staves to arrest Jesus, Jesus said to them, "Do you think that I cannot now pray to My Father, and He will provide Me with more than twelve legions of angels?" (NKJV). Jesus knew that He was a righteous servant and for this reason, He was confident that God would have answered His prayer. You can also be confident.

If there are people on your job who are trying to form weapons against you, all you have to do is pray to God and remind Him of His promise. He promised that no weapon formed against His servant would prosper. as long as you are serving Him and living a life according to His righteousness, you can be confident of this.

Countless times I have heard it said, there is not a certain way to pray and prayer is merely talking to God. I must admit that I agree with this for those of you who just choose to merely talk to God. But if you want Him to manifest His promises in your situation, it will behoove you to check the way you pray.

Helping Others Cope with Death

**Proverbs 4:7
The beginning of wisdom is this: Get wisdom.
Though it cost all you have, get understanding.**

Our incarceration does not stop life from going on, neither does it stop death. The death of a loved one is very difficult to deal with and even more difficult when we are in prison. If one of your fellow inmates receives a death notification, please have some understanding.

You need to understand that when someone loses a loved one this is a very emotional time and you are in a position to be there for this person. You can do this by listening if they want to talk and by removing yourself if they choose to be alone.

One thing you need to understand is that we all are different. You may not handle death the way others do and vice versa. Therefore, you should never tritely say 'I know how you feel'. Why? Because you don't.

Both of my parents are deceased. Yet, if one of the ladies got a call informing her that one of her parents had died, I would be lying if I said I knew how that person felt merely because I had lost mine; I only know how I felt. Still, I wouldn't dare compare the relationship I had with my wonderful parents to someone else's because all relationships are different and when it comes to death feelings certainly are not mutual.

The best thing we can do to help someone who loses a loved one is to be whatever they need us to be. Be a friend if they need a friend. Be a listener if they want to talk, but more than anything be understanding.

Don't Ignore Hygiene Issues

Proverbs 27:5
Better is open rebuke than hidden love.

It is wrong to keep from doing good to others, even when the good is embarrassing. When you see that someone has hygiene issues don't keep this to yourself but go to the person and openly rebuke them.

For months I watched my roommate hang out with people she called her friends. Some she would even call her momma or sister. This led me to believe she was very close to these people. While my roommate were hanging out every day with these people, her hair was usually all over her head, her clothes were unclean, and she had a bad body odor. Ironically, the people she hung out with were the opposite. It was very sad to see my roommate walk around looking the way she did, it was even sadder that these so call friends of hers didn't tell her a thing about her hygiene. I tried talking to my roommate when she first moved into the room with me, but it was obvious she was embarrassed and immediately she took my concern for her welfare as being judgmental. I could only assume that she didn't believe she had hygiene issues. After all she hung out every day with people she claimed to be close to and they never said a word. At least not in her presence.

I'll be the first to say it's difficult to approach someone about their hygiene. We still need to do it anyway whether they take heed or not. It is important that we let the person know we are telling them because we love them. The person may get angry with you just like my roommate did, but it is okay because you lovingly did your part; now pray and let God do the rest.

Look to Jesus

Ecclesiastes 7:20

Indeed, there is no one on earth who is righteous, no one who does what is right and never sins.

It is okay to look at certain people as role models. Nothing is wrong with this, but we must remember that role models are people, and people are human. There are some really good people in prison, but even good people sometimes miss the mark, so keep your eyes on Jesus.

It is very common to hear an unbeliever ridicule a backslider, who was faithfully following the Lord. This often causes others who may have looked up to this person to become discouraged. If they are babies in the Lord, they may decide to turn away themselves. If they have not accepted the Lord, someone turning away may cause them not to accept Him.

There may be people in prison you look up to and respect. These people may be role models and have exemplary characters, yet no one is sin-proof. We are all capable of sinning and this is why we shouldn't trust in people to the point that their falling will cause us to fall, too.

We must look to Jesus. He is where our help come from (Psalms 121:2, KJV). Jesus is the just man. The only man who walked this earth without sinning. He is the perfect role model. He will never let us down. Therefore, we should keep our eyes on Him and not man.

One Day at a Time

Proverbs 27:1

Do not boast about tomorrow, for you do not know what a day may bring.

I consider myself to be an organized person who loves to make plans. Nothing is wrong with making plans as long as God is included. We should never make plans for tomorrow without consulting with God; after all, he has the power to change our plans.

In Jesus' parable on the rich fool, this man thought to himself, saying, what shall I do, because I have no room where I can bestow my fruit? And he said, this will I do. I will pull down my barns and build greater; and there will I bestow all my fruits and my goods. And I will say to my soul, soul, thou hast much goods laid up for many years; take thine ease, eat, drink, and be merry. But God said unto him, thou fool, this night thy soul shall be required of thee: then whose shall those things be, which thou hast provided? (Luke 12:18-20, KJV). This man was rich. He trusted in his riches. This man had so much that he was making plans to build bigger places to contain all his things. However, he never saw tomorrow when it came because he died the same day.

All too often I hear inmates say they are going to do what they want while they are serving time in prison. They say they will do it their way and when they get home they will get saved. In the meantime, they live to stock up on canteen because the devil has deceived them into thinking this makes them important in prison. It is extremely dangerous to be on this earth and not be saved. It is even more dangerous to think you can live your life playing around with sin, trying to gain more and more, only to leave it behind. Don't think you can wait until you get home to live for Christ. Tomorrow is not promised to anyone. Now is the time.

No Resemblance

1 John 3:10

This is how we know who the children of God are and who the children of the devil are: Anyone who does not do what is right is not God's child, nor is anyone who does not love their brother and sister.

I was very adamant about not relating to everyone in prison as my sister or brother in Christ. Before I did, I had to be absolutely sure we had the same Father. I was able to distinguish these people by their characteristics.

God created man in his own image, in the image of God created him; male and female he created them (Genesis 1:27, KJV). There is no question about how we as human beings came to existence. The Bible makes it clear that each and every one of us are a creation of God Almighty which means we all have the same Creator. Although this is true, this does not mean that He is the Father of all His creation.

I am blessed to have a beautiful daughter. My daughter has some of my features, but she resembles her father more. My daughter resembles her dad so much it is obvious who her father is.

As children of God it should be obvious that God is our heavenly Father. Children of God should resemble Him. God is righteous and our lifestyle should be righteous. Not righteousness by the world's definition, but our righteous lifestyle should be based on every scripture in the Word of God. 'You'll know a tree by its fruit' (Matthew 12:33, KJV) means you will know if someone is a Christian by the way they live. Their lifestyle should reflect the love spoken of in 1 Corinthians 13:4-7. They should be operating in the fruit of the Spirit spoken of in Galatians 5:22-23. Although as a child of God you should live a lifestyle of righteousness, this does not mean that you won't fall, but when you fall, you must repent, get right back up and strive to practice scriptures so you may start resembling your Father.

Surrender All

1 Samuel 15:3
Now go, attack the Amalekites and totally destroy all that belongs to them. Do not spare them; put to death men and women, children and infants, cattle and sheep, camels and donkeys.

When we make the decision to serve Jesus, we have to serve Him wholeheartedly. We cannot do this by getting rid of some of our sinful practices and keeping the rest of them. We must get rid of every trace of sin.

God is a jealous God (Exodus 20:5, KJV). He will not tolerate us serving other gods. He wants to be the only one. In fact, He will be the only one. I heard it said several times that God will be God of all or not at all. This is so true.

Saul was commanded to destroy the Amalekites. This went for men, women, and children and everything they possessed (1 Samuel 15:3). However, Saul disobeyed God and spared King Agag, and the best of the sheep, and of the oxen, and of the fatlings, and the lambs, and all that was good, and would not utterly destroy them: but everything that was vile and refuse, that they destroyed utterly (1 Samuel 15:9, KJV). Because of Saul's disobedience, God rejected him as being king (1 Samuel 15:23, KJV).

Maybe your problem is slandering others or gossiping, if this is the case, then it will behoove you to stay away from people who don't have anything better to do than tear others down. You must do whatever it takes to refrain from sin.

We all know that sin is pleasing to the senses. It makes us feel good. It looks good. It smells good. It tastes good. Regardless of what we feel we must get rid of all traces of sin. If we don't, we will end up giving in to temptation.

What Manner of Man Is This?

Mark 4:41
They were terrified and asked each other, "Who is this? Even the wind and the waves obey him!"

As Christians we should live our lives so far from the natural that people began to question who we are. Although we are in this world, we should be different. After all, we are a peculiar people. (1 Peter 2:9, KJV).

It is not uncommon to be in the midst of a storm. Storms are natural and we all expect them from time to time but never would we expect someone to speak to a storm, as Jesus did, then see the storm behave immediately (Mark 4:35-41, KJV). This caused the disciples to ask the question: What manner of man is this? (Mark 4:41, KJV).

We too can live our life in a way that people began to wonder who we are. This will happen if we stop living life in the natural and start living in the supernatural. We live in physical bodies. It is natural for our physical bodies to get hungry, but it is supernatural to decide to be hungry instead of compromising, just to get something to eat. It is natural to want to respond when someone is screaming ugly things about you in your face, but it is supernatural to keep your mouth closed and walk away. It is natural to skip everyone in line so you can be sure to get some of the last of the peach cobbler before it's gone, but it is supernatural when you take your chances and go to the end of the line.

When people know you are a Christian they begin to watch you. After they watch you enough, and see that you consistently live a supernatural life they will began to ask themselves: What manner of man is this?

Keep Your Hands and Mouth off God's Children

Psalm 105:15
"Do not touch my anointed ones; do my prophets no harm."

God will not tolerate you putting your hands on a child of God, neither will he allow you to put your mouth on them. This is extremely dangerous. It will be in your best interests not to do this.

Moses was criticized by his sister Miriam and by his brother Aaron for marrying an Ethiopian woman (Number 12:1). However, jealousy was their real reason for speaking against their brother. They were envious because God spoke through Moses and not through them (Numbers 12:2). As a result, Miriam became leprous, but Aaron did not; perhaps this was because he confessed and repented.

Little children teased Elisha. They called him bald-headed as he was going up by the way of Bethel. Elisha turned back and cursed the children and two she-bears came out of the woods and tore up forty-two of the children (2 Kings 2:23-24, KJV).

In my own life I have seen people put their mouths on a child of God and thereafter these same people end up in trouble. While eating in the cafeteria, a lady began saying ugly things to me because of my Christianity. Although I was tempted to respond, I did not say a word. About a month later this same inmate, who was an unbeliever, was punched in the eye for mouthing off at another unbeliever. Then I witnessed one of my co-workers suffer one health problem after another after she assassinated my character. I am not saying God makes people sick because this is not true, the God I serve is a healer. Yet, I am saying that God does allow things to happen without intervening when you put your mouth on his children.

Christianity is not forced on anyone; you have to choose this route. If you do not want to be a Christian that is your right. Yet there are those of us who do, and it will be in your best interests to let us be or you will be sorry.

Things Made Should Not Make You

Isaiah 17:8
They will not look to the altars, the work of their hands, and they will have no regard for the Asherah poles and the incense altars their fingers have made.

Prisons are filled with many talented people. Many of these people are able to make many different things with their hands, yet all too often they allow the things they have made to become idols.

Many of the images spoken of in Isaiah 17:8 were of Asherah. The Bible warns against worshipping Asherah. (Exodus 34:13, Deuteronomy 12:3, 16:21, KJV). These images were made by the hands of man and were considered idols because people worshipped these things.

I had the opportunity to see fish tanks, sofas, tables, chairs, artwork, jewelry, purses, beautiful grandfather clocks and much more made by the hands of inmates. Many of these things are sold for profit. Inmates often allow the things they have made to become idols. They spend all their time making these things and then they take the credit for it instead of giving the credit to the only one who deserves it.

It is a gift to be able to create beautiful things with your own hands, but we cannot allow these things to become idols. If you have been blessed with such a talent remain humble and be sure to give all the glory to the one who gave you the gift.

What Do You See?

Numbers 13:33
We saw the Nephilim there (the descendants of Anak come from the Nephilim). We seemed like grasshoppers in our own eyes, and we looked the same to them.

For the most part inmates share the same circumstances. Yet, we don't all view these circumstances the same. This is because most of them are looking from a worldly point of view.

Moses sent out 12 men to spy on the land of Canaan (Numbers 13:1-17). Although the 12 men spied on the same land they did not all see victory. Ten of the men saw defeat but Joshua and Caleb saw victory. Caleb's attitude was let us go up because we are well able to overcome it (Numbers 13:30, KJV). The other 10 men reported that they were not able to go up against the people; for they are stronger than we (Number 13:31, KJV).

You are in prison. I'm in prison. Yet, ironically our perceptions of the prison experience are different. You see prison as the end, but I see it as a new beginning. You see prison as a bad thing, but I see it as all good. You see prison as being locked up, but I see prison as being free.

Let's get real, prison has taken some people away from a life of drugs, running the streets without taking a bath for days or maybe weeks at a time, from prostitution, drug dealing, fornication, and whatever else. If prison took you away from any of these things, then how could you not see prison as anything but a blessing in disguise.

Be Led to Altar Call

1 Thessalonians 4:11
And to make it your ambition to lead a quiet life: you should mind your own business and work with your hands, just as we told you.

We all must work out our own salvation (Philippians 2:12, KJV). This has to be done individually. If we are doing this then we shouldn't be worrying about who's not going to the altar.

There are many different church services at the Louisiana Correctional Institute for Women. Most of the same volunteers come every week to hold church services, yet there are times when there may be a speaker from another state visiting for the first time. Whenever we would have such speakers come, the pews were usually empty when an altar call is given for salvation, backsliding, prayer and whatever else. Most of the time I wouldn't get up. Whenever I didn't I would get many looks from some of the inmates who went to the altar. I discerned from their spirits they were bothered because I stayed in my seat instead of going to the altar. It was also revealed to me that these inmates were judging me as having it all together, which certainly was not the case. I went to the altar many times but I wasn't going to go merely because a new speaker ministered, as if that person had some type of magic potion. The only time I went to the altar is when I was led to do so.

The Bible tells us to mind our own business (1 Thessalonians 4:11). We are not obeying this when we are worrying about why a certain individual didn't go to the altar. It's none of your business if someone else doesn't get up for prayer. You should only be concerned with getting there yourself.

Locked Up but Free

John 8:36
So if the Son sets you free, you will be free indeed.

Sin had me so messed up I could not even think straight. In fact, it caused me to think that I was straight. It wasn't until God allowed me to go to prison and see the life I chose for myself, that I was made free.

The prodigal son requested that his father give him his inheritance. After he received it he went on his way to do any and everything he could think of, yet he ended up out with the swine, even wanting to eat the slop they ate (Luke 15:16, KJV). This was the last straw for the prodigal son -- he could not take anymore and at that moment he was set free and returned to his father.

In so many ways I was just like the prodigal son. I did anything I wanted to do. I lived my life like it was actually mine (1 Corinthians 6:19) until my choices resulted in me being confined to a holding cell filled with women from all walks of life. Some of these women were strung out on drugs, some were beat up and bloody. This little cell contained one deplorable little toilet for all of us to share. This cell had trash everywhere, and it smelled horrible. I could not believe this was the life I had chosen. It did not take any more, I knew there was something better for me, and at this very moment I was made free.

I will never forget what I was forced to experience in that disgusting holding cell. That place was not fit for any human being, yet it was in that place that I was made free.

What Are You Really Throwing Away?

Acts 3:6
Then Peter said, "Silver or gold I do not have, but what I do have I give you. In the name of Jesus Christ of Nazareth, walk."

Money is very beneficial and having it makes life better. However, the Word of God is much more beneficial. No amount of money you may receive will ever benefit you more than the Word of God, so stop throwing away your blessings.

When Peter and John went into the temple there was a certain man, lame from birth, who was carried and laid at the gate of the temple to ask alms (Acts 3:1-2, KJV). When the lame man saw Peter and John he asked them for alms: then Peter said, silver and gold I have none; but such as I have I give thee: in the name of Jesus of Nazareth, rise up and walk (Acts 3:6, KJV). Sadly, this man was carried to the gate every day to beg for money, for he was more concerned about money than he was the Word of God which brought him healing.

I am sure that all inmates would agree that they look forward to mail call. Unfortunately, most inmates are looking for someone to send them money. They relate to mail containing money as good mail and to mail from different ministries as junk mail. This junk mail is usually thrown in the garbage can immediately. The mail that can't benefit much is what the inmates want, but the Christian mail which can benefit them far beyond this life is rejected. The lame man probably received money every day, yet it didn't do a thing for him. It wasn't until he was given Jesus that he was healed.

Are you waiting for God to answer your prayers? Then stop going to mail call every day looking for alms. God may have an answer to your prayer in the Christian mail you keep throwing away. That thing you have been seeking from God may very well come by way of Christian mail, but you will never know if you keep throwing it away.

What Are You Willing to Sell for Canteen?

Genesis 25:33
But Jacob said, "Swear to me first." So he swore an oath to him, selling his birthright to Jacob.

We can't allow our flesh to have its way. When we allow this to happen our flesh will control us. As Christians we need to learn how to dominate the flesh and make no provision for it (Romans 13:14) or else we will make poor choices just to satisfy ourselves.

Esau, the eldest son of Isaac and Rebekah, sold the rights he had as the firstborn son to his brother Jacob because he was hungry. As the first born son, Esau was to be given a double portion of all Isaac had (Deuteronomy 21:17b, KJV), yet he chose to sell this right to his brother for a meal that will only bring him temporary satisfaction.

I am so qualified to write this particular devotion. At the time of this writing, I am sitting up on the top bunk that I am assigned to at 9:54 p.m. and I am hungry. I don't get much money from home and I don't have anything to eat in my locker. Although I don't have food, I do possess many nice things that I could sell to someone for something to eat. Many inmates resort to selling their things when they don't have any food. I have a brand-new robe and pajamas, new panties, socks, bras, jeans, jewelry, and several other things. However, I am not willing to sell. Don't get me wrong, I am not trying to cling to these material things, but neither am I trying to sell them to temporarily please my flesh. It would be a different story if I was about to go home, but as I have yet to see relief from the courts I decided to say my prayers, go to sleep, and thank God for the breakfast I'll be served in the morning, Lord willing.

Inmates in America are blessed with three meals a day. If you do happen to get hungry at night like I am now, don't allow your flesh to cause you to sell your possessions for temporary satisfaction. Hold fast, this is only a test, and remember breakfast will be provided in the morning.

Learn to Love Yourself

Psalms 139:14
I praise you because I am fearfully and wonderfully made; your works are wonderful, I know that full well.

Some of us may have a complex about our bodies, yet we have to pray about this and begin to love ourselves the way we are. God did not make a mistake when He made you. You are fearfully and wonderfully made and need to start seeing yourself as such.

It is common not to want to undress in front of other people. Our bodies, of course, are very personal. Yet in prison we have no other choice than to share a shower area with other inmates. This is something I always hated, but still I adjusted. It wasn't because I was ashamed of my body but because my nudity was exposed to others against my will. It's okay to feel the way I do about getting undressed in front of others. However, if your reason for not wanting to get undressed in front of others is because you are ashamed of your body then you have a serious problem. I know there are people who struggle with weight problems. Some believe they are too big and some believe they are too small. Although with self-discipline you may be able to lose or gain weight, in the meantime you have to learn how to love yourself. You may not have to live with others, but you have to live with yourself, so practice loving every part of you.

Do not allow the stares and foolishness of others to cause you to condemn yourself. The ugly things people may say about your body says more about them than it does about you. You did not make you, God did. The next time you get in the shower, do so with no shame or regret. After God made man, He said very good (Genesis 1:31) and this is how you should see yourself.

Refrain from Retaliating

Romans 12:19
Do not take revenge, my dear friends, but leave room for God's wrath, for it is written: "It is mine to avenge; I will repay," says the Lord.

Several times throughout my incarceration I heard inmates talk about something bad they planned to say to a guard on their way out and a few inmates do carry out their plans. Just because your time is up and you are on your way out the prison doors, don't allow Satan to use you to mouth off something ugly at a guard who mistreated you; bless them instead.

Paul and Silas were in jail. They were bound, both hands and feet. Yet after an earthquake shook the prison, Paul and Silas were both freed from their chains. When the jailer saw that Paul and Silas were freed he was about to take his own life until Paul and Silas screamed for him not to, telling him they were still there.

When you are blessed with your freedom, do not waste your time thinking about ugly things you can say or do to a guard who was ugly to you throughout your incarceration. You can thank that guard for everything he or she did, knowing that their mistreatment made you stronger in the Lord and brought you to a higher level in Him. Tell the guards you pray the blessings of God over their life and that you wish them the best.

You don't have to retaliate. God knows everything that went on between you and this guard and He'll make sure He avenges for you.

God's Children Are Untouchable

1 Corinthians 6:20
You were bought with a price. Therefore, honor God with your bodies.

Whatever you purchase belongs to you and no one has the right to touch what is yours without your permission, neither can Satan touch a child of God without God's permission.

As prisoners, we are allowed to purchase things from the canteen; whatever we purchase is ours. We get to store our stuff in our lockers. Although we can't store much in the lockers, whatever we keep in there belongs to us and no one has the right to touch it.

If you are a child of God you are bought with a price (1 Corinthians 6:20). This means you were purchased. This means you are not your own. You have an owner. You were not purchased with money; you were purchased with blood. God gave His life to purchase you. This means you belong to God and unless God allows it, Satan can't touch you. You don't belong to you. You have no control over your life but God does, so stop allowing Satan to use people to move you. Remember, you don't belong to yourself and can do nothing to help yourself. Leave your conditions in the hands of the one who cared enough to purchase you with His blood.

Broken Promises

2 Corinthians 1:20
For no matter how many promises God has made, they are "Yes" in Christ. And so through him the "Amen" is spoken by us to the glory of God.

There are people who may make promises to you and go back on their word. If someone makes a promise to you, you should hold on to it lightly because sometimes these promises are not kept. However, the promises of God are a sure thing.

Joseph was in jail along with Pharaoh's butler and baker. While in jail, Pharaoh's butler and baker both dreamed a dream the same night. After they told Joseph their dreams, Joseph gave them the interpretation. He told the butler that he will be restored back to his position in three days. He told the baker that he would be executed in three days. Both interpretations came to pass (Genesis 40:1-22). Joseph also told the butler to put in a good word for him to Pharaoh so that he could get out of jail, but the butler forgot about Joseph (Genesis 40:23).

I believe most inmates could testify about all the promises made to them by other inmates that were never carried through. 'I'm going to write you.' 'I'm going to send you something.' 'I am going to accept your calls.' These are just a few of the most common promises inmates make to other inmates.

God has promised us so much and his word will not return to Him void. You may not be able to depend on the promises of others, but every promise God has made will come to pass in your life.

Don't Bother Answering

Proverbs 26:4
Do not answer a fool according to his folly, or you yourself will be just like him.

To everything there is a season, and a time to every purpose under the heaven (Ecclesiastes 3:1, KJV). There is a time to love and a time to hate. There is a time to reap and a time to sow. There is even a time not to answer fools and we have to know when this time comes.

After Jesus was betrayed and arrested, two false witnesses said, this fellow said I am able to destroy the temple of God and to build it in three days (Matthew 26:60-61, KJV). The high priest asked Jesus if He was going to answer in response to the accusations against him, but Jesus did not say a word (Matthew 26:63). Jesus knew the carnal mind was not able to understand spiritual things. The people would never have grasped that Jesus' body was the temple He was speaking of that would be destroyed and raised from the dead three days later. Jesus knew that it did not make any sense to answer the high priest. Jesus' answer would just have been the start of a debate.

Just like Jesus, you will encounter people who you will not be able to answer according to their folly. Many inmates have accused me of living for Jesus only because I am in prison and went on to say I would leave my Bible behind when I went home. It did not make sense to answer these people because nothing I said or did would convince them to believe otherwise. Just like the high priest would not have believed that Jesus himself was the temple that would be destroyed and rebuilt in three days until after it came to pass. No one is going to believe you are going to live for Jesus once you are released until you are out there doing it, so do yourself a favor and do not say a word.

We do not have to respond to every foolish remark people make about us. Although there may be times when we are led to respond, learn to decipher when it is appropriate for you to respond to fools or you will find yourself foolishly responding to any and everything.

A Time to Answer

Proverbs 26:5
Answer a fool according to his folly, or he will be wise in his own eyes.

There are times when it would be best for you to ignore the foolishness of another. However, we may sometimes have to answer fools. If we do not, our silence may be misconstrued.

Jesus was led up of the Spirit into the wilderness to be tempted by the devil (Matthew 4:1, KJV). The devil used physical desires, power, and pride to tempt Jesus. Yet, Jesus did not give in to any of these temptations. The devil knew that Jesus had fasted for 40 days and 40 nights (Matthew 4:2). Therefore, he told him to command the stones to be made bread, if he be the son of God (Matthew 4:3, KJV). But Jesus answered and said it is written, man shall not live by bread alone, but by every word that proceeded out of the mouth of God (Matthew 4:4, KJV). Each time Jesus was tempted he responded with the word of God (Matthew 4:4, 7, 10) We all know that the devil was kicked out of heaven because of his own conceit (Isaiah 14:12). Jesus could have ignored Satan but did not. I believe Jesus wanted Satan to know that even though He was physically weak from lack of food that He was not going to utilize his power to turn the stones into bread, because the bread his father had was far greater. This had to sound strange coming from a hungry man. Satan was wise to tempt Jesus with bread at a time like this, but Jesus' answer was wiser.

Numerous times I have had people tell me something negative about one of my sisters. Whenever this would happen, I always saw the need to answer these people, because I did not want them to think for one second that it was okay to discuss my Sister-n-Christ. If what they were accusing my sister of was in line with the Word of God I would show them in the Bible. If it was not in line, I would tell this person I was willing to go with them to bring this matter to my Sister-n-Christ. Of course, they did not take me up on my offer, neither did they approach me with any more foolishness.

Evil Assumptions

Philippians 2:5
In your relationships with one another, have the same mindset as Christ Jesus.

Assuming things about others is not bad in itself. However, when we act on our assumptions this can be a problem. If you are always making negative assumptions about others, then this is clear evidence you do not have the mind of Christ.

From the day I received a 20-year sentence and was remanded to prison I was on a mission to do everything I could to attempt to regain my freedom. This resulted in doing a lot of reading, studying, and researching law materials. It also resulted in keeping on the lights.

When I entered the Louisiana Correctional Institute for Women, I found myself sharing a room with one or two other inmates. No matter which room I was assigned to or who my roommates were, I often kept the lights on until curfew at 10:30 p.m. Sadly, my decision to keep the lights on at night were often mistaken for trying to vex my roommate(s). There were even times I was looked at as being evil simply for using the light during the acceptable times.

There are many people who take things personally. This mindset causes them to think that everything someone does is an attack against them. A Christlike mind does not think this way but on whatsoever things are true, honest, just, pure, lovely and of good report (Philippians 4:8, KJV). Every time I stayed up with the light on and then later in the dark it wasn't because I wanted to, I wanted to go to sleep but I needed to be there for my daughter and this was my only reason for sacrificing my sleep. This was not done to aggravate another individual. No one has that type of control over me and should not have it over you.

The Dishonest Borrower

Matthew 25:21

His master replied, 'Well done, good and faithful servant! You have been faithful with a few things; I will put you in charge of many things. Come and share your master's happiness!'

We must take good care of things entrusted to us. When someone is kind enough to allow you to use their belongings, you should be faithful enough to inform them of any potential damage you may have caused; failing to do so is dishonest.

There are many people who often misconstrue Christianity. They hold the belief that if you are a Christian, they can get over on you. Some people think Christians are doormats.

One day one of my roommates borrowed an iron from one of the ladies on the hall and accidentally dropped it on the floor. It was obvious the iron was still working after it was dropped because my roommate continued to iron her clothes. However, when she returned the iron, she never once mentioned anything about the incident. Yet, she was obligated to do so because the lady was nice enough to trust her with the iron in the first place, so she should have been faithful enough to let the lady know that it had been dropped.

It always pays to be faithful. People will respect you when they see you consistently practice honesty. We must always be willing to glorify God and this is exactly what you are doing when others hear you admit to someone, something they would never have known, if it was not for your open admission.

If Finders Don't Keep Losers Won't Weep

Matthew 5:16
In the same way, let your light shine before others, that they may see your good deeds and glorify your Father in heaven.

Throughout life you will encounter many opportunities to let your light shine before men. This can even happen in prison. Be sure to take advantage of every opportunity to do this and God will be glorified.

One day while out in the yard, one of my sisters-in-Christ found an envelope containing eight postage stamps, and the envelope had a name on it with which we were both familiar. This person lived in my dorm, so my sister gave me the envelope so I could return the stamps to their rightful owner. To make a short story shorter I gave the envelope to the compound manager who gave them to the person they belonged to, after telling her who found them. When the girl went back to her living area, she began to scream repeatedly that the Christian girls found her stamps and turned them in. She then said, 'those girls are real' and thanked God for allowing the Christian girls to find her stamps.

We did not go around bragging that we found stamps and turned them in, because we were not looking to be praised. We just wanted to be the honest people Christians are supposed to be and see God get the glory as a result. Both myself and my sister-in-Christ were indigent and always in need of stamps, yet the stamps we found were not ours to keep. and we were not about to give in to lack and keep them. We were more concerned with using this opportunity to let our light shine so that our Father in heaven could be glorified.

Resist Dishonest Gain

Philippians 4:11
I am not saying this because I am in need, for I have learned to be content whatever the circumstances.

As Christians, we need to learn how to be satisfied with whatever we have. Many of us have more than the next person and still are not satisfied. If we don't learn how to be content, we will find ourselves trying to gain more by unjust means.

One of my sisters-in-Christ obtained her GED after trying for some time, after which she was blessed to be accepted in the Upholstery program. To some, this sister appeared to be very strong in the Lord. She was known for walking around ministering and passing out scriptures. Not long after this girl had started Upholstery, I witnessed her selling bags to other inmates. When I saw this, I was very disappointed, because bags made in Upholstery and sold by inmates was created with stolen material. Unbelievers made things in Upholstery all the time and I expected such behavior, but I did not expect this from my sister-in-Christ.

We must learn how to be content. It is a little easier to be content when we have what we want but regardless of our situation, we must make every effort to be content.

Sadly, this girl who appeared to be a mature Christian allowed the unjust gain of the unbelievers to entice her to sneak bags out of her class to sell them. This was done to get extra canteen items here and there, not due to need but merely because she just wanted more.

We have to be determined not to compromise. We must learn how to be content. This is extremely important. If you compromise in here just to gain a few extra snacks, there is no telling how you will compromise when you get home in order to obtain a few extra dollars. Do not allow yourself to succumb to such practices instead be content and resist dishonest gain.

No Reason to Steal

Ephesians 4:28
Anyone who has been stealing must steal no longer, but must work, doing something useful with their own hands, that they may have something to share with those in need.

Stealing is a very serious crime. Not only is it a crime, it is also a sin, a sin which is commonly practiced in the prison system. Sadly, much of the stealing is done by those who are in prison for this very thing.

One day a sister-in-Christ was placed in maximum security for stealing from her job. When I learned what had happened, I was saddened but not at all surprised because I had witnessed others asking this lady to help them smuggle something stolen; instead of telling them no and letting them know she's delivered, she talked in circles giving an indirect response.

This lady did not get much money from home. The enemy used this fact to tempt her into stealing food from the kitchen. After she would steal the food, she would sell it to get some of the things she wanted.

You must get it through your head that God allowed you to come to prison to clean you up. However, once you are clean, you jump right back into the same mess just because you are experiencing lack. And you are wondering why your prayers regarding being released from prison have not yet come to pass. God knows that as soon as your children are in need or as soon as you are in a financial bind you will revert to the same thieving behavior you practice in prison. Then back to jail you go.

At the time of this writing, I am experiencing lack and have been for some time, yet stealing is not an option. If it isn't for me it doesn't have to be for you, either because there is no reason to steal.

Hate Mail

Proverbs 23:17a
Do not let your heart envy sinners.

Inmates practice many bad things in prison. However, this does not give you the right to write their family to tell them what they are doing, for this is information you should not be volunteering.

One day an inmate made a phone call to her husband and found out that he had received a letter from her roommate. In the letter, the roommate had informed him that his wife was involved in a homosexual relationship. She also told him all the money he was sending her was being spent on the person she was in the relationship with.

It is not hard to see that the roommate was envious of the girl. She resented the fact that she had a husband who was taking good financial care of her. It was her intention to cause this man to stop helping his wife financially.

Envy and jealousy are two very strong emotions and we must avoid them. When we live in the same room or stay on the same dorm with someone who is financially comfortable, it is very easy to fall into temptation and start coveting what these people have. However, you won't be tempted to do so if you keep your eyes on the one who is able to give you so much more.

Borrowing Schemes

Romans 13:13a
Let us behave decently.

It does not matter how much you read your Bible or how much you go to church; you will be tempted. Every day of our lives, Satan will try to get us to fall. However, we must stand strong and not give in to any of his attacks.

Every night I would sit in bed and listen to different Christian stations on the radio. One day my headphones stopped working so I ended up using someone else's. After I put them on, I noticed they were exactly like my headphones. Immediately an evil thought came to me telling me to switch the headphones I got from the girl with the broken ones I had in the room. No one would have known right? Wrong! The one who sees all knows, and He is the one I'm trying to please. Without wasting time, I cast down the thought and thanked God for giving me the strength not to act it out.

It would have been quite easy for me to switch the headphones. Yet, I did not want them badly enough to sin. Yes, I used them to listen to Christian stations and I was grateful that the lady was kind enough to let me use them, yet they were not mine and I had no right to gain them through deceit.

We need to be forever mindful that God is all-knowing and omnipresent. We need to remember this every second of every minute. When we do, we won't think twice about committing dishonest acts.

A Time to Tell

Matthew 10:16
**I am sending you out like sheep among wolves.
Therefore, be as shrewd as snakes and as innocent as doves.**

There may be occasions when we have to report another inmate to the authorities. When we do, it may cause us to experience light affliction. Still, some things just have to be done.

I was housed in Aquarius dormitory at the Louisiana Correctional Institute for Women. The rooms in Aquarius contain one set of double bunks, four lockers and a toilet for two people to occupy. One day I walked into my assigned room and noticed brown paper was lodged in the toilet. It was obvious it had been flushed but didn't go down. This was the second time I'd found brown paper in the toilet and I wanted to bring this issue to my roommate. However, I decided not to because my roommate was a very evil person and I knew it was best not to go to her. Instead I went to security and reported this problem. I did so because if the toilet were to have stopped up and it was discovered that brown paper was being flushed down, we both would have been written up for property destruction. I didn't want to bring this to security, but I knew I didn't have any other choice. My only reason for reporting this was to protect myself, not to hurt my roommate.

My decision to report my roommate to security made her very upset with me. I didn't want to anger her, nor did I want to get in trouble. Therefore, I weighed the odds and did what I had to do to cover myself.

Christian Until Sentenced

1 Samuel 16:7
But the Lord said to Samuel, "Do not consider his appearance or his height, for I have rejected him. The Lord does not look at the things people look at. People look at the outward appearance, but the Lord looks at the heart."

Man is limited in knowledge, but God is all-knowing. He knows more about us than we can ever know ourselves. He even knows what everyone sees about us, and if it is an act or the real deal.

While housed in the Parish Prison I was surrounded by many women who appeared to be deep in the Word of God. These ladies were constantly ministering to others, acting as peacemakers, leading praise songs on the dorm, conducting prayer circles, and calling people together for Bible study. Yet, after these people went to court and discovered they wasn't going home they stopped doing all those things.

We are not and never will be smarter than God, neither can we fool Him. It is impossible to fool the God who can see our hearts. We are only fooling ourselves and maybe a few others. We cannot deceive the Almighty God. He knows the end of a thing at the beginning (Isaiah 46:10, KJV), this is how he knows you are acting like a Christian, hoping that this will give you the outcome in court that you desire.

If you have been acting like a Christian thinking you can fool God, stop it now. God couldn't care less about what we are doing, because he knows why we are doing it. If it is God's will, he has the power to change the outcome of our situation, but first we must be real.

What Good Can You Remind God Of?

Isaiah 38:3
"Remember, Lord, how I have walked before you faithfully and with wholehearted devotion and have done what is good in your eyes." And Hezekiah wept bitterly.

God is a good God. We should also be people who practice doing good. One day we may need to remind God of the good we have done, which could very well keep us out of trouble.

Hezekiah was sick unto death. Isaiah the prophet, the son of Amoz, came unto him and said Thus saith the Lord, set thine house in order for thou shalt die, and not live (Isaiah 38:1, KJV). After Isaiah told Hezekiah that the Lord said he was going to die, Hezekiah turned his face to the wall in prayer, reminding God of all the good he had done and as a result God added 15 years to Hezekiah's life (Isaiah 38:2-5). Hezekiah was able to remind God of all the good he had done because Hezekiah kept his commandments (2 Kings 18:6).

What about you? What can you remind God of? Are you able to honestly tell God that you were kind to strangers without a motive? Are you able to remind God of how well you walk in integrity when He is the only one in the audience? Are you able to remind God that you never complain? If you are not able to remind God of anything, then obviously you have not been doing anything good.

God Is Why We Testify?

John 7:18
Whoever speaks on their own does so to gain personal glory, but he who seeks the glory of the one who sent him is a man of truth; there is nothing false about him.

It is good to go before the church and give testimony. However, we should never do so to bring ourselves glory. Testimonies should be given for no other reason than to give God glory by testifying about what God did in your life.

While in church one night, one of my sisters-in-Christ asked to give a testimony. Before she began, she pointed at a lady and asked her to come up. After the lady came up my sister began to testify. She talked about how she and the lady were in the same prison some years ago. She said she was constantly attacked by this lady and her gang. She said that they cussed at her often and she never said a word. My sister said one day she called her pastor and told him about this lady and asked him to please send the woman some money, and he did. This was really a good testimony, but unfortunately it was told by the wrong person.

Whenever we give a testimony, it should be done to help others. Our testimony should never bring embarrassment to anyone and should always bring glory to God. If your testimony is all about lifting up yourself then you are the only one who received the glory.

Bothered but Not Moved

1 Corinthians 10:13
No temptation has overtaken you except what is common to mankind. And God is faithful; he will not let you be tempted beyond what you can bear. But when you are tempted, he will also provide a way out so that you can endure it.

Prisons are filled with people who will do things to try to get you to fall, however their tricks are not uncommon so do not give in to the temptation by reacting negatively.

Presently, I find myself in a very trying situation. The roommate I have is constantly spitting in the sink she and I both shares. My roommate does this about 30 times a day. After I saw her do this repeatedly and leave it there without sanitizing the sink, I was tempted to give her a piece of my mind. Yet, I didn't because I realized I could not afford to do so. Instead, I decided to stay in the bunk and not react at all. If I had, my roommate would have known her actions bothered me. Although I thought what my roommate was doing was absolutely disgusting, I knew if I had said something, it would have shown her she was bothering me and may have caused her to do it even more. Therefore, I had to remind myself not to be moved by my roommate's disgusting ways. Although on the inside I was sick to my stomach, on the outside I didn't allow her to see how disturbed I was. I also avoided using the sink in the room, as a way of escape.

If you are tempted to argue with someone who has been doing things to provoke you don't do it. God sees exactly what's going on and has provided a way out. God has promised us an escape plan when tempted. Although it will temporarily satisfy our flesh to give in to the temptation, we shouldn't. Besides, it shows that you are a strong person to be bothered but not moved.

God Is More Concerned with the End Results

Isaiah 53:10a
Yet it was the Lord's will to crush him and cause him to suffer.

God loves us all very much. He cares about you just like He cares about me. However, God is more concerned about the end results than what you went through to get there.

Joseph was sold into slavery by his brothers (Genesis 37:27). This pleased the Lord because God knew that the outcome was going to cause him to be second to the king (Genesis 41:40). And all countries came to Joseph to buy food because the famine was great (Genesis 41:57, KJV). God wasn't moved by what Joseph had to go through because he knew the end result.

The Roman soldiers platted a crown of thorns, then put it upon Jesus' head (Matthew 27:29, KJV), they spit on him, took a reed, and smote him on the head (Matthew 27:30, KJV). One of the soldiers with a spear pierced his side (John 19:34, KJV). Everything Jesus went through was cruel, but yet it pleased God because He knew that Jesus' blood had to be shed to save humanity.

God loves you so much. He doesn't love me anymore than He loves you or anyone else. God is not saddened by your incarceration, He is pleased with it. It doesn't matter to God that you are away from your family, locked up in some cell with no or limited communication from your friends and loved ones. What matters to God is that the experience draws you to Him. What matters to God is that your soul is eternally secure when it's all over and done. It doesn't matter to God what you have to go through for His mission to be accomplished.

Stand on the Whole Scripture

Psalm 37:4
Take delight in the Lord, and he will give you the desires of your heart.

Too often we like to stand on part of a scripture without taking heed of the other parts. If God has not been giving you the desires of your heart then check yourself, maybe you will find that you are standing on part of a scripture.

I believe it would be safe to say all prisoners desire to be set free from their incarceration. I myself had many desires and being set free from prison was one of them. I had no doubt in my mind that God would give me the desires of my heart, but I wasn't sure if I was delighting myself in Him. Then I was led to a scripture that said: If thou turn away thy foot from the Sabbath, from doing thy pleasure on my holy day; and call the Sabbath a delight, the holy of the Lord, honorable, and shalt honor him, not doing thine own ways, nor finding thine own pleasure, nor speaking thine own words: then shalt thou delight thyself in the Lord (Isaiah 58:13-14a, KJV).

I was determined to delight myself in the Lord. Instead of doing those things that pleased my flesh, I did those things that pleased the Lord. Instead of slamming lockers to get back at my sleeping roommate, I did things God's way and tried to be as quiet as possible. Whenever I was faced with a choice to do or say what I wanted to say, I decided to say thus saith the Lord. I did all these things not because I wanted to but because I desperately wanted to delight myself in the Lord.

Prayer Can Uncover Corruption

James 5:16d
The prayer of a righteous person is powerful and effective.

Prayer is a very powerful tool that we are free to practice. We should never forsake the freedom we have to communicate with God. In fact, if you are trying to be relieved of the sentence man handed down, nothing can assure relief like the power of prayer.

Esther 6 tells a story about a king who ordered the records of the daily journal brought and read to him because he could not sleep. Through this reading the king found out that Mordecai exposed a plot to assassinate King Achashverosh, which had saved his life. Previously, the king had granted Haman's wish to have Mordecai hung on the gallows, but after finding out Mordecai was never honored for saving the king, the king decided to honor him by relieving him of this sentence.

Man sentenced me to 20 years for theft of goods valued at $179.00. I was guilty as charged, but everything in me said both my sentence and the habitual offender law were unconstitutional. For years I filed motions, appeals, and wrote everyone I could think of regarding this injustice. One day an inmate showed me an article from the newspaper about a Fifth Circuit court employee committing suicide in his office. This man left behind a suicide note stating that back in 1994 the court adopted the illegal practice of automatically denying all indigent inmates who filed anything into the court, due to the court's high case load. The ironic thing is that I was representing myself and therefore possessed three letters from this court employee that all turned out to be lies.

According to the newspaper approximately 2,000 inmates were affected by the decisions of this man, and several judges, but I didn't lose hope. I never stopped fasting. I never stopped praying. I was persistent and consistent and prayed until the corruption was exposed and my sentence was overturned.

It was a tragedy for this man to commit suicide. However, God allowed it because His child was fervently praying that justice be done in her case. This man was at his end. He had lost all hope and could have taken his life without leaving a note behind, but when the righteous is in communication with God through prayer, God is going to make sure that the guilty one does whatever it takes, such as leaving a note that sets His child free.

Love Your Enemies

Matthew 5:46
If you love those who love you, what reward will you get? Are not even the tax collectors doing that?

It is so easy to hate those who hate us, and very difficult to love those who hate us. The only way to accomplish this is to allow God to do it through us.

Throughout my lifetime I met many people who were kind, peaceable, mannerly, selfless, and teachable. These people were very easy to get along with. It was also no problem to walk in love with these people because they were loving. On the other hand, I also encountered people who were bitter, with nasty attitudes, and couldn't get along with anyone. These people were always gossiping and trying to find fault with others. No one wants to be around people like this let alone love them, however we are commanded to do so (Matthew 5:44).

Jesus is the most perfect example of love. In fact, Jesus is love. When Jesus died on the cross He died for the sins of the world, not just for his immediate family. He didn't just die for his disciples. He didn't just die for his followers but also for His enemies (Matthew 27:30). Jesus died for those who cast lots for his clothes (Matthew 27:35, KJV). Jesus died for those who drove nails through His hands and feet. Allow Jesus to be your example the next time you are tempted not to love those who hate you. Using him for an example will help us to do away with any poor excuse we can think of not to love.

One on One Time

1 John 2:27
As for you, the anointing you received from him remains in you, and you do not need anyone to teach you. But as his anointing teaches you about all things and as that anointing is real, not counterfeit just as it has taught you, remain in him.

I have encountered some really good Bible teachers. However, most of these teachers are only allowed to teach in the chapel. If you are prohibited from enjoying fellowship with other believers or partaking in a Bible study because you are bed-ridden, in the infirmary, or presently on lockdown, don't let this discourage you and allow the one who lives within you to teach you instead.

I love going into the prison chapel to enjoy fellowship with other believers. I am so blessed to sit down and participate in Bible studies so I can learn more about the Word of God. You may be in a position where there is no one available to teach you, but the Holy Ghost, whom the Father will send in Jesus' name, shall teach you all things, and bring all things to your remembrance, whatsoever Jesus have said unto you (John 14:26, KJV).

It does not matter where you are right now. It doesn't matter if you are in some cell by yourself or lying sick in the infirmary. If you are saved born again believer, then you have the anointed one, the Holy Spirit living inside you. Don't neglect picking up your Bible because you don't understand it, ye have an unction from the Holy one, and ye know all things (1 John 2:20, KJV). The Holy Spirit will make those things you don't understand clear to you. This may or may not happen all at once but it will happen, you just need to take advantage of the time you have alone to allow the Holy Spirit to teach you. After all, there is no greater teacher.

Don't Just Wait

Isaiah 40:31
But those who hope in the Lord will renew their strength. They will soar on wings like eagles; they will run and not grow weary, they will walk and not be faint.

Prisoners are not strangers when it comes to waiting. Some of us are waiting on one thing and others on another but we all are waiting on something. Whatever it is you are waiting for, be sure not to simply wait.

Paul and Silas were both thrown in prison (Acts 16:23). I can only assume that Paul and Silas were being held in prison until their trial, yet while they waited, they prayed and sang praises to the Lord (Acts 16:25, KJV). They did not just wait, they worshipped while they waited.

Paul was imprisoned again on another occasion (Acts 21:33). While he waited for trial and appeals, he witnessed to King Agrippa (Acts 26:1-28) and wrote a letter to Philemon trying to convince him to forgive his runaway slave Onesimus (Philemon). These great men of faith refused to do nothing while they waited in prison and we should be the same way.

Maybe you are waiting on the governor to sign your pardon. Maybe you are waiting for the parole board to rehear you or for the court to send the ruling you need to release you from incarceration; whatever it is you are waiting on, just be sure to wait wisely.

At the time of this writing, I have been incarcerated for almost nine years. My sentence was vacated over a year ago, but I am still sitting in prison waiting to be released. Although I have no other choice but to wait, I do have a choice when it comes to what I do while I wait. One of the things I am doing, is answering God's call to write this devotion.

There are so many inmates who need you to minister to them. Some need you to lead them in the prayer of salvation and there are other inmates who just need you to listen. Whatever you can do to serve, do it, and don't just wait.

God Knows That You Are in Prison

Philippians 4:6
Do not be anxious about anything, but in every situation, by prayer and petition, with thanksgiving, present your requests to God.

Most high school students are anxious to graduate. A new mother is anxious to hold her newborn baby. I believe that most people are anxious about something, but I am sure no one is more anxious than those who are incarcerated.

One of the first scriptures I learned when I went to jail was Philippians 4:6. When I read this scripture I thought it couldn't possibly be for prisoners, because we all are anxious to go home and move on with our lives. Then I realized that Paul was the writer of Philippians and when he wrote it, he himself was a prisoner.

I'll be the first to admit I had a big problem with being anxious. I was anxious to get my release papers from the court, I was anxious to live life as a Christian outside of prison walls, and I was anxious to be reunited with my daughter. Suddenly I understood that being anxious was lacking trust in Jesus Christ and I had to ask God to help me with this.

The Children of God were anxious to have a king, wanting to be like other nations (1 Samuel 8:5). Although God knew it wasn't good for them to have a king, he gave them one anyway. Saul was not God's choice of a king but he allowed it to teach the people a lesson.

I don't recall meeting an inmate who wasn't anxious to get released. Some would go home and end up right back in prison. Sadly, some would go home and get back on drugs or end up murdered.

God knows where you are right now and what is best for you. He knows what awaits you on the other side of the prison doors. If you believe this and if you trust God like you say you do, then be anxious for nothing, not even your freedom.

Orderly Prayer

Matthew 6:5
And when you pray, do not be like the hypocrites, for they love to pray standing in the synagogues and on the street corners to be seen by others. Truly I tell you, they have received their reward in full.

There is absolutely nothing wrong with praying out loud. If you are doing this, make sure your motives are pure. However, God is so awesome He will still hear you even if you pray silently.

Everything we do should be done decently and in order (1 Corinthians 14:40). There are always different activities going on in prison at the same time; some inmates are watching television, some lying down reading, some studying or doing homework, and some may just be sleeping. It would be totally inappropriate for someone to begin praying out loud, causing many problems. We must remember that God is not the author of confusion, but of peace (1 Corinthians 14:33). If you are praying aloud, this will certainly stir up confusion and is proof that your actions are not Spirit-led.

As inmates, we have the right to freely exercise religion which means we can pray aloud if we choose to, but this is not necessary. Christians are obligated to live right before others. We are obligated to walk in love with everyone and we are not doing this if we are stirring up mess on the dorm by praying aloud.

The next time you want to pray in the dorm, don't do it out loud. Instead, go pray in your prayer closet. God will still hear you.

Strong Foundation

Matthew 7:24
Therefore, everyone who hears these words of mine and puts them into practice is like a wise man who built his house on the rock.

As long as we are on this earth we will be faced with storms. Throughout our lives storms will come and go; how well we endure these storms will all be based on our foundation.

Growing up, I always enjoyed reading Goldilocks and The Three Bears. If my memory serves me correctly, one of the bears lived in a house made of straw, one was made of wood and the other house was made of brick. There was a wolf that came by, trying to attack the bears. The wolf huffed and puffed and blew down the house of straw and the wooden house. However, no matter how much the wolf huffed and puffed he could not blow down the brick house. The brick house was simply too strong for the wolf to destroy.

We may not have to deal with wolves in this life, but as sure as we are living, we will have to deal with something. Our wolves will come as tribulations that we refer to as storms. The storm may be the death of a loved one, an estranged family, or perhaps it is your incarceration. Whether in prison or out of prison we will be faced with storms. It is much harder to deal with storms while in prison, but it can be done. When the storms come, we have to be sure our foundation is strong. We must stand on the Word of God because it is the strongest foundation.

The word of God says that Jesus will not put more on us than we can bear (1 Corinthians 10:13, KJV). This means we can deal with being denied by the courts. This means we can bear being denied work release. Whatever it may be that we are going through, it is not uncommon to man (1 Corinthians 10:13, KJV) and as long as we are standing on the Word of God as our solid foundation, just like that brick house, we will continue to stand.

Final Hour

Revelation 18:19
They will throw dust on their heads, and with weeping and mourning cry out: Woe! Woe to you, great city, where all who had ships on the sea became rich through her wealth! In one hour she has been brought to ruin!

If you are currently living your life led by the flesh, it will behoove you not to continue this way. Start allowing the Spirit to lead you before it is too late. After all, this could very well be your last hour.

Babylon symbolizes anyone who is opposed to God (Revelation 14:8). 2 Kings 20:14 tells how this great city grew to a world power. Babylon invaded Judah three times (2 Kings 24:1, 24:10, 2 Kings 24:14). Babylon relied on its own greatness (Isaiah 47:8-9), and their riches came from the misfortunes of others (Hebrews 2:913). Regardless of how powerful Babylon was, this great city was destroyed just like Isaiah prophesied (Isaiah 13:1, 13:20, 47:1), and it all happened in just one hour (Revelation 18:19).

If you are doing any and everything your flesh tells you, this means you are not walking by the Spirit like you should be. This also means the life you are living is opposed to God. We are in prison because we did it our way, yet God gave us all another chance. Use this chance wisely and allow God to turn your life around. I know it's possible because I allowed God to do it for me and I know he can and will do the same for you.

Don't be fooled into thinking you have time to get your life right with God. The only time you have is NOW. You can't afford to play around with sin. Don't be like Babylon, depending on yourself as if you don't need God. It will behoove you to turn away from such a lifestyle. Don't wait, do it now, as this could be your final hour.

Resist Remaining Angry

Ephesian 4:26
"In your anger do not sin": Do not let the sun go down while you are still angry.

Anger is something we all experience from time to time. Sometimes the anger we are experiencing is righteous, however it shall still be dealt with before the sun goes down.

If we go to the altar to bring a gift and recall that we have an issue with someone, then we need to leave the gift at the altar and go and be reconciled with our brethren (Matthew 5:24, KJV). This must be done first. If we don't get it right, then we are wasting our time at the altar.

I've heard inmates stress that God has not moved in their lives. In reality, he is hindered from moving because of the anger we often hold in our heart for someone else. God knows your coworker did you wrong. He also knows about the person who lied about you, but these people are not worth our peace. God wants to bless us, He wants to answer our prayers, He wants to meet our needs and will do so if only we get rid of the anger.

Don't allow whatever someone did to you to allow you to harbor anger in your heart for them. You should make it your business to deal with that anger. The Lord already knows you have anger in your heart and the quicker you deal with it, the sooner God will begin to work in your life. Don't allow anger to linger on and on, and certainly don't let the sun go down before you make it right.

Bad Security Guards

Micah 2:1
Woe to those who plan iniquity, to those who plot evil on their beds! At morning's light they carry it out because it is in their power to do it.

Inmates often have to deal with security guards abusing the authority they have over them. This is quite common. Yet, not even this should move you.

Queen Jezebel abused the power she had and wrote letters in King Ahab's name, sealing them with his seal and sending the letters unto the elders and the nobles who were in his city, dwelling with Naboth (1 Kings 21:8). King Ahab asked Naboth for his vineyard (1 Kings 21:22). After Naboth refused to give it to him, King Ahab became depressed (1Kings 21:22). As a result, Queen Jezebel decided to write a letter to have Naboth killed (1Kings 21:13-15). This was done just so Ahab could take possession of Naboth's vineyard.

Fortunately, I have never encountered a guard who went to the extreme of taking a life. However, I have witnessed guards abuse their authority by planting contraband on inmates or making false accusations against them just so the inmate will be placed on lockdown. I even experienced security guards yelling in an inmate's face. I know it's not easy to deal with this, but I know it is possible because I endured some of the same abuse and was not moved.

When the wicked are in authority, the people mourn (Proverbs 29:2, KJV). You can rest knowing God sees everything that happens and He will take care of it for you (Romans 12:19). It may be tempting to handle the problem yourself but if you just step aside and let God handle it, you won't have to deal with it anymore.

Live Like You Trust God

Micah 7:5
Do not trust a neighbor; put no confidence in a friend.
Even with the woman who lies in your embrace guard the words of your lips.

We say with our mouths that we trust God. This is easier said than done. With our actions it is clear to see who and what we really trust.

Meteorologists are trusted a great deal and I believe people who are incarcerated trust them even more. Whenever the inmates who work outside hear the weather person predict rain in the forecast, they all get happy and make plans to be off from work. It's evident they have confidence in this human being. Some of them take off their uniforms and get back in the bed. Their actions clearly supported their beliefs. Nothing is wrong with trusting the report of the weatherman, but if we can trust man then we shouldn't have a problem whatsoever in trusting God.

If someone comes to you and tells you that your former bunkmate is back on the streets doing drugs, don't believe such negative reports. Reports like this spread through prisons often and most times they are not true. You should never believe negative reports brought to you (Proverbs 14:15). You can show you are doing this by not allowing the negative report to change your actions.

We are so quick to trust everyone but God. In our minds we begin to think that we trust him, then we go to the mailroom and find out the court denied all our appeals. Instead of thanking God for what He is doing in our lives, we begin to question why God let it happen. Well, this is a good question; God allowed it to happen because He sees the big picture. We, on the other hand, can't see it which is why we must trust God and also live like it.

Free but Bound

Philippians 4:6
Do not be anxious about anything, but in every situation, by prayer and petition, with thanksgiving, present your requests to God.

Many inmates have been blessed with the opportunity to participate in work release. Although work release allows inmates to earn some money before going home, this is not the only benefit; work release also gives us a chance to prove to society that we can hold a job and be a productive citizen. If we are given this chance, we should not ruin it by doing something foolish.

It is a great opportunity to be allowed the chance to attend work release. Unfortunately, I was never blessed with the opportunity and many of those who were, chose to abuse this blessing. They went from being housed behind a barbed-wire fence 24 hours a day to being able to freely go back and forth to work in the free world. Some are even allowed to go shopping. Although work release gives the residents much more freedom, for some that is not enough, which is why they decide to escape. Most people in work release have only months left before going home, yet they still decide to make such a foolish move.

There is not anything or anyone important enough to cause you to get more time by leaving work release. In prison you were free, at work release you were free, but if you decide to escape from work release you will no longer be free. You will have to dodge police officers, you won't be able to buy anything in your own name or even go near your relatives because you will be a wanted person. Eventually you will be found and taken right back to prison with additional time to serve for escaping.

Don't be so anxious to get back to your old life that you escape to rush the process. Even if your reason for doing so is because you want to be with your kids, this is understandable but still you should not even do it for them. You have been away from them this long, and your escape will only cause you to be away from them longer.

Don't Go Back

Ephesians 4:28
Anyone who has been stealing must steal no longer, but must work, doing something useful with their own hands, that they may have something to share with those in need.

Some criminal act landed most of us in jail. My crime of choice was theft of goods. Unlike myself, you may not be serving time for theft, but this just may be a bad habit of yours. Whatever the case may be, it is time for us to stop engaging in criminal activity.

Before my incarceration, shoplifting from merchants was a lifestyle. This was not something I wanted to do, but I believed I had to do it to survive and to help support my family. This was a very miserable lifestyle; most of the time I didn't bring my daughter to the store with me because I didn't want her to witness me stealing. I thought everyone I encountered was plain-clothed security and in my mind, everyone was following me. The very sight of a police officer sent my heart racing. This was absolutely no way to live. The Lord allowed my life of stealing to come to an end when I went to prison, but first God allowed someone to steal all my nice things and I had the audacity to get angry.

From the time I was sentenced and remanded to jail, I made up my mind that I didn't want to steal anymore. I realized that I have a good head on my shoulder and that Jesus had equipped me to make an honest living. The devil tempted me many times. There were times I wanted stamps and the devil would put some in my path and tell me to steal them. There were times I was hungry and the devil constantly tempted me to steal food. However, by the grace of God, I was able to stand and not give in to temptation. Glory be to God. I had made up my mind that I would work for what I needed or wanted and never go back to my old lifestyle.

God Is Waiting on You

Nahum 1:3
The Lord is slow to anger but great in power; the Lord will not leave the guilty unpunished. His way is in the whirlwind and the storm, and clouds are the dust of his feet.

Inmates often say they are waiting on God; in fact, I made this statement myself. Then I was quickened in my Spirit. When Jesus was on the cross He said, "It is finished". This is because He had done everything He was sent to do. Jesus came to earth to show us the way -- now He is waiting on us to follow his example.

God is all-knowing. He knows what you are going through right now and He knows what you will go through later. He knows which commands you are keeping and the ones you have not. Remember, God knows your heart. He knows exactly what it is you need to do before you are released and is waiting for you to do it. I don't know what it is God wants you to do, but in my case, he had been preparing me to write this book. God was also preparing me to take a stand against an injustice. After I did what God led me to do and received victory, God showed me in a dream that I was going to court for 8 a.m. I didn't see a date in my dream, but I knew in my Spirit that this dream would come to pass. It took a few more years, but my dream finally came to pass.

There is no need for any of us to wait on God. His work is done. We just need to seek His face so He can show us the work He wants us to do, and when he does make sure you don't keep him waiting.

Misbehaved but Sorrowful

Romans 7:15
I do not understand what I do. For what I want to do I do not do, but what I hate I do.

Many times, we do things we really don't want to do and later regret. Don't become discouraged because you find yourself doing some of the same old stuff you were doing before you became a believer. This only means that you live in a flesh suit.

Paul was a powerful man of God, very bold and not one to mince words. He was sold out for the Lord. Despite all Paul had going for him, he still struggled within. This struggle was between the Spirit and the flesh, between good and evil. You should not doubt your salvation if you are faced with the same struggle. We don't know exactly what it was that Paul struggled with because the Bible doesn't say, however I believe Paul was not talking about a lifestyle of practicing sin, but instead of occasionally succumbing to it.

Living in this world we will encounter people with many different personalities. I often struggle with being humble. Sometimes I find myself telling some rude person who skips ahead of me in line that I'm standing in it for my health. I also find myself foolishly responding to someone who accuses me of being a hypocrite. I know Satan is the accuser of the brethren (Revelation 12:10, KJV). I also know that holding my peace is a good thing and I should always practice doing good. Yet, I still find myself giving in to my flesh sometimes. I don't want to give in to my flesh, I don't like to give in to my flesh, neither is it my intentions to give in to my flesh, yet I still fail at this sometimes.

The word of God does not condone sin, neither does the word of God give us a license to sin (Romans 6:1-2). However, we still fall and sometimes commit sinful acts. When we do, our actions should clearly show that we are deeply sorrowful for our behavior.

Don't Break Family Ties

1 Corinthians 13:7d
Love always perseveres.

We are all in prison. Our loved ones are not, they are physically free. I know it seems like your life is on hold because you are incarcerated, and in some ways, it is. However, life goes on for our loved ones so please be mindful of this.

The devil will try to disrupt our lives in any way he can. Don't let the devil plant negative seeds in your head about your family. If you are doing your time with little to no family support like I was, this is a perfect time for you to practice one of the several characteristics of love. Through this, learn how to endure and continue to express your love for them.

It's easy for me to stop communicating with my family because of their failure to help me or support me in any way while I'm serving time. However, I refuse to do so and would rather walk in love by enduring everything my family does or fails to do. I choose to do this because I love them.

Serving time in prison is not easy. It is even harder when you don't get visits, can't call home, or seldom receive letters. We must remember, our family has to continue to live their lives and we must continue to love them despite of their lack of support. To do this we must endure all they do or don't do and continue to love them.

Jesus loves us so much. He loves us when we do what we are supposed to do as well as when we don't. Jesus endures all we do and He still loves us, so be a good disciple and follow His example. Continue to show your loved ones how much you love them. Endure all when it comes to loving your loved ones. After all, our love for our family should not be based on what they do for us.

Deadly Choices

Jeremiah 8:3
Wherever I banish them, all the survivors of this evil nation will prefer death to life, declares the Lord Almighty.

You may not engage in certain activities because doing so could lead to death, yet you make other choices that lead to death. When we don't obey the Word of God, the result is death. God doesn't want us only to know His Word, He wants us to obey His Word, so that we may live.

In Leviticus 26:3-13 you will find the rewards for obedience. In Leviticus 26:14-46 you will find the results of disobedience. Your lifestyle will determine the one you choose. Most people wouldn't do anything to cause their own death, not literally anyhow. Yet everyday your actions prove that you choose death.

AIDS is a serious disease that presently has no cure. Considering this fact, one would think people would do their part not to contract such a disease; instead, every day people make conscious choices to engage in a promiscuous lifestyle which can potentially lead to AIDS, and eventually leads to death.

The choices we make in this life can impact our lives and often, the lives of others for good or bad. Therefore, I pray that you stop choosing death. Stop choosing to steal, stop choosing to slander others, stop choosing homosexuality. Don't continue to operate in the same old mindset that caused you to make the choice resulting in your imprisonment. Instead, choose the word of God so that you may live.

Money Can't Help You

Zephaniah 1:18
Neither their silver nor their gold will be able to save them on the day of the Lord's wrath. In the fire of his jealousy the whole earth will be consumed, for he will make a sudden end of all who live on the earth.

Money is extremely important when it comes to living in this world. We need money to buy food, clothes, and to purchase other basic needs. Having money makes life easier, yet there are some things that money just can't buy.

Solomon was a very rich man and there was no other king like him (1 Kings 3:13). Regardless of how rich Solomon was, he concluded that money wasn't everything and was therefore meaningless (Ecclesiastes 1:2, KJV).

It doesn't matter if you have all the silver and gold in the world, this will not deliver you in the day of the Lord's wrath. Nothing can stop God's will from going forth.

I believe God allowed me to come to prison to get my attention. I didn't have any money so I couldn't afford to take chances with an attorney. Unlike myself, there were some inmates whose families were well off and though they tried every attorney money could buy, they were unsuccessful in obtaining the freedom of their loved one. Don't allow this to discourage you. God knows what He is doing. For our own good, He has us right where we are.

Don't think your money can help you out of every situation you get yourself into. If this were true, you wouldn't be in prison. The will of God must be done. If your situation is the will of God, don't waste your money because you can't buy your way out of God's will.

Possible Peace

Romans 12:18
If it is possible, as far as it depends on you, live at peace with everyone.

In this life we will encounter difficult people. We still must try hard to live at peace with them. Unfortunately, no matter how hard we may try to be kind to others the fact remains that there will be some with whom we cannot live peaceably.

Saul was very jealous of David and made sure he kept his eyes on him (1 Samuel 18:9). Saul hated David so much he wanted him dead (1 Samuel 19:1). It was impossible for David to be around Saul because it would have cost him his life. David was not able to live at peace with Saul because Saul would not allow it. Yet, David was at peace with God (Psalms 4:8; 37:11).

Jesus could not live in peace with the self-righteous Pharisees and Sadducees. He would have loved to do so but they would not allow it. They hated Jesus. He was hated so much that they nailed him to the cross (Matthew 27:35).

Prisoners do not have a say in who they get to live amongst. You may be moved near someone who is quite easy to live with or you may be forced to live with someone who is very difficult. Regardless of how hard this person may be to get along with, you must still live peaceably. However, if it's not possible to live in peace with someone, try hard to avoid that person while continuing to walk in peace yourself. It is important that you stay in peace with God.

Try to do everything in your power to live peaceably with others. If you see that this is not possible, avoid them and pray for them. We can try to live at peace with people, but we cannot make them live at peace with us.

Safe Haven

John 3:16
For God so loved the world that he gave his one and only Son, that whoever believes in him shall not perish but have eternal life.

God loves us all so much. Do not think for one second that He doesn't love us because we are in prison. In fact, if He did not love us, He would have let us die out there in our sin.

If you have not yet praised God for your present situation, then it is long overdue. We are where we are because God loves us. We are where we are because God has a plan for our lives (Jeremiah 29:11). We are where we are because God has work for us to do. He knows as long as we would have allowed ourselves to self-destruct out there in society, we would never have done the work He has for us to do. God knows about all we were doing. He knows about all those shameful activities we engaged in, yet He still loved us enough to save us from all of it. Even while we were sinners, Christ loved us enough to die for us (Romans 5:8). God did not spare His son but delivered Him up for us (Romans 8:32).

The next time you want to complain about your imprisonment, think about everything you were spared from and rejoice instead. God did not want you to end up prematurely in the grave, so He blessed you with another chance to get it right. This has nothing to do with what you did but because He loves you and wanted to put you in a safe place.

Give a Soft Response

Proverbs 15:1
A gentle answer turns away wrath, but a harsh word stirs up anger.

Arguments are common in a prison setting, but you can avoid them if you make it a daily practice to answer softly. It is extremely hard to argue with a person who gives a soft response.

When Stephen was martyred by stoning because of his faith, he could have cursed at those who stoned him and yelled out all sorts of ugly words. Yet he did not, and instead he kneeled, crying with a loud voice, Lord, lay not this sin to their charge. After he said this, he fell asleep (Acts 8:54-60, KJV).

Jesus was crucified not because of something He did but for our sins. He could have lashed out verbally, but as hard as it had to be for him to speak, he managed to say, 'Father, forgive them for they know not what they do' (Luke 23:32-34, KJV). Wow! Can you imagine asking for forgiveness for someone who is trying to kill you? I cannot imagine it either, but Jesus did it. If Jesus could give such a response in his situation then it should be nothing for us to give a soft answer to those who lightly afflict us.

When I first went to jail, I did not want to give a soft answer to someone who was treating me in an ugly manner. I failed at this many times, but finally was able to do it. I must say, being able to respond calmly to someone who was screaming in my face made me feel much stronger.

It does not matter what someone may say to you, neither does it matter if it is true or not; the only thing that matters is your response. There is nothing someone can say to you that should cause you to respond inappropriately. If you do not remain calm then they will know what makes you lose your patience, so put an end to the foolishness with a soft answer.

Keep Looking

Jeremiah 29:13
You will seek me and find me when you seek me with all your heart.

God did not instruct us to seek Him as if He's lost because God is not lost. Regardless of where we are, God wants us to find Him in our situation. Whether we are housed in an open dorm or confined to a cell, God is also there so look for him.

As a young girl, I can recall losing one of my earrings in a park near my home one night. Although I tried looking for my earring that same night, it was just too dark for me to see. The next morning, I returned to the park and soon found my earring. My earring was there the entire time, but my vision was impaired due to the darkness.

It does not matter how bad things may appear; they are not as bad as they seem when Jesus is with you. You do not have to do your time alone, just begin seeking the Lord. In order to do this, we have to push past how things seem. In the midst of it all we must be able to find Jesus when we search for Him. We cannot find Him if our spiritual sight is impaired. God is ready to open your eyes through the Word of God. After all, Jesus is the word (John 1:1). Search the scriptures so you will know how to find Him.

The next time you find yourself in a bad situation, start seeking and searching so you can find the only one who can bring you out. It does not matter how bad your situation may appear, Jesus is in your midst. Just look past your mess and you will see that Jesus is there, seeing you through.

What's Coming out of Your Mouth?

James 3:10
Out of the same mouth come praise and cursing. My brothers and sisters, this should not be.

Every part of you belongs to God. You are not your own (1 Corinthians 6:19, KJV). You were bought with a price (1 Corinthians 6:20, KJV). If you didn't know this it's okay, but now that you know, start allowing blessings, not cursing, to flow from your mouth.

Our heavenly Father is the creator of everything. He is the creator of the heavens and the earth (Genesis 1:7-10). He is the creator of light (Genesis 1:16). He is the creator of great whales and every living creature that moves (Genesis 1:21, KJV). Yet, we are His most precious creation. I know this because He loved us so that He made us in His own image (Genesis 1:27, KJV).

Sweet and bitter water cannot flow from the same fountain (James 3:11, KJV); neither should both sweet and bitter words flow from the mouth of a Christian. We should not be speaking foul language from the same mouth we use to bless the Lord. We all go through things from time to time, but this should not affect how we speak. Our speech should always be pleasing to God.

God is not pleased when you are in church singing praises to him and blessing His holy name, then using profanity as soon as you walk out of the church. No one needs to use bad language; there is nothing anyone can do or say to provoke you to allow cursing to part from your lips. Throughout my incarceration I was lied on, my name slandered, I had been accused of horrible things, yet I never allowed myself to let vulgarity come from the mouth with which I praise God. Don't get me wrong, I wanted to, but I didn't; I put my feelings aside. I was more concerned with my witness and pleasing the awesome God I serve even with my words.

Faith Works

James 2:20
You foolish person, do you want evidence that faith without deeds is useless?

Life is not always what we hope it would be. There are times when things may look dim and problems appear unsurmountable. God knew we would sometimes see things this way, which is why it is not always best to give attention to our surroundings. Instead, practice living by faith.

Now faith is the substance of things hoped for, the evidence of things not seen (Hebrews 11:1, KJV). Without faith it is impossible to please God (Hebrews 11:6, KJV), because a lack of faith shows a lack of trust.

We are living in perilous times; however, we cannot focus on what is taking place all around us. If we do this, we will not make it. We must keep our faith in Jesus Christ and what He did for us on Calvary.

Although we cannot please God without faith, this faith must be evidenced with works. Abraham's works were evidence of the faith he had in God. When God told Abraham to sacrifice his son Isaac, Abraham did not question God. He just obeyed and proceeded to the place where he was to kill his own son. Abraham did not have a problem making a move because he had enough faith to believe that God was going to spare his son somehow (Genesis 22:1-13). Moses did not allow his surroundings to cause him to lose faith.

I was sitting in prison with a 20-year sentence. However, everything in me told me I was not going to serve my entire sentence. I gave some things away to clear out my locker. I also packed most of the things I would have taken with me because I had faith that I was about to be released from prison. I was not sitting around paying attention to the time man gave me. I knew I would be relieved of that sentence and I spoke it into existence every day. I had faith that I would one day receive immediate release and I did, after serving nearly 14 years.

You may be serving a long prison sentence that looks like an impossible situation. It does not matter how much time man gave you, you just need to walk by faith and not by sight (2 Corinthians 5:7, KJV). Allow your works to be evidence of that faith. Remember that the same God who opened the doors for me can open the doors for you, too.

No Patience, No Love

1 Corinthians 13:4a
Love is patient.

There are several characteristics of love, and patience is just one of them. We must allow patience to manifest in our lives, otherwise, we are not walking in love.

I am very grateful to know that we serve a patient God. If you have loved ones who are not saved, then you and I have something in common. The good thing about this is that God knows they are not saved. This is why the Lord is not slack concerning his promise as some men count slackness, but is longsuffering to us, not willing that any should perish, but that all should come to repentance (2 Peter 3:9, KJV).

God wants those who are lost to be saved so badly that he is willing to patiently wait until it happens. He does not do this because He has to, He does so because He loves us. God himself is love and we must walk in it. If our lack of patience is hindering us from doing so, then we should write down those situations that cause us to be impatient and practice being longsuffering.

Personally, I noticed that I do not operate in patience whenever my daily plans are interrupted. You would think inmates would be the most patient people on the face of the earth, considering we have to stand in line for everything. Yet, this is not the case.

There have been times when I wanted to go to the library to do legal research on my case and would have to change my plans because count did not clear timely, or some other unusual occurrence takes place preventing me from doing so. I realized that every time something like this would happen it caused me to be very impatient. Then I reminded myself that I am in a controlled environment and cannot allow interruptions to move me. Once I realized this, I was able to work on this characteristic of love.

We are all in prison. We must understand that things we do not like will happen. We may be expecting to go to court, but the date is reset, or maybe someone promises they will visit but they do not show up. Whatever the case may be, we must be determined to walk in love and remain patient.

Be Kind Regardless

1 Corinthians 13:4b
Love is kind

As an inmate forced to live in close proximity with many people, it is not uncommon to run across those who are difficult to get along with. Yet, we are still obligated to show them love through our kind acts. I am qualified to write about kindness not because I am living it, but because this was something with which I struggled.

At this writing, I am in a room with someone who is very evil. She says vulgar things to me. She slams her lockers while I am sleeping and complains about everything I do. I could go on and on, but I believe you get my point. Whenever she would do these things I chose not to respond. My flesh would tell me to do the same to her, but then the Spirit reminded me that I am a Christian and commanded to do unto others as I would want them to do unto me (Matthew 7:12, KJV). Although I was obedient in this area, I was failing every time I went to breakfast and refused to give my roommate my sugar, although I was not using it, merely because I did not want to be kind to someone who was so evil to me. Boy, was I convicted.

As Christians, we are obligated to walk in love. If we pass up the opportunity to be kind to the one who is evil toward us, we are not walking in love with this person. However, we can start anew the next time we see that person by showing some kind act. It is not easy, but I am a witness that it's possible.

Boast About God

1 Corinthians 13:4d
Love does not envy

The very air we breathe is possible because of Jesus. For in Him we live, and move, and have our being (Acts 17:28, KJV). Unless God allows us to, we cannot do anything. It does not matter what we have earned or achieved, Jesus is our true source of all, and our only boast should be in Him.

I literally had to train myself to give credit to Jesus, the only one to whom credit is due. We can do nothing in and of ourselves. You are not the reason you have the ability of your limbs. You are not the reason you achieved your GED. You are not the reason you were able to learn a trade or earn your degree. You did not give yourself that beautiful voice. You did not give yourself the gift to draw. This is why we have no room to boast.

There is no way someone who is boasting can walk in love; when you boast, you are exalting yourself. When you are doing this, you are not exalting the only one worthy of being exalted.

You must grasp that we were created to praise God (Psalm 102:18, KJV) and you must be forever mindful of this. This will help you to give glory to God for your abilities and your accomplishments. This will help us not to get a big head and start thinking we are better than the next person.

When I worked in the prison garment factory, I met women who were very good at sewing. Sadly, most of them bragged about how they worked better than the next person. They acted as if they were doing all they did on their own. It was obvious these ladies believed they were the reason they sewed so well. These ladies took all the credit for the skill that God enabled them to have.

We have all been given capabilities and they may or may not be the same. Even if they are, they are still unique. Whatever your capabilities, they are blessings from God and should always be considered as such. Remembering this will help you not to boast.

It's Not About You

1 Corinthians 13:4e
Love does not boast.

I believe if we are truthful, we will admit that we have some pride. I advise you to do a self-inventory to see if you have it and if you find that you do, you must overcome it in order to love others.

Since the time I began my Christian walk this has been a struggle for me most of the time. Fortunately, I was able to identify the reason I continued to fail at this: I still battled with pride in several areas of my life. When it came to asking for something, my pride would not allow it, even if it was a need. When it came to asking for help, my pride hindered me from asking. When it came time for to take my shower and I chose to use state soap, my pride told me to also bring along a bar of Dial so people would not think all I had was state soap. Pride really had me bound. Pride prohibits us from walking in love because pride makes one think that they are too important to have to depend on the aid of another. After the Lord dealt with me on this subject, I did not allow it to keep a hold on me any longer.

In prison it is common for an inmate to be prideful because they hold a certain position. These people have a certain walk, a certain talk. They are puffed-up to the highest degree.

Joseph had good reasons to walk in pride, but he didn't. His jealous brothers sold him to the Ishmaelites (Genesis 37:28). Then these same brothers had to depend on Joseph for food during the famine (Genesis 42). This was the perfect time to be puffed up, but Joseph refused to give in to pride. Instead, he looked at his brothers and told them, 'you intended what you did to me for my harm, but God meant it for my good' (Genesis 50:20).

If you have a roommate or someone on your dorm who can help you study for your GED, do not allow pride to prevent you from asking for assistance. Maybe you are out of soap or deodorant and pride has you to embarrassed to ask for some. Do not be embarrassed, everyone needs help from time to time. If you have been blessed with an executive position inside the prison, do not allow this to puff you up; go ahead and humble yourself. Make it a constant practice. If you cannot walk in humility, then you are not walking in love.

God Can Save Anyone

1 Corinthians 13:7c
Love always hopes.

We should have confidence in others if we love them. Giving up or letting go should not be options when you love someone. Love will always keep hope alive.

Throughout my incarceration I encountered people who appeared to be bad. I am talking about those people who are always cursing others, the ones who fight with other inmates and disrespect the guards. I am talking about the type of people who do most of their time on lockdown. I am sure you know people like this. The best thing you can do is pray for them and show them the love of Christ through your lifestyle.

Do not ever think that troublemakers are too far gone; when you begin to think this way, you look at those people as hopeless. Once you see them as hopeless you will not see the need to pray for them, because in your mind they are at the point of no return.

The Word of God states that love hopes all things (1 Corinthians 13:7c, ESV). This means when you encounter such people, that you continue to believe in them even when they do not believe in themselves. If you love them, you will tell them how low you were and how God never gave up on you. Then, if this is not enough, show them in the scriptures how God never gave up on David who committed adultery and murder (2 Samuel 11:4, 15), how He never gave up on Rahab the prostitute (Hebrews 11:31) and last but certainly not least, how He did not give up on Saul who persecuted and killed Christians (Acts 9:1-2).

God did not give up on David, Saul, and Rahab, nor did He give up on us. He did not give up on us because He loves us. We need to follow his example and show love for others by not giving up on them.

Love No Matter What

1 Corinthians 13:8a
Love never fails.

Heart and kidney failure are all too common. Many of us often fail Spiritual test, and some of us may have failed in school. At some point in our lives, we will all experience failure. Yet, the love we have for others should never fail.

Anyone can say 'I love you', but not everyone can show it through their lifestyle. One good thing that came from my incarceration is, through it, God showed me who loved me and who did not. Unfortunately, I discovered that some who I called my friends did not love me. Yes, my girls, the ones I knew for years and hung out with all the time, forgot all about me. I am not saying they forgot me because they did not send me money, that wasn't important, but a letter from time to time would have meant so much (1 Corinthians 13:8).

We owe it to everyone to love them even if sometimes doing so may not be easy. God did not say love only when it is easy, He just said 'love'. In doing so, we cannot fail because love never fails (1 Corinthians 13:8). When love fails, that means it did not endure the test of time. It means you failed to forgive the wrong that person did when they lied about you, stole from you, or maybe even slandered your character and rejected you. Regardless of what your roommate did to you, you must love him or her. You must love the guard who had you falsely locked up. Regardless of what someone may have said or done to you, do not give in to the temptation to let your love for them fail. After all, the suffering our Lord and Savior went through is no comparison, and yet the love He has for us never fails.

Weigh All Advice

2 Chronicles 10:8
But Rehoboam rejected the advice the elders gave him and consulted the young men who had grown up with him and were serving him.

Christians are a group of believers who make up the body of Christ. None of us can function alone, we all need each other. Sometimes we need to go to another part of the body for advice. It is good to take advice from others at times, because no one person knows it all. Taking advice from someone can only affect you if you take heed of it, so be sure to only take heed of godly advice.

After the death of King Solomon, his son Rehoboam reigned in his stead (2 Chronicles 9:31, KJV). And it came to pass that Jeroboam and all Israel came and spoke to Rehoboam, saying, thy father made our yoke grievous: now therefore ease thou somewhat the grievous servitude of thy father, and his heavy yoke that he put upon us, and we will serve thee (2 Chronicles 10:3-4, KJV). Rehoboam went seeking advice from the old men that stood before Solomon (2 Chronicles 10:6), and then he went to the young men whom he was brought up with (2 Chronicles 10:10, KJV). Unfortunately, Rehoboam decided to forsake the counsel of the old men and take the counsel of his peers instead (2 Chronicles 10:13-14, KJV).

It is no secret that a lifestyle of illegal activities usually leads one to prison. Many times, some of those same people you ran with in your life of crime will either meet you there or beat you there. It is dangerous to get caught up with those same people. If they have the same street mentality and have not been transformed, then you have no business taking advice from them. It does not matter that they are people you know from the street, none of this is important. Just know that any advice you decide to take should be backed up by scripture; any other advice will only cause division, just like the poor advice Rehoboam followed divided his kingdom (2 Chronicles 11:1).

Nothing is wrong with asking for advice when you are led to do so, but make sure your decision to follow any advice given is based on the Word of God. Knowing someone from the street is not a reason to follow their advice -- the Holy Scriptures should be your only tool for weighing any advice.

Costly Complaints

Numbers 11:1a
Now the people complained about their hardships in the hearing of the Lord, and when he heard them his anger was aroused. Then fire from the Lord burned among them and consumed some of the outskirts of the camp.

When I first arrived at the Louisiana Correctional Institute for Women, there were several privileges available to inmates. Unfortunately, some of these privileges have since been taken away, most of the time this was because of the foolishness of one person.

God told Moses He would give the children of Israel the Promised Land (Exodus 3:8). However, due to their complaining they never saw it (Deuteronomy 1:34-35). Their own complaining cost them everything.

Inmates housed at LCIW live two- and three to a room, behind a door that we can open and close when we want to. Most prisons are open dorms; therefore, it is a blessing to live with no more than two other inmates.

One day a memo was placed on the bulletin board, informing inmates that an open-door policy would soon be instituted. Anyone caught in violation of this policy would be subjected to disciplinary action. This rule resulted from inmates constantly complaining that security guards opened and closed their doors all night, disturbing their sleep. These inmates acted as if they had forgotten they were in prison. They acted as if they had forgotten they were prisoners and security is paid to watch them every second of every minute. These inmates tried to use psychology, thinking that the warden would stop guards from opening the doors at night; instead, he ordered that the doors remain open at all times, so that the security can continue to do their job without disturbing sleeping inmates through the night. This complaint cost all the inmates at LCIW what little privacy they had.

Sometimes making a complaint is necessary, but we need to be able to distinguish when it is not. The next time you decide to complain about something, make sure your complaint is not frivolous and make sure you count the cost.

God Knows What He's Doing

Revelation 3:8
I know your deeds. See, I have placed before you an open door that no one can shut. I know that you have little strength, yet you have kept my word and have not denied my name.

We are all required to obey the Word of God. Do not allow the enemy to trick you into believing that your obedience to God is in vain. Ofttimes it may seem like it, but this is never the case.

Have you ever felt like the more you obey God and try to live a lifestyle pleasing to Him, the more he blesses those who are disobedient and live contrary lifestyles? This is where I am right now. I desperately longed for my freedom, yet I saw those who could not care less about serving God get released over and over again. This really bothered me at first. I felt these people were so undeserving, then I was reminded that God rains on the just and the unjust (Matthew 5:45, KJV). I remembered that the Word says fret not thyself of evildoers, neither be thou envious against the workers of iniquity (Psalms 37:1, KJV).

The worst thing you can do is stop obeying God, as this is what the devil wants you to do. God knows your works (Revelation 3:8a, KJV). He knows how faithful you are. He knows that your motives are all pure. God knows how badly you want to go home, and He also knows when to open the door to make it happen. Besides, he is God and we are not -- this is why we have to trust Him, not just with our words but also with our actions.

Do not be discouraged the next time God allows an unbeliever to get an unexpected release. Instead, release your faith and began to believe God for yours. In the meanwhile, be sure to rejoice for them while you await your own release and remember: God knows what's He is doing.

We Are All in Debt

Romans 13:8
Let no debt remain outstanding, except the continuing debt to love one another, for whoever loves others has fulfilled the law.

I do not owe anyone anything is what one of my sisters-in-Christ often said. Her reason for saying this was because she did not want to share with other people. She admitted that sharing with others was a big struggle for her and that God was still working on her in this area.

As Christians, we are obligated to live a lifestyle that is pleasing to God. When others see us, they should be able to recognize us by how we live; it is hard to see a person who is stingy as a loving person.

Today one of my sisters disclosed to me that when she and another sister sit out and fellowship in the dayroom area, that this mature sister, sits in her presence at the same table and eats a full course meal in her face without offering. She went on to say that this sister made it a point to inform her when she first moved in the same dorm with her that she had a problem with giving. She also said she felt what she was doing was okay because she did not owe anyone anything. Boy, was she wrong.

The believers who became the first church openly expressed their love for fellow believers by giving to the needs of others (Acts 2:44, KJV). Literally speaking, they did not owe them anything, but we are commanded to love, which cannot be done if we are overlooking the needs of others. Look not every man on his own things, but every man also on the things of others (Philippians 2:4, KJV). Christians should be given to hospitality and eating in front of your sister without offering is not hospitable at all.

You are not blessed for yourself, you are blessed to be a blessing to others. This does not mean that you must give all your food away -- let wisdom be your guide. If you still find that you have a problem with giving, ask God to help you be as generous as the believers in the first church (Acts 2:42-47).

Your Purpose in Prison

Romans 8:28
And we know that in all things God works for the good of those who love him, who have been called according to his purpose.

At times we all go against what God has for us and decide to do our own thing. Often, as a result, what we choose to do turns out badly. We are where we are because we were living outside of God's purpose for our lives. God wants all of us to use this time to work in accordance to His purpose.

The Word of the Lord came to Jonah telling him to go to the city of Nineveh and cry against it for their wickedness (Jonah 1:1-2, KJV). God had called Jonah to go to this great city, as this was his purpose for Jonah at the time. Instead of Jonah doing what God told him to do he decided to run away from God and as a result boarded a ship, was thrown off, and found himself in the mouth of a very large fish (Jonah 1:1-17). Things were not going well for Jonah. Jonah was not called to get on a ship going to Tarshish, he was called to go to Nineveh. Things were not working for his good, because he was outside the purpose of God.

It does not matter what you have done or where you are in your life, God can and will begin to work in your situation until He turns the mess you made around for good. He will not do so until you are living according to His purpose, so you may not see your situation turning around for good because you're still doing what you want to do. If this is the case, you may need to check your purpose; it should be in correlation with the Word of God. If by chance it is not, then your calling is not according to His purpose and will not turn out for good until you begin to do as you were called to do.

Your incarceration is not a bad thing, although it may seem that way. God is only trying to get you back to the purpose He called you for, so put yourself in His presence and find out what God's will is for your life and stop running away from your purpose.

Never Stop Spreading the Good News

Ezekiel 2:5
And whether they listen or fail to listen for they are a rebellious people they will know that a prophet has been among them.

I find it is not easy spreading the gospel from one inmate to another because often the inmate who is being preached to is doubting the person's authority; this does not shock me one bit. After all, many inmates fake it to make it.

I had the advantage of ministering to other inmates around the clock. Doing so had its pros and cons; pros because they had the opportunity to observe my walk and see the life, I lived day in and day out. It is much easier to minister when others see that you practice what you preach and usually, this makes them more receptive. It has its cons because often Christian inmates are stereotyped and placed in a class with those who are practicing jailhouse religion. For this reason alone, some may not want to hear what we have to say. Whether they choose to listen or not, you are called to preach the word; be instant in season and out of season; reprove, rebuke, exhort with all long suffering and doctrine (2 Timothy 4:2, KJV).

Do not waste your time and energy concerning yourself about whether you are being heard, just focus on what God will have you say and say it. This is what Ezekiel was told to do. Ezekiel was sent to a rebellious people (Ezekiel 2:5, KJV). God was not as concerned about these people hearing, as he was about the Word going forth. It is His will for the gospel to be brought to everyone whether they receive it or not. Speaking the word is on you and hearing is on them. Just do your part.

Heavens Point of View

Ezekiel 2:6

And you, son of man, do not be afraid of them or their words. Do not be afraid, though briers and thorns are all around you and you live among scorpions. Do not be afraid of what they say or be terrified by them, though they are a rebellious people.

Fear stops many people from fulfilling their purpose. As Christians, we should not be walking in fear, but this is what we are doing whenever we allow looks to prevent us from doing the will of God.

Goliath was a giant. He was a champion out of the camp of the Philistines. Goliath's height was six cubits and a span (nearly ten feet tall!) (1 Samuel 17:4, KJV). Goliath challenged the Israelites to fight him, but everyone feared Goliath because of how he looked (1 Samuel 17:8-11). David on the other hand did not allow Goliath's appearance to cause him to be afraid (1 Samuel 17:32). Not only did David fight against Goliath, but he killed him (1 Samuel 17:50). David was able to defeat Goliath because he did not see what everyone saw. You see, David was looking from heaven's point of view. When we look from heaven's point of view everything looks smaller. You may still be confused, so let me elaborate: if you get on an airplane, as long as that plane is on the ground you will see people as they are but when the plane takes off and begins to ascend, those same people will begin to look as small as ants. When we change our view, the problem gets smaller and smaller. Glory be to God!

We may not have to fight with giants like Goliath, but we all deal with giants in our lives. The problems you are faced with could be your giant. Whatever it is that appears so daunting is your giant. If you walk by faith, and not by sight (2 Corinthians 5:7, KJV), then everything will look small to you, and you will see that God is so much bigger than any problem you may have.

Evil Plots Do Backfire

Proverbs 26:27
Whoever digs a pit will fall into it; if someone rolls a stone, it will roll back on them.

It is an evil thing to dig a pit for someone else. It is also unwise. If you allow the enemy to use you to dig a pit thinking it is for someone else, it will behoove you to measure it to fit yourself because eventually, you will be the one to fall.

King Ahasuerus promoted Haman and set his seat above all the princes with him (Esther 3:1, KJV). All the king's servants in the king's gate bowed and paid reverence to Haman. However, Mordecai, a Jew, refused to bow down or show reverence to Haman. Haman was so furious over Mordecai's refusal that he decided to have gallows made to hang Mordecai (Esther 5:14). Unfortunately for Haman, he himself was hanged on the gallows he prepared for Mordecai (Esther 7:10).

I had seen many pits dug before my incarceration. Sadly, living in a penal institution among different people from different walks of life had caused me to see even more. As Christians, we should not be going around digging pits. Someone may be digging one for you, and you may have found out about it. Yet, this still does not give you the right to dig one for them. Instead, sit back, pray without ceasing, and trust God. You will see that person fall in their own pit.

God does not sleep. He knows when you have been lied on by a jealous individual. He knows about the person who is trying to set a trap to hurt you. God is everywhere at the same time. He sees the pit that has been dug for you, and in His perfect timing He will allow you to see it backfire.

Include God in All Future Plans

James 4:15
Instead, you ought to say, "If it is the Lord's will, we will live and do this or that."

God has made us many promises in his Word. However, seeing tomorrow, or knowing what will happen when it comes, is not one of them. Therefore, we should not talk like we have such abilities.

God's mind is infinite, and our minds are finite. For my thoughts are not your thoughts, neither are your ways my ways saith the Lord (Isaiah 55:8, KJV). Many of us are familiar with this scripture, but we are still talking like we know God's thoughts. We talk like we know His ways when the scripture clearly states we do not. We should not talk like we know what is going to happen tomorrow. To do so is boasting.

Haman sent for his friends and his wife Zeresh (Esther 5:10). Once they arrived, Haman bragged to them about all the king would do for him the next day. Haman anticipated tomorrow, never knowing that when it came, he would be killed (Esther 7:10).

I am not telling you that we should not talk about tomorrow but when we do, we should do so humbly and not with any certainty. When we talk about the future, we must consult with God first. I have seen many inmates brag about going home on a certain day, yet as that day quickly approached, they were informed they still had more time to serve.

To confidently speak about any time past this moment as if you know the future is bragging. When you decide to talk about tomorrow or the future, be sure to say, 'if God is willing'. If you practice this, God may not have to change your plans.

When Anger Controls

Hebrews 12:15
See to it that no one falls short of the grace of God and that no bitter root grows up to cause trouble and defile many.

I will be the first to admit that I have met some people who are unlikeable. However, these people should not anger us every time we see them; if they do, they control us. God did not create us so that He can control us. He wants us to have free will. If God does not control us, then why are we yielding control to someone else?

In the book of Esther, it is recorded that Haman was filled with joy. Haman had a glad heart. Yet, as soon as Haman saw Mordecai, and saw that Mordecai showed him no honor or respect, he became furious (Esther 5:9). In seconds, Haman allowed another individual to turn his joy into sorrow. Make no mistake about it, Mordecai had complete control over Haman.

There is absolutely nothing wrong with getting angry. It is normal to get angry when we see someone mistreated but not to the degree that it causes us to sin. It is not a sin to get angry. Jesus got angry (Mark 11:15); however, He did not allow His anger to cause Him to sin. Jesus' anger was for righteousness sake. The word of God teaches us to be angry and sin not (Ephesians 4:26, KJV).

In Haman's case he was angry because Mordecai refused to bow down to him. The anger Haman had for Mordecai turned into hatred. Haman hated Mordecai so much he wanted him killed and made preparations to have it done (Esther 5:14).

We cannot continue to allow the root of bitterness to stay planted deep inside. This root must be plucked up by applying the Word of God to our lives. I know there are security officers who lie on you and cause you to be put on lockdown, and I know about the inmates who do and say ugly things to you because of your stand for Jesus Christ. Do not allow any of these things to cause you to walk in bitterness. If you do, every time you see these people you will allow them to ruin your day which means they control you. If you make up in your mind right now that you will no longer allow anger to move you it will no longer control you again.

Why Are You Surprised

Matthew 7:12
So in everything, do to others what you would have them do to you, for this sums up the Law and the Prophets.

We are commanded to do unto others as we would have them to do unto us, but yet when this practice is manifested in our lives, we are surprised. If this surprises you then you obviously do not believe the Word of God.

If you go around lying on people, then why are you surprised when someone lies on you. If you are a gossip and love slandering the character of others, then do not be surprised when this same gossip and slander comes your way. If you are a thief going around stealing from your job, you are saying with your actions that you want people to steal from you. Yet, when you find out that your clothes are missing from the laundry or something is missing from your locker you are surprised.

Doing time in prison is hard enough. Do not allow Satan to use you to make someone's time harder by violating them. If you allow yourself to be used, expect Satan to use someone else to violate you.

Just because you do right by others does not mean they will do right by you. You should do right by others because you expect the same, although we do not always get what we expect. Remember that you reap what you sow (Galatians 6:7), so sow good seeds.

Be mindful of how you treat people. Ask yourself if you are doing to them what you want done to you. If you do not want whatever it is done to you, then stop what you are doing.

Love Based Giving

1 Corinthians 13:3
If I give all I possess to the poor and give over my body to hardship that I may boast, but do not have love, I gain nothing.

Giving does not make you good. Still, it is good to give. Christians should always be ready to give and should always do so with pure motives. If our act of giving lacks love, then we are wasting our time.

You would think that a person who gives their body to be burned is walking in love. You would think someone who gives all they have to feed the poor is a loving person. However, our heavenly Father knows better. He knows that people give for selfish reasons and when we do, we are not walking in love, neither will we profit anything (1 Corinthians 13:3, KJV).

People give for many different reasons. Unfortunately, most of those reasons are not good. Although I was in prison and surrounded by many people, I tried really hard to give in secret. I did not want any attention just because I gave something to someone. It is possible to give in secret in prison. Jesus commanded us in his Sermon on the Mount not to do alms before men, to be seen of them (Matthew 6:1, KJV). It is a must that we give in love.

Not all people give to be seen, some give because they expect something from you in return. It is good for someone to go out, get food for someone else and serve it to them. This is exactly what Jacob did. Such a good deed appeared to be honest and pure; however, since we know the whole story, we know that it was not. We know that Jacob's only reason for serving food to his father Isaac was so he could pretend to be his brother Esau and trick his father out of his brother Esau's blessing (Genesis 27:17-30). Jacob's giving was not an act of love.

It is wrong to give of your time or finances for any other reason than it is the Christlike thing to do. If you have an impure motive for doing so, then you are giving out of an impure heart. The next time you decide to give something to someone, check your giving and make sure it is motivated by love.

A Little Helps Too

Ruth 2:7
She said, 'Please let me glean and gather among the sheaves behind the harvesters.' She came into the field and has remained here from morning till now, except for a short rest in the shelter.

Often, I heard inmates say they did not want to go to work release. They claimed this was because 'the people take all your money'. If you are left with a few dollars, then all your money has not been taken. Moreover, you will earn much more money at work release than you will ever earn in prison.

I just love the book of Ruth. She was such a noble woman. She was a very responsible person who was willing to work hard for what she wanted. Ruth refused to be a burden to her mother-in-law; she knew they needed to eat, and she was willing to make it happen. No job was too lowly for Ruth. She earned a living by following behind the maidens, picking up whatever dropped from their baskets (Ruth 2:9). It did not matter to Ruth that the other maidens took most of the grain. She was grateful to receive the leftovers.

Work release is set up for inmates to earn some money to go home with. I know we hear inmates saying they take all your money, but this is not the truth. I realize they take most of your money, but even if you get $100 from each paycheck, this is yours and it will allow you to have money when you are released.

It will benefit you to go to work release. You will not have to be a burden to your family if you take advantage of the work release program. It does not matter if you only get a small amount from each paycheck it will all add up to a nice savings and will make things a little easier when you are released.

Reaping the Noise You Make

Luke 6:31
Do to others as you would have them do to you

When people hear you claim to be a Christian, they will watch you. They will observe your talk. They will observe your walk. They will watch to see if both your walk and talk line up with one another or if they contradict.

One night, one of the ladies who lived on the hall with me yelled down the hall, telling some of the other ladies to turn to a certain radio station. It was obvious she was constantly changing the stations because every time her definition of a good song would come on, she would yell out the station so others tune in. However, a few mornings later this same inmate came out of her room fussing because some of the ladies in the dorm were loud and disturbing her sleep. This woman went on and on about how she was off and trying to rest, yet she was not thinking about who was resting when she was yelling on the hall a few nights prior.

We are commanded to do unto others as we would have others do unto us (Matthew 7:12, KJV). I heard the same noise on the hall that the other girl heard, although I am not one to make noise on the hall. This scripture does not mean that others want disturb my sleep because I do not disturb theirs, it means I should not disturb another person's sleep if I do not want my sleep interrupted. On the other hand, if you are a noisemaker yourself, you have no right to get angry when someone else is making noise while you are sleeping.

I know it is not easy doing time in prison, however time can be a little easier if we all learn to respect one another. Everyone on the hall may be loud and boisterous, but you do not have to be the same way. Use this as an opportunity to minister by saying you cannot join with the singing or other noise because you want to respect those who are sleeping or just trying to study. Explain to them that you are doing so because you expect the same courtesy from others and because it is the right thing to do. Taking this stand may cause others to follow and may very well lead to a noise-free dorm.

Don't Accept All Help

Malachi 2:9
"So I have caused you to be despised and humiliated before all the people, because you have not followed my ways but have shown partiality in matters of the law."

Everyone who offers you their help is not doing so from the kindness of their heart. It is essential that you know whose help to accept and whose to refuse. It will behoove you to know the difference.

I came across many people at the Louisiana Correctional Institute for Women who appeared to be nice. Some would offer to help me with my canteen bags, or voluntarily pick up my laundry when I was not there to get it myself. There were others who would offer to help someone write a letter, or to push someone in a wheelchair. These same nice people would then ask you to do something illegal or continuously ask you for things and expect you to give them whatever they ask because of all the 'nice' things they've done for you.

Do not allow yourself to become like the priests who are mentioned in the book of Malachi 2:1-9. These priests began to accept help from people who obviously had a motive for giving it and ultimately became dependent on them. As a result, they began to be partial because they felt beholden to these same people (Malachi 2:9).

We are commanded to be as wise as serpents and as harmless as doves (Matthew 10:16). Being wise will lead you to say 'no thank you' to all those nice people who mean you no good. Do not get me wrong, it is okay to accept help sometimes, but we must know when we should and should not. After all, help is not help if it hurts you in the long run.

What's More Important?

Luke 10:41
"Martha, Martha," the Lord answered, you are worried and upset about many things.

Ecclesiastes teaches that there is a right time for everything (Ecclesiastes 3:1-8). Although it does not mention a time to clean up, there is such a time. It will behoove you to know when this time comes.

One evening while talking with a few of my sisters-in-Christ in the chapel after a church service, a co-worker approached me and said for me to help her empty the trash cans in the inmate bathrooms. This is something she took upon herself to do. However, I never understood why she did this when we were both chapel housekeepers who were scheduled to work the very next day from 8-3. There was nothing else going on in the chapel, and the bathrooms were an area I cleaned every morning I worked. Usually after service I spent my time saying my goodbyes to the volunteers and fellowshipping. I am commanded not to forsake this assembly (Hebrews 10:25) and this is what I would have been doing if I had run from service to empty trash that could wait until I got to work the next morning.

My co-worker was someone who worked hard to please man. We both were chapel workers and we had both finished with our housekeeping duties for the day. My only reason for being back in the chapel was for the church service. It would have been a different story if the trash was overflowing or something else had required immediate attention, yet this was not the case.

Chores are very important, but even Jesus had to tell Martha that at the present time she was worried about the wrong thing. Spending time with Jesus was more important than doing chores.

At my job I do my work as unto the Lord (Colossians 3:17, KJV). It is the Lord I live to please and it will benefit you to do the same. However, you will not benefit if you forsake what is important for what is not, simply to please man. No matter what, be sure to always choose Jesus, because he is the most important choice.

INDEX

Accountability - 111

Anger - 89-112, 237, 238, 303, 315, 334

Anointed - 124, 268

Authority

- Obeying - 17, 26, 61, 196
- Walking In - It-94, 174

Backsliding - 122, 133, 176, 252

Believers - 244

- Approaching Believers - 28, 52, 76
- New Believers - 54 28, 52, 54, 76, 244

Blessing - 96, 165, 177, 219, 235, 270

Business - (Mind Yours) - 2, 32, 271

Character - 23, 50, 70, 77, 86, 88, 90, 100, 107, 109, 162, 171, 175, 209, 222, 224, 265, 290, 317

Children - 27, 217

Choices - 3, 19

Church - 14, 24, 35, 92, 110, 121, 184, 198, 201, 205

Considerate - 11, 20, 56, 64, 87, 215, 229

Content - 22, 118, 140, 149, 156, 245, 258, 284,

Counsel - 43, 325

Count time - 30

Death - 45, 129, 239, 261, 311

Deliverance - 272

Difficult People - 137, 279, 280

Diligence - 41, 199, 247, 337

Discipline - 17, 26

Drug Abuse - 36, 37

Enemy - 93, 131

Endurance - 73, 80, 82, 147, 148, 301, 326

Faith – 10, 68, 77, 115, 119, 318

Faithfulness – 121, 138, 180, 213, 223, 227, 282

Family (Victim's) – 39

Fasting – 145, 232

Fears – 170, 331

Forgiveness – 39, 57

Friends – 4, 40, 69, 172

Giving – 130, 146, 153, 212, 336

Glory – 38, 65, 143, 202, 253, 269, 291

Gossip - 79

Hate – 46, 151, 228, 246, 255, 286

Holiness – 97, 142

Homosexuality – 40, 47, 81, 122, 124, 221

Honesty – 7, 34, 168, 282, 283, 287

Hope – 44, 53, 117

Humility – 51, 206, 250, 333

Hypocrites – 127, 243, 289

Idols – 65

Integrity - 79

Jealousy – 55

Judging – 31, 52, 123, 207, 240

Laziness – 56

Life – 12

Lockdown – 233, 251, 254

Love – 8, 28, 59, 64, 91, 128, 159, 191, 262, 296, 310, 314, 319-324, 328

Loved Ones – 6, 155 - (Separation from) – 1, 186

Lord – 104, 242

Lying – 74, 144, 145, 241, 255, 257

Merciful – 9, 72, 120

Ministering to Others – 21, 95, 108, 141, 214, 330

Neighbors – 60

Obedience – 13, 17, 28, 88, 166, 200, 230, 234, 249, 266, 327, 329,

Patience – 16, 220, 274, 306

Peace – 67, 194, 203, 256, 313

Peculiar – 135, 179, 182, 188, 248, 267

Prayer – 27, 62, 225, 260, 300

Priorities - 19

Privacy - 84

Promises – 101, 116, 185, 278, 294, 316

Prophesying – 66

Rejection – 190

Respect – 105

Revenge – 276, 304

Righteousness – 125, 160, 164, 178

Rights vs. Privileges - 25

Salvation – 264, 302

Shower Time - 16

Slander – 58, 79, 134, 210

Sick Call – 29, 31, 218

Sickness - 42

Sowing & Reaping – 71, 152, 103, 332, 335, 338

Spiritual Gifts – 48, 51

Stealing – 5, 115, 173, 285, 307

Temptation – 15, 99, 132, 183, 192, 292, 309

Trust God - 75, 83, 98, 113, 119, 158, 167, 169, 187, 189, 204, 236, 263, 297, 299, 305, 312

Temple of God – 114, 136, 150, 157, 161, 208, 277

Thoughts – 93, 211, 216, 281

Tithing – 146

Tribulation – 63, 102, 106, 226, 293

Unrighteousness – 181, 193

Waiting – 16, 298, 308

Wisdom – 18, 78, 85, 99, 139, 197, 259, 273, 288, 339

Worrying – 126, 299, 340

www.ingramcontent.com/pod-product-compliance
Lightning Source LLC
Chambersburg PA
CBHW070300010526
44108CB00039B/1408